FIXING LAW SCHOOLS

FIXING
LAW
SCHOOLS

FROM COLLAPSE TO THE
TRUMP BUMP AND BEYOND

BENJAMIN H. BARTON

NEW YORK UNIVERSITY PRESS

New York

NEW YORK UNIVERSITY PRESS
New York
www.nyupress.org

References to Internet websites (URLs) were accurate at the time of writing. Neither the author nor New York University Press is responsible for URLs that may have expired or changed since the manuscript was prepared.

Library of Congress Cataloging-in-Publication Data
Names: Barton, Benjamin H., 1969–   author.
Title: Fixing law schools : from collapse to the Trump bump and beyond /
Benjamin H. Barton.
Description: New York : New York University Press, [2019] |
Includes bibliographical references and index.
Identifiers: LCCN 2019004716 | ISBN 9781479866557 (cl : acid-free paper) |
ISBN 1479866555 (cl : acid-free paper)
Subjects: LCSH: Law schools—United States—History—21st century. | Law schools—
United States—Finance. | Law—Study and teaching—United States. | Law—
Vocational guidance—United States.
Classification: LCC KF272 .B37 2019 | DDC 340.071/173—dc23
LC record available at https://lccn.loc.gov/2019004716

New York University Press books are printed on acid-free paper, and their binding materials are chosen for strength and durability. We strive to use environmentally responsible suppliers and materials to the greatest extent possible in publishing our books.

Manufactured in the United States of America

10 9 8 7 6 5 4 3 2 1

Also available as an ebook

CONTENTS

INTRODUCTION

THE LOST DECADE

In 1887 an intrepid group of Quakers founded the town of Whittier, California, in a lovely spot tucked in between Los Angeles and Anaheim. That same year they also founded the Whittier Academy, which eventually became Whittier College. Both the town and the school were named after the Quaker poet and abolitionist John Greenleaf Whittier. From these humble origins Whittier College was born. Whittier is no longer formally associated with the Society of Friends but is still Quaker adjacent in its spirit. Its website proclaims that "the College remains proud of its Quaker heritage and deeply committed to its enduring values, such as respect for the individual, fostering community and service, social justice, freedom of conscience, and respect for human differences."[1]

Whittier College's most famous alumni are Richard Nixon and the Quaker novelist Jessamyn West.[2] The school's sports teams are called the Poets after John Greenleaf Whittier, and their mascot is a running fountain pen toting, "Johnny Poet." It is unclear how the actual poet Whittier would have felt about this likeness, but given the contemporary photos of an unsmiling and uncompromising lifelong warrior against slavery who also suffered from intermittent poor health, let's guess that Whittier might have mixed feelings.

It does seem likely that Whittier would be pleased with the college as a whole though. Whittier remains a relatively small school, with an undergraduate enrollment of 1,615 students in 2016 and boasting a twelve-to-one student-faculty ratio.[3] It is a school that treasures its intellectual and moral heritage, as well as its namesake.

Whittier's Mascot "Johnny Poet."

Unless you have closely followed American law schools, you may be wondering why this book starts by discussing Whittier College (let alone the poet Whittier). It is because Whittier's law school is exhibit A for the lost decade that law schools suffered from 2008 to 2018. On April 14, 2016, Whittier Law School celebrated its fiftieth anniversary.[4] A year and five days later, on April 19, 2017, Whittier College's trustees announced that the law school would be closing its doors for good.[5]

Whittier Law School started as the Beverly College School of Law in Los Angeles in 1966.[6] Beverly College was a night-only law school explicitly tailored to second career and underrepresented law students.[7] The school was a throwback to the old, night-only YMCA law schools of the early twentieth century. It focused on practical skills and bar passage, not scholarship or other higher-minded pursuits.[8] In the boomtown Los Angeles of the 1960s, there was a significant and unmet demand for a school like Beverly, and its role in advancing nontraditional and underrepresented lawyers was salutary and necessary.

Whittier College purchased Beverly in 1975.[9] From the outset, Whittier hoped to operate a law school that fit its educational mission. Beverly College School of Law was a night school. After Whittier took over, the law school graduated its first day class in 1976, the first of many moves meant to up the law school's academic profile, while still maintaining its original mission of diversifying the legal profession and offering a leg up to its graduates.

Beverly operated without accreditation by the American Bar Association Section of Legal Education and Admissions to the Bar (ABA). Then and now, ABA accreditation carried important psychological and logistical advantages. Most American states require graduation from an ABA-accredited law school to sit for the bar (California is a notable exception, thus the existence of the Beverly College School of Law). Moreover, any law school that aspires to any kind of academic footprint eventually seeks ABA accreditation.

In 1978, the ABA granted Whittier Law School provisional accreditation. Full ABA accreditation came in 1985. Whittier gained membership in the Association of American Law Schools (AALS) in 1987.[10] The decision to pursue AALS membership as well as ABA accreditation demonstrated Whittier's desire to have a first-class, academic law school. ABA accreditation is critical because it is a key part of lawyer licensing. AALS membership is voluntary and only for academically oriented law schools that seek to "uphold and advance excellence in legal education."[11]

As of the mid-1980s Whittier Law School looked poised to succeed. It was the first ABA-accredited law school in the booming Los Angeles suburbs of Orange County, California. But by the 1990s and early 2000s, the ABA was warning the school about low bar passage rates.[12] By 2005, the ABA had seen enough and placed Whittier on probation for two years.[13] This was an aggressive and unusual move by the ABA at the time. In order to place Whittier on probation, the ABA had to find Whittier out of compliance with its accreditation standards. The problem was that in 2005 the ABA standards did not include any explicit language on what was or was not an acceptable bar passage rate. The ABA claimed that Whittier's bar passage rates violated Standard 301, which states, "A law school shall maintain an educational program that prepares its students for admission to the bar, and effective and responsible participation in the legal profession." The ABA's current, more specific Standard 316 covering bar passage (which we discuss at length in chapter 6) was not included in the standards until 2014–15.[14]

Whittier promptly sued, claiming that the ABA's enforcement of the standard violated due process and was too vague.[15] The ABA won on Whittier's request for a temporary injunction, but the lawsuit bought Whittier time to improve its bar passage results, and in 2008 when the ABA lifted the probation, Whittier dropped the suit.[16]

But the probation period itself was quite costly. Whittier lost twelve full-time faculty members, and enrollment dropped from 1,000 to 600.[17] The school faced significant financial pressures but eventually rebounded, getting off of probation and temporarily raising its bar passage rates to more acceptable levels. Whittier's first-time bar passage rates were 70 percent in July 2012 and 65 percent in July 2013, which were decent in California.[18] For these two years Whittier looked as if it was going to be able to thread the needle and deliver on the promise of both Beverly College and Whittier College: it was admitting a diverse class of traditionally underrepresented students and preparing them for success on the bar.

Unfortunately, the bottom fell out again after 2013, and first-time bar passage rates in July 2016 fell to an unimaginably awful 22 percent.[19] This was the worst bar passage rate in the State of California among ABA-accredited schools and a low-water mark even for a school that had a spotty record of bar passage.

The July 2016, results were likely at least partially due to falling admissions standards implemented during the great law school application collapse of the post-2011 period. In 2010, the median Law School Admission Test (LSAT) score for Whittier's incoming class was 152, and its median undergraduate grade point average (GPA) was 3.02. By 2016, those numbers had fallen to 146 and 2.85.

Despite these declines in admissions standards, the entering class size shrunk from 303 to 132 over the same period. Whittier was hardly alone: the collapse in student credentials and class sizes across law schools over this period are a theme of this book. But note Whittier's hardship. Between 2010 and 2016, Whittier moved to an almost open admissions schema by lowering LSAT and GPA targets substantially, and their first-year enrollment still fell by more than half!

Whittier's other indicators were likewise troubling. One hundred twenty-eight students graduated from Whittier in 2016, and six months after graduation only thirty-eight of them had a full-time, long-term job that required a JD. Whittier's tuition was $45,350 in 2016, and the school estimated living expenses at another $32,136 per year—$77,486 a year! High tuition leads to large loans, and in 2016 Whittier's graduates carried a crushing average debt load of $179,056, the second highest in the country.[20]

Pause for a minute to let that debt figure sink in. The debt carried by Whittier (and many other) law grads is perhaps the most upsetting legacy of the lost decade. Over the same period of time that job placement was deteriorating, law schools all over the country relentlessly raised tuition and asked students to borrow more to pay for law school. For a struggling law school like Whittier, the strategy was necessary for survival. Whittier needed to boost revenue any way it could, so they accepted even marginally qualified applicants and asked them to borrow a fortune to support their education.

This raises another question: why would the students take this risk? There are three reasons. First, starting in 2005 the federal government agreed to allow graduate students to borrow the entire cost of their education (plus reasonable living expenses) from the Grad Plus Program. Congress did this because the existing caps on federal loans had not changed in years and some students were being priced out of graduate school. Despite this salutary goal, the result has been that Whittier (and many other law schools) can saddle their students with massive debt loads on loans that no private bank would consider underwriting.

This helps explain why tuition prices and debt loads at Whittier (and almost every other law school in the country) continued to rise much faster than inflation, despite the worst market for law school applications in a generation.

Second, many of the students who applied to and enrolled in Whittier Law School came from challenging economic backgrounds and hoped that a law degree might be a ladder into a middle-class or upper-middle-class existence. After all, most Americans think that lawyers do quite well financially and that law school is a good bet. At one time this was unquestionably true. Median private law school tuition in 1960 was $475 (roughly $4,000 in 2017 dollars). Median public law school tuition was $204 ($1,700 in 2017 dollars).[21] The available census data suggests that even the graduates of the Beverly College of Law (who likely paid well below the average tuition) made a fine living as lawyers. Unfortunately, job prospects have deteriorated and tuition expenses have exploded, so what was once a well-paved road into a professional, upper-middle-class life has transformed into a dangerous risk.

Nevertheless, this was *still* a rational risk for the Whittier students who came from disadvantaged backgrounds. If things worked out and they passed the bar and got a good-paying job as a lawyer, the gamble would be worth it. If not, they would default on their loans and not be much worse off than they were already. After all, many of these students already carried an undergraduate debt load they were going to have a hard time repaying. Studies have shown that disadvantaged Americans are much more willing to take long-shot financial risks to improve their circumstances than are middle-class Americans, even when the downside risk is substantial.[22] This explains the enduring (and unfortunate) existence of payday loans or layaway for furniture. The business model of law schools like Whittier's is, in fact, closer to a payday-loan operation than what we think of when we imagine a typical professional graduate school.

Third, Whittier actually appeared to be a relative bargain among California's private, ABA-accredited law schools. Stanford Law School charged $58,236 in tuition in 2016. Loyola Law School's tuition was $52,760. California Western School of Law cost $48,900. Thomas Jefferson School of Law's tuition was $47,600. Struggling law schools like Whittier were able to jack up their tuition in a bad market because other law schools, especially America's best law schools, normalized high tuition. This is another part of the lost decade: when employment opportunities flagged, the cost of attending all law schools rose heedlessly and continuously.

Still, with Whittier showing such poor results and such high costs the question remains: why did it fall to the trustees to close the school? Why didn't market forces or regulators strike the final blow? How could a school struggling as much as Whittier keep its doors open?

Weirdly, at the time Whittier closed it was not in any immediate financial or regulatory peril. Whittier College's president admitted that the law school was not running a deficit at the time of the announced closure, although future deficits were projected.[23] Moreover, Whittier had just sold the land the law school occupied for $35 million (at a $13 million profit), so Whittier College certainly could have floated a deficit for a while if it had been so inclined.[24] Whittier Law School's faculty was so sure that the trustee's decision was not defensible fiscally that in 2017 they sued to keep the school open.[25]

How could Whittier still break even despite the collapse in enrollment? The same way any other business does: cut costs and boost revenues. Cutting costs was simple. Whittier had already cut the faculty and the staff in response to their previous crisis of ABA probation, and another round of cuts kept costs low. Boosting revenue came from a combination of open-enrollment admissions and convincing their students to max out on their federal loans.

But wouldn't these strategies create the potential for more trouble with the ABA? Sure! Whittier had to know that regulatory trouble was a possibility. But the ABA is hardly a lightning-quick body, and when your choices are to fold immediately in financial distress or face a later regulatory problem, Whittier (and every other law school faced with this dilemma) rationally chose to risk later ABA troubles. In fact, Whittier was fully accredited and not in hot water with the ABA (at least publicly) in 2017. As for the collapse in bar passage rates, ABA Standard 316 allows a law school to use a five-year period to comply, so Whittier's decent bar passage numbers from 2012 to 2013 might have bought it time.

Since 2017 we have seen an uptick in ABA activity, including a successful effort to close/disaccredit Arizona Summit Law School, but as of 2017 the ABA was still relatively quiet. In fact, the attempt to disaccredit Arizona Summit is the first time the ABA has *ever* attempted to remove accreditation from a fully accredited school. Whittier (and many other schools) assumed they would get time (and maybe a long time) to address any ABA issues. The ABA has historically been pretty generous in dealing with schools on probation. Even in the case of Arizona Summit the ABA put the school on probation in March 2017 and did not announce an attempted disaccreditation until June 2018. In between the announcement of probation and disaccreditation, Arizona Summit posted disastrously low bar results. Its July 2017 passage rate was 20.1 percent, and its February 2018 pass rate was 19.8 percent.[26] At first Arizona Summit announced plans to appeal and to try to survive, but after canceling classes for 2018 and facing eviction for nonpayment of rent, the school announced a teach-out plan and eventual closure.[27]

The trustees of Whittier College did not wait for the law school to run at a deficit or for the ABA to place Whittier back on probation. They pulled the plug preemptively. If the decision was not financial or regulatory, why did Whittier close? It closed because the trustees had seen enough from the law school. Whittier College is a small, academically minded Quaker liberal arts school. Whittier Law School had devolved into a headache and an embarrassment, if not a financial or accreditation risk. Whittier College seems like a poor host for a struggling law school with a collapsing bar passage rate. The law school fit the school's overall diversity mission, but every other aspect of the program was discomforting to a small, intellectually oriented school.

When your law school is graduating a diverse class that is mostly passing the bar and mostly gaining employment, you can look the other way at high tuition and a less academic bent. When the law school is saddling students with an unconscionable debt load and offering neither bar passage nor employment in return, it is a different institutional and moral calculus. At some point the Whittier trustees likely concluded that they were propping up a student loan scam. Given the optics and the law school's long struggles with bar passage, at a certain point the trustees were bound to pull the plug.

WHITTIER IS HARDLY ALONE

Whittier's story is especially emblematic of the lost decade, but it was hardly alone. Other law schools closed or are near closing. Arizona Summit appears to be finished following an ABA disaccreditation action. In chapter 7 we cover the closure of the Charlotte School of Law at length. Indiana Tech decided to close its provisionally accredited start-up school in October 2016, noting $20 million in losses during just four years of operation.[28]

Valparaiso University Law School suspended admissions in November 2017. At first the school was careful to note that it was not closing and would be looking to relocate the law school if possible.[29] In 2018 it looked as if Valparaiso Law might merge with Middle Tennessee State University, but the Tennessee Higher Education Commission rejected the move, sparing Tennessee a seventh law school on top of the recent additions of Belmont and Lincoln Memorial University law schools. Valparaiso Law is scheduled to close in 2020. Western State's owner, the private higher education company Argosy University, filed for bankruptcy in 2019, temporarily throwing that school's survival into doubt. Westcliff University bought Western State, apparently keeping it in business going forward.

Several law schools have closed branch campuses. John Marshall (Atlanta) abruptly pulled the plug on Savannah Law School in March 2018.

They fired most of the Savannah faculty and staff and encouraged their students to finish up in Atlanta.[30] Cooley Law School likewise closed its Ann Arbor campus in 2014.[31]

The struggle has hardly been limited to bottom-tier law schools. This book argues that *all* American law schools have suffered through a lost decade in two different ways. The first is easy to see in Whittier's tale: employment results have been historically bad. Applications and enrollment cratered. Revenue dropped precipitously, and several law schools closed. Almost all law schools shrank in terms of students, faculties, and staffs. Despite these bad results, law school tuition outran inflation, and student indebtedness exploded, creating a truly toxic brew of higher costs for worse results.

We have seen a "Trump Bump" in applications since 2017. The election of Donald Trump in 2016 and the subsequent role of hero-lawyers in the "resistance" have made going to law school cool again.[32] Signs of a turnaround abound. Since 2017 more people are taking the LSAT. More LSAT takers applied to law school, with a special increase among applicants who did well on the LSAT. Matriculation rose modestly in 2018. The media narrative changed from "don't go to law school" to "law school is the place to become a future lawyer-hero."

Trump has also assisted law schools (especially for-profits and other struggling schools) by greatly loosening Department of Education (DOE) oversight. The Obama DOE basically closed the Charlotte School of Law in 2016–17. The Trump DOE has signaled a much friendlier tone, although the ABA has since picked up where the Obama DOE left off.

Consider for a moment the irony of President Donald J. Trump assisting mightily in saving law schools where few, if any, professors or administrators voted for him (at least if records of campaign donations can be used as a proxy for voting). President Trump rarely likes to assist his enemies, but here we are.

Despite the strong early returns, we still have no idea whether law schools are out of the woods or not. If the Trump Bump is temporary or does not result in further increases in enrollment, especially for struggling, lower-ranked schools, we will see more closures. But if it does last, we face our second danger. We tend to hope that crises bring needed reforms. This is the entire point of the process of "creative destruction," where a downturn causes some businesses to fail and other businesses to adapt. Unfortunately, the opposite has happened for law schools. Brian Tamanaha's excellent *Failing Law Schools* came out in 2012 and well chronicled a century or so of problematic law school management. This book does not try to duplicate that book's feat. But *Failing Law Schools* came out before the full scope of the damage from the lost decade became clear, so while it detailed past failures, it could not foresee the ways that law schools would exacerbate the exact problems that led them to the precipice.

That's the irony of the lost decade. Law schools have suffered a harrowing, near-death experience, and the survivors look as if they're going to exhale gratefully and then go back to doing exactly what led them into the crisis in the first place. The main point of this book is to convince law school stakeholders (the faculty, students, applicants, graduates, and regulators) *not* to just return to business as usual if the Trump Bump proves to be permanent. We have come too far, through too much, to just shrug our shoulders and move on.

This book starts by explaining the underlying causes of the law school downturn and then describes just how hard it has been for law schools to survive in a very tough market since 2011. More importantly, the book shows the way that all law schools, from top to bottom, have failed to address the root causes of their challenges. Rather than make the value proposition of law school better by improving the product and lowering the price, law schools of all stripes did little to improve (and many got worse through deep cuts) but much to raise prices.

Isolating this decade also draws our attention to how law schools have behaved selfishly in ways that have devalued the entire institution. In this way the story of American law schools is a small part of a larger deleterious trend: long-standing American institutions profiting off of the shine of their past performance. Generally speaking, Americans think that lawyers make a very good living and that law school is a gateway to an upper-middle-class life. Some (many?) law schools ask their students to borrow a fortune based on this assumption, despite the reality that a great number of their students will not graduate, pass the bar, or get a job that requires a law degree. Even America's finest law schools have relentlessly raised tuition, again because of the idea that their graduates will earn a fortune in private practice, so it will be worth it. But outside of a handful of top schools, graduates of even very storied law schools have faced a challenging job market.

WHAT HAPPENED

The lost decade starts with the Great Recession, which was the worst economic contraction since the Great Depression across any number of measures.[33] It lasted sixteen months, the longest continuous contraction since the 1940s. From May 2007 until October 2009, America shed more than 7.5 million jobs, and the unemployment rate grew from 4.4 to 10.1 percent. Long-term unemployment also grew sharply, and the total number of adult Americans working fell sharply as well. The Dow Jones Industrial Average fell from a high of 14,164 in October 2007 to a low of 6,547 in March 2009, a 54 percent decline.

The downturn was likewise brutal for lawyers. By one estimate, 14,347 people were laid off from jobs in major law firms (5,632 lawyers and 8,715 staff members).[34] Law firms cut salaries, the earnings of partners fell, hiring freezes were common, and the employment of law graduates fell sharply. Federal, state, and local governments likewise cut lawyers or instituted hiring freezes. Small firm and solo practitioners faced clients with less disposable income and new competition from online companies offering legal services, such as LegalZoom and Rocket Lawyer. Disbarments rose because more lawyers were caught stealing client funds.[35]

At first the Great Recession was a boon for law schools. Recessions are traditionally good times for professional schools. College graduates have a hard time finding work and decide to get a graduate degree rather than face unemployment or underemployment. The Great Recession was no different. In January 2010 the *New York Times* ran an article entitled "Recession Spurs Interest in Graduate, Law Schools" that reported on more people taking the LSAT and attending law school during the Great Recession.[36]

The admissions boom and good press was not destined to last, however. As other areas of the economy improved, the legal employment market remained stubbornly poor. When the law graduates in the classes of 2008 and 2009 faced a tough market, law schools assumed it was a cyclical problem associated with the downturn in the entire economy. When the classes of 2010 and 2011 faced even worse results, prognosticators like Bill Henderson concluded that these changes were structural. The knives came out, and law schools faced a tsunami of bad press. The *New York Times*, the *Washington Post*, and the *Wall Street Journal* (among many others) all published extremely unflattering portraits of the cost and value of a legal education.[37] Articles began to appear noting a collapse in applications and attendance, as well as arguments that multiple law schools were bound for closure.[38]

This book takes a close look at what caused the lost decade, how law schools have addressed—and failed to address—the crisis, and then asks what should be done and what is actually likely to be done, noting sadly that what's likeliest is more of the same. This book is not an attempt to take a long view on what has ailed American law schools for decades— Brian Tamanaha's masterful *Failing Law Schools* has already cornered that market. Instead, we take a deep dive into the remarkable events of the last ten years to prove that law schools faced (and still face) exceptional challenges and to argue that more must be learned from the experience.

◆ 1 ◆

THE ORIGINAL SIN

LAW SCHOOLS TEACH LAW BUT NOT LAWYERING

For as long as there have been organized law schools in the US, critics have complained (accurately) that law schools do a relatively poor job of teaching students the nuts and bolts of law practice. Law schools have always chosen to focus on broader theory and "thinking like a lawyer" instead. This is the oldest of the old-school critiques, but it has gained new salience after 2011 as the "law schools in crisis" narrative has really taken off.

If you are in the mood to read an eloquent, and still amazingly timely, version of this critique, consider reading the legal realists Karl Llewellyn and Jerome Frank. Frank wrote the seminal 1947 *Yale Law Journal* article "A Plea for Lawyer-Schools."[1] Llewellyn wrote the more influential, and equally devastating, 1944 Association of American Law Schools (AALS) report on law school curriculums that noted that the case method was failing to produce "reliable professional competence."[2] If you are among the readers who pooh-pooh this critique as largely the product of lawyers who have an insufficient understanding of the value of great legal scholarship, consider that two of the greatest legal scholars of the twentieth century strongly disagree with you.

You can read the fullest current version of this critique in two exhaustingly researched and well-written 2007 publications, Roy Stuckey's *Best Practices for Legal Education* and the Carnegie Foundation report entitled *Educating Lawyers*.[3] Brian Tamanaha's excellent *Failing Law Schools*, Paul Campos's blogs and books, and Steven Harper's *The Lawyer Bubble* offer more recent and quite pointed critiques as well. Law schools spend too much time on academic pursuits and training students to "think like a lawyer" and too little on actually teaching students the nuts and bolts of the practice of law.

These same critiques have leaked out into the popular press. In 2011, the *New York Times* ran an article entitled "What They Don't Teach Law Students: Lawyering" that gave a brisk and damning summation of law school deficiencies on this front.[4] The article noted that one survey found that almost half of the recent hires at top law schools had *never* practiced law before joining academia. The article also took a pot-shot at abstruse and overly academic law review articles, singling out a particularly goofy, word-salad article entitled "Future Foretold: Neo-Aristotelian Praise of Postmodern Legal Theory." Picking on silly law review articles is shooting fish in a barrel of course, and the story itself was hardly breaking news for the *Times*: they published nearly identical articles in 1983 and 2014.[5]

This critique is surely correct, but it faces two ironies. The first is that due to the growth of clinical legal education, externships, and simulation programs in American law schools, there are now *more* opportunities to learn how to practice law while in law school than ever before. In fact, the American Bar Association (ABA) changed its accreditation requirements in 2014 to address this specific complaint, requiring that law school graduates take a mandatory six hours of "experiential" learning before graduation and allowing students to work more outside of law school.[6] Six hours is hardly a cure-all, but that requirement is a beginning, and it is true that more law schools expend more energy and effort on practical training than they have since before World War II, if ever.

The second irony is that the experiential complaint is as old as law school itself and misunderstands the fundamental nature of American law schools. We turn first to a brief history of how we ended up with the lawyer-training/legal education model we have and then a brief discussion of the problems that flow naturally from that history. Law schools did not back into this problem, and it did not happen accidentally. They were born this way.

THE "EXPERIENTIAL" PROBLEM: LAW SCHOOLS' ORIGINAL SIN

History is written by the winners, and humans have always attempted to arrange it into a tidy narrative with good guys and bad guys, and the triumph of the right side over the wrong one. This explains much of the generally accepted history of law schools. In the original narrative, law schools played a key part in creating the modern legal profession and creating order (the scientific study of law) from chaos (apprenticeships).

Consider former Harvard Law School dean Roscoe Pound's excellent (if heavily slanted) 1953 history of the American legal profession, *The Lawyer from Antiquity to Modern Times*. Pound describes the period of 1836–1870 as "the era of decadence" because bar associations, and thus the legal profession in his telling, had fallen into disrepair.[7] The country was saved by the "revival of professional organization" after the Civil War.[8]

The replacement of apprenticeship with legal education plays a key role in this story of the triumph of professionalism.[9] In this version, American lawyers used to train for the profession by serving a set term of years as an apprentice to a practicing lawyer. Following the Civil War and during the Industrial Age this process was recognized as primitive and inadequate and wisely replaced by the more scientific law school program we have today.

This version of the story focuses too hard on just one of the three formative battles that law schools have faced along the way and thus misses exactly why law schools look the way they do now. A closer examination of the history shows that the first battle was indeed against the deprofessionalization of Jacksonian democracy. The elite bar's first job was not to support law schools in a battle against apprenticeships. Instead they fought to reinstate any formality into the requirements for entering the profession.

Law schools did, indeed, eventually have to beat back apprenticeship, but that was only half of the battle, because while law schools tried to replace apprenticeship with the elite, academic Harvard model, they faced an even greater threat from their other flank: much cheaper and much less academically oriented proprietary schools. Proprietary law schools presented a different threat: inexpensive legal education for the masses. In the first three decades of the twentieth century, it was unclear which model would triumph.

Below we take a brief trip through these battles because the strategies that led to the triumph of elite-model law schools also explain much of the puzzling nature of current law schools. If you are wondering when and why law schools became too focused on the scientific and academic study of law, the answer is that they have always emphasized the academic study of law over the practical, because that was their main differentiation from their twin enemies: apprenticeship and proprietary law schools. The overly academic nature of law schools is thus neither an accident nor peripheral to their existence. The overly academic study of law is in fact the raison d'être of the elite model.

MODERN LAW SCHOOLS ARRIVED INTO DEPROFESSIONALIZATION

In the early nineteenth century there were a handful of American law professors and the beginnings of what might later be called a law school (William & Mary and Harvard were early examples), but the vast majority of American lawyers were trained in formal apprenticeships.[10] Twelve of the thirteen original states required some period of apprenticeship before entering the practice of law, and none required any formal legal education.[11]

The election of Andrew Jackson in 1828 launched Jacksonian democracy, a period when governments of all levels tried to change their laws to disempower American elites. The legal profession was a natural and juicy target. The years from 1828 until the Civil War brought a number of reforms that were hostile to the formalized legal profession. Legislatures made great efforts to simplify pleading standards and codify the common law in order to break the lawyer's monopoly in the law and courts.[12] States also moved toward elected judiciaries to rein in judicial power.[13]

Most importantly for our purposes, legislatures made every effort to lower barriers to entering the legal profession, and over this period apprenticeship requirements melted away.[14] New states joined the union with few entry requirements, and existing states rolled theirs back. This effort was remarkably successful. By 1860, only *nine* of thirty-nine jurisdictions had any fixed apprenticeship requirements. None required law school.[15]

This led to a predictable collapse in interest in bar associations and formal legal education. It is too strong to say that the legal profession was completely deprofessionalized. There were still influential and wealthy lawyers who maintained a professional identity. But it is certainly fair to say that the profession hit a nadir in terms of formality.

THE BAR ASSOCIATION REPROFESSIONALIZATION PROJECT

It is important to understand the nature of the legal profession (such as it was) in the middle years of the nineteenth century because the struggle to reprofessionalize informed every step of the creation of the modern law school. In the 1870s and 80s, the choice was not between a functioning apprenticeship system and a resurgent or redesigned law school system. To the contrary, Jacksonian democracy essentially killed law schools, formal apprenticeship, and even bar associations themselves, so the reprofessionalization movement arrived with a relatively blank slate, but also a steep hill to climb.

In many ways, doctors set the model for lawyers. Doctors faced similar challenges during Jacksonian democracy, but they started their reprofessionalization project sooner. Lawyers followed their lead repeatedly. A select group of elite doctors formed the American Medical Association (AMA) in 1847.[16] A similarly elite group of lawyers formed the ABA thirty years later in 1878.[17]

The AMA railed against the results of low-entry standards, claiming the medical profession had become "corrupt and degenerate."[18] The ABA felt similarly about the legal profession, arguing that low standards had led to a generation of lawyers "believing themselves immune, the good or bad esteem of their co-laborers is nothing to them provided their itching fingers are not thereby stayed in their eager quest for lucre."[19] Both the ABA and AMA recommended that each state form a central licensing board and that entry to the respective professions be through formalized and required professional schools rather than apprenticeship.

Why did the ABA not return to set periods of apprenticeship rather than pushing for law schools? After all, apprenticeship had previously been required in the United States, and law school had never been. Given that it was likely to prove difficult enough for the ABA and local bar associations to fight back against forty successful years of Jacksonian democracy, why raise the degree of difficulty more by skipping over apprenticeship and moving right to formal law school training?

A separate trend sweeping American elites (like the lawyers who formed the ABA) explains why the reformers favored law schools over apprenticeships. The Industrial Age's push for standardization in all pursuits suggested that a rigorous and scientific educational program would always be preferable to an ad hoc apprenticeship approach.[20] This era also saw the birth of the modern American university, and law schools, not apprenticeships, fit the trend. The ABA was thus enthusiastic about the "scientific" study of law, favoring German and French university-style models.

Not coincidentally, in 1870 Dean Langdell of Harvard Law School introduced a new, more scientific study of the law: the case method.[21] This set the model for the study of law and is still dominant today. The case method was explicitly scientific and argued that law could be best understood by the distillation and study of judicial opinions.[22] This model is now so ingrained in our minds that it is worth pausing for a moment to explicitly recognize what a massive shift it was. Rather than focusing on the work of the lawyer, as apprenticeship naturally would, the case method focused on the work of the judges. Why? Because that was where we could find the academic/scientific study of the "law." The work the lawyers did was merely a byproduct of the law and hardly worth covering, at least not during formal education. This change of focus alone explains the main difference between the elite-model of law schools and apprenticeships and proprietary law schools. It also explains much about law schools today. This one change of focus set the course of our destiny.

Harvard also set the model for the position of the law school within a modern university. The law school was an academic department like other departments, using scientific tools to study and explain just another phenomenon in the world. Law students were expected to study full time, for a set period of years, with a set curriculum.[23]

The Harvard model was controversial at first but gained steam over time and eventually became the dominant model among all law schools. How dominant? Robert Stevens's excellent history of law schools has two separate chapters explaining the rise of the modern, academic-style law school entitled "Harvard Decrees the Structure and Content" and "Harvard Sets the Style."[24]

Humorously, the weaknesses of this approach were obvious even at the very outset. During an early debate over requiring law school, one ABA delegate carped that law schools resembled the "education of priests and monks" and that "students of law schools are not generally as proficient as others in drawing pleadings, deeds, and the like, and in the knowledge of actual practice."[25] Surely *that* would get ironed out over the years. Not so much.

LIMITED INITIAL SUCCESS

It took roughly sixty years to get from the founding of the ABA to a clear victory for the Harvard model, and there were several inflection points where the outcome was far from clear. Significantly, the single most important factor in the eventual victory was not a triumph of marketing hustle by the elite law schools, nor was it the political muscle or savvy of bar associations in gaining legislative favor. Instead, the single biggest factor was the decision of state supreme courts all over the country to wrest control of lawyer regulation from state legislatures as a matter of their "inherent authority" to govern lawyers as officers of the court.[26]

It is far too long a story to cover here, so a few highlights must suffice. At first, bar associations tried to follow the AMA's model of lobbying state legislatures, but, unsurprisingly, they found state legislatures less enthusiastic about helping lawyers than doctors, especially elite lawyers. It also didn't help that so few lawyers in America had any formal higher education at all. When the ABA was founded, there were more lawyers in the United States than college graduates, let alone law school graduates.[27] So for the first twenty years or so, bar associations found themselves swimming upstream against hostile legislatures.

At the turn of the twentieth century, state supreme courts began to step in, which eventually made all the difference. State supreme courts shared the elite bar's interest in higher standards and more barriers to entry. After all, nothing makes a common-law judge's job easier than better lawyers. Further, all of these justices were themselves lawyers, so they were especially susceptible to arguments for "improving" the status and nature of the bar. Nor should nativism and racism be discounted. Every time a bar association railed against a greedy and unprincipled wave of new lawyers, they were often using code for Jewish immigrants or other disfavored minorities. Jerold Auerbach's masterwork *Unequal Justice* lays out this shameful history at length.[28] This is not to say that legislatures did not remain involved in lawyer regulation; they did. But lawyers are the only American profession that managed to appeal to state supreme courts (staffed by lawyers) in their reprofessionalization mission.

PROPRIETARY VERSUS ELITE VERSUS APPRENTICESHIP

By the turn of the twentieth century, bar associations had accomplished a lot: more than two-thirds of American jurisdictions required some formal period of apprenticeship or study, and a formal written bar exam was quickly becoming the norm.[29] The informal and easy access to the profession of Jacksonian democracy had been replaced by a much more formal and difficult process. Mission accomplished? Not so for the elite-model law schools, which found themselves engaged in a two-sided cage match for supremacy. On one side, the traditional route of apprenticeship was being reestablished. On the other side sat a completely different model: the proprietary/night law school.

Proprietary schools were a natural reaction to the move toward legal education as a route into the profession. The elite-model law schools were relatively expensive to run. They typically had some or many full-time faculty members, law libraries, and dedicated buildings. The students were often required to have some level of formal or undergraduate experience before entering, and they were expected to study law full time and also pay comparatively expensive tuition.

It does not take a cost-cutting wizard to recognize that there is some fat in that recipe, especially if the goal is simply to prepare the students for a bar examination. Proprietary schools popped up all over the country, running on a vastly cheaper model. These law schools were often freestanding part-time or night law schools intended to serve poorer or working-class students. These schools had smaller or nonexistent full-time faculties. Classes were mostly taught by what we would call "adjunct professors" today, practicing lawyers and judges working part time for limited remuneration.

Money was also saved on facilities. To give you the full flavor, many of these law schools were located in YMCA gymnasiums at night. If you have played basketball in a YMCA gym, picture that space filled with folding chairs and a podium and you get the idea. Consider the relative bargain on overhead: these schools only needed to pay the rent on a YMCA gym and enough to get a few part-time practitioners to come in and lecture.

The Nashville YMCA School of Law, founded by four young lawyers in 1911, is a great example. It offered night classes at the downtown Nashville YMCA, taking advantage of underused facilities at night.[30] The school continued to hold classes at the Y until 1990 and still operates as a non-ABA-accredited law school, solely licensed by the State of Tennessee. This makes the Nashville School of Law one of the very few remaining enemy combatants from the great lawyer-training war. From the 1940s forward, most proprietary law schools followed one of two well-trod paths. Either they bit the bullet and did the work to become ABA accredited (like John Marshall [Chicago] or Brooklyn Law School), or they went out of business. A few in Tennessee, California, and other states continued on as nonaccredited anomalies.

ABA + AALS + THE GREAT DEPRESSION = VICTORY

How did the Harvard model triumph? The Association of American Law Schools (AALS) is a big part of the story. Founded by elite law schools and their faculties in 1900, the AALS was created under the aegis of the ABA from twenty-five "reputable" law schools, with an explicit mission to boost the requirements for operating a law school and to discourage night and proprietary law schools.[31] The elite law schools decided to found the AALS as a separate entity because while the ABA generally favored law school over apprenticeships, elite schools felt the ABA was not doing enough in the battle between the Harvard model and proprietary law schools.

Unlike the ABA, whose members were individual lawyers, the AALS was a law school, not law professor, organization. Its membership consisted only of law schools that met relatively challenging requirements. Initially AALS membership consisted of only law schools that (1) admitted students with a high school degree; (2) required at least a full-time, two-year course of study over thirty weeks per year; (3) established final examinations as a prerequisite to graduation; and (4) had access to a law library.[32]

The AALS strengthened these requirements almost immediately, requiring a three-year program in 1905 and barring schools with day and night programs of equal length in 1912.[33] These changes actually drove AALS membership down as membership requirements outstripped the number of law schools willing/able to comply.[34]

The AALS was a voluntary organization, and while it had some success in raising the requirements for its members, its membership fell behind proprietary law schools. From its founding until the end of the 1920s, AALS member schools continuously shrank as a percentage of law schools and law students, while night law schools flourished.[35] Between 1920 and 1929, the number of law students more than doubled and many new law schools opened, but almost all of the growth went to proprietary schools.[36] Apprenticeship shrank, but the bulk of the gain went to the "wrong" schools.[37]

While the AALS and the ABA had an on-again, off-again romance before the 1920s, the explosion in proprietary law schools and the concomitant growth in the size of the profession drove them to get on the same page. The ABA created its own accreditation standards in 1921.[38] These standards were slightly slacker than the AALS's but still left the great majority of law schools noncompliant. How close were the ABA and AALS standards? By 1927 the list of ABA- and AALS-accredited schools was almost identical.[39]

And yet the effect was minimal. In 1927, no state required graduation from law school as a prerequisite for joining the bar, let alone graduation from an ABA-accredited law school.[40] The battle lines were more clearly drawn than ever, with the Harvard model pitted against proprietary schools. Unsurprisingly, proprietary schools showed little interest in capitulating to moral suasion from either the ABA or the AALS. Why would they? Students were flocking in.

The Great Depression changed the calculus altogether. The Depression hit the legal profession especially hard. Increasing the requirements for entering the practice of law changed from an aspiration to an existential emergency. Between 1927 and 1941, the number of states requiring graduation from an ABA-accredited law school as a prerequisite for entering the legal profession rose from zero to forty-one.[41]

From the late nineteenth century forward, the elite bar had tried its best to close proprietary law schools through professional opprobrium with limited success. Would requiring graduation from an

ABA-accredited law school to sit for the bar be different? The answer was a resounding yes. Between 1930 and 1950, seventy law schools went out of business. Sixty-nine of them were unaccredited.[42]

By the time the 1950s arrived, the battle was largely over and the Harvard model had won. Some proprietary schools survived, and a few states still allow apprenticeship in lieu of law school. Notably, in 2019 Kim Kardashian announced her plan to become a lawyer via California's apprenticeship program rather than through a law school. That route is actually pretty challenging. She will have to "read the law" for at least four years, for at least eighteen hours a week, file biannual compliance reports, and pass a difficult mini bar exam after her first year of study. Perhaps inveterate fans of *Keeping Up with the Kardashians* will follow Kim's lead and spark an apprenticeship revival. Notwithstanding Kim's trailblazing, it is now clear that for the vast majority of Americans there is one, and only one, route to becoming a lawyer: an ABA-accredited law school.

TAKEAWAY ONE: LAW SCHOOLS' PEDAGOGICAL WEAKNESSES ARE NOT NEW

The first takeaway is that the complaints about the educational flaws in the elite-model law school have always been obvious and have hardly changed over the years. Modern law schools do too little to prepare law students for the actual practice of law. That problem is neither new nor accidental.

Consider Alfred Zantzinger Reed's 1921 classic, *Training for the Public Profession of the Law*.[43] The Carnegie Foundation underwrote Reed's study. The Carnegie Foundation had established itself as an expert in professional education by publishing an earlier study of medical schools called the Flexner Report. The Flexner Report arrived in 1910, a time when the AMA and state medical boards were trying to close down a significant number of medical schools as substandard diploma mills.

The Flexner Report covered 155 different medical schools and lambasted most of them. It concluded that America needed "fewer and better doctors" and thus fewer and better medical schools.[44] The AMA leveraged the report and its own growing political muscle into becoming the accrediting body for medical schools.[45] Predictably, AMA control of accreditation thinned the ranks substantially. In 1920, just ten years after the Flexner Report studied 155 medical schools, there were only 85 medical schools in America.[46]

As you can imagine, the ABA and AALS were encouraged by the AMA's experience with the Flexner Report and asked the Carnegie Foundation to create a similar report on law schools. Surely a study of law schools would, like the Flexner Report, excoriate proprietary law schools and hail the Harvard model.

Ironically, this was not the case. Reed had a scathing critique for law schools of all stripes: "The failure of the modern American law school to make any adequate provision in its curriculum for practical training constitutes a remarkable educational anomaly."[47] Nor did Reed recommend mass closures of law schools. Instead, he noted that lawyers themselves were a stratified profession and that each of three different types of law schools had a role to play:

The scholarly law dean properly seeks to build up a "nursery for judges" that will make American law what American law ought to be. The practitioner bar examiner, with his satellite schools, properly seeks to prepare students for the immediate practice of law as it is. The night school authorities, finally, see most clearly that the interests not only of the individual but of the community demand that participation in the making and administration of the law shall be kept accessible to Lincoln's plain people. All these are worthy ideals. Taken together, they roughly embrace the service that the public expects from its law schools as a whole. But no single institution, pursuing its special aim, can attain both the others as well.[48]

Needless to say, the ABA and AALS were not pleased.[49] Instead of recognizing the inherent benefits of the Harvard model and the obvious deficiencies of any other model, Reed called the lack of practical training in the Harvard-model schools a "remarkable educational anomaly" and defended the roles that cheaper and leaner law schools might play.

To anyone familiar with the current critiques, Reed will sound right on point. Remember that in 2007, eighty-six years after Reed's report, a second Carnegie Foundation report entitled *Educating Lawyers* made essentially the same point about the desperate need for more practical training.[50] Current debates over the value of legal scholarship also echo Reed's idea that while there is certainly a place for a "scholarly" law schools, why should every potential lawyer in America be required to attend one?

TAKEAWAY TWO: LAW SCHOOLS' EXPERIENTIAL WEAKNESSES ARE NOT ACCIDENTAL

The history of the battle for supremacy in legal education explains crisply and clearly why law schools emphasize scholarship and theory over more practical pursuits. First, the most basic DNA of current law schools, including their structure and educational program, came from Harvard in the nineteenth century. Apples rarely fall far from their trees, and this provenance alone predicts an academic and theoretical bent.

Second, the Harvard model faced three different opponents, and each of them pushed law schools farther away from more practical legal education. The first two, loose admissions standards and apprenticeship, were easy to differentiate from a new, scientific, and university-based learning style. Just as we who are living in the Information Age have placed our hope in computers and algorithms to finally solve the world's puzzles, the Industrial Age hoped that scientific- and university-based inquiry would do the same. Bar associations and elite-model law professors argued that untrained or ill-trained lawyers were a hazard to the public and our system of government itself. By contrast, lawyers that studied law systematically would be demonstrably superior. This logic requires a particular type of law school, however: one where the faculty and students spend their time in the academic study of law, not how to actually practice law.

The location of these law schools also contributed to their mindset. While not all elite law schools were connected to a broader university, most were, and certainly the elite paradigm considered law schools an *academic* unit within a broader university community, rather than a freestanding trade school. In this way geography determined destiny. Attaching law schools to universities meant they were naturally more academic.

The battle against proprietary schools sharpened the purely academic focus even more. The history of the early AALS and ABA accreditation stories is one of continuous upward ratcheting. Every aspect of running an accredited law school grew more challenging: the pre–law school educational requirements, the length and nature of law school itself, the requirements of full-time faculty and a law library, and so forth. Each of these changes was defended as an improvement, but they were also clearly meant to widen the divide between the proprietary law schools and the Harvard-model law schools. Rather than try to meet proprietary law schools in the middle, the elite schools made the savvy strategic decision to go the other way and widen the gulf between the elites and everyone else. Consider the fact that for thirty years or more proprietary schools flourished by offering a simpler, cheaper, and faster product. Doesn't the strategy of becoming *more* expensive, lengthy, and academic seem puzzling?

Elite law schools may have hoped that ratcheting up accreditation standards (and the expense to students in time and tuition) might have a market advantage of differentiation from proprietary schools, but there is limited evidence that it worked out that way. To the contrary, before state supreme courts and bar associations required graduation from an

ABA-accredited law school as a prerequisite to sitting for the bar, proprietary schools were growing much faster than their university-based competitors.

But maybe rising accreditation standards had a different aim than appealing to law students. Perhaps, instead, they were meant to appeal to state supreme courts and other lawyer regulators. Increasingly academic law schools had at least two features that appealed to the legal elites that largely ran (and still largely run) the regulation of lawyers. First, then and now, elites have had a soft spot for high-minded and academic-sounding rhetoric. When you tell a state supreme court that requiring university-style law schools will result in a better class of lawyer going forward, that is an appealing message. Further, the "better class of lawyers" rhetoric also verged into explicit xenophobia and dislike of Jews and other immigrants. Night schools were associated with these allegedly less ethical lawyers, so eliminating them served a nativist purpose as well.

But these appeals were tried repeatedly from 1900 to 1929 with limited success. What actually swung the battle? The Great Depression. When the depression hit and lawyer incomes collapsed, any system that limited the number of new lawyers sounded good. As long as the new requirements were facially defensible (and the high-minded defenses of the scientific study of the law filled that need), the longer and more expensive the better.

Making law school longer and more expensive, but still not very practically focused, fit this conscious or unconscious anticompletive goal perfectly. Not only would law school be longer, harder, and more expensive, but also the graduates would need a few years of experience before they could begin to truly compete. The timing of the triumph of the Harvard model is not coincidental at all. It took an existential crisis for state supreme courts and bar associations to finally accede to the AALS and the ABA and require elite law school education.

It is often dangerous to ascribe motivations to past actors, and it is certainly likely that the players in this drama sincerely believed they were doing the best thing for themselves and the country. Nevertheless, if the elites of the legal profession and the elites of legal academia had gotten together and planned out a system of mutual benefit, it is hard to imagine a system better suited to that goal than the one we wound up with. The continuous growth in lawyer and law professor earnings and social status after World War II alone establishes the success of this imaginary plot.

◆ 2 ◆

THE NEW PROBLEM

THE JOB MARKET FOR LAW GRADS,
1990S TO THE PRESENT

In the symphony of recent bad press for law schools, there was a single motif that dominated all the others: the job market stinks. The stories in this vein were most prevalent in the 2011–2013 period, but the first bubblings started earlier and continued into 2017.

Here is just a smattering of headlines, including a prescient *Wall Street Journal* article from 2007, before the Great Recession really hit:

- 2007, *WSJ*, "Hard Case: Job Market Wanes for U.S. Lawyers."[1]
- 2009, *WSJ*, "As Students Fret over Jobs, Law Schools Get Creative"[2]
- 2011, *NYT*, "Is Law School a Losing Game?"[3]
- 2012, *WSJ*, "Law Grads Face a Brutal Job Market."[4]
- 2012, *Forbes*, "Why Attending Law School Is the Worst Career Decision You'll Ever Make."[5]
- 2013, *Slate*, "The Real Problem with Law Schools: Too Many Lawyers."[6]
- 2013, *Time*, "Just How Bad Off Are Law School Graduates?"[7]
- 2014, *Bloomberg*, "The Employment Rate Falls Again for Recent Law School Graduates."[8]
- 2016, *NYT*, "An Expensive Law Degree, and No Place to Use It."[9]
- 2016, *WSJ*, "Law School Graduate Employment Data Shows Decline in Legal Jobs."[10]
- 2016, *NYT*, "Too Many Law Students, Too Few Jobs."[11]
- 2017, *USA Today*, "Why You Might Want to Think Twice Before Going to Law School."[12]

There has been a pretty steady drumbeat of negativity on this issue. Has the critique been fair? This chapter argues that, by and large, yes, the coverage has been fair, with two significant caveats. The first is that the media narrative tended to treat the employment issues as if they were new after the recession. In reality, the market for law grads, and especially law grads at less prestigious schools or in the bottom half of their law school class, has been rough since the 1990s.

Second, the media has occasionally conflated the job market at large corporate law firms (so-called BigLaw) with the job market for all law graduates. This explains why the coverage turned so negative after the recession. The first wave of stories was actually about associate and partner layoffs in BigLaw, combined with a series of "the end is near for BigLaw" pieces and then "hiring collapses in BigLaw."[13] Since BigLaw was conflated with the overall market for lawyers, the starting date for the hiring downturn was set at the Great Recession. Over time the attention widened to encompass the weakness in the entire market, but BigLaw led the way. Now the situation in BigLaw seems to be stable to possibly improving, with hiring flat or up slightly and some firms raising first year salaries to $190,000.[14] This has meant that some of the harsher coverage of the job market has lightened up, though despite some improvement the overall market remains relatively slow.

This chapter presents data on the number of American lawyers, the market for legal services, and employment outcomes since the 1990s. The point of this overview is to convince you that we have had too many law graduates crowding into a saturated market for about thirty years or so. There is substantial disagreement about this claim, and I'll cover some of the dissenting voices at the end of the chapter. But first, here's my case.

AMERICA HAS A LOT OF LAWYERS

The first thing to note is that America has a lot of lawyers. Every year since 1880 the ABA has gathered a count of the number of American lawyers.[15] The count starts at 64,137 in 1880 and rises to 1,335,963 in 2018. Figure 2.1 graphs the data over the last 137 years of growth.

The growth rate accelerated substantially over the last sixty-five years. Between 1950 and 2018, the number of American lawyers increased by 503 percent.

For most of the years over this period, the legal profession grew faster than the population as a whole. Figure 2.2 is a graph that shows the number of Americans per lawyer from 1930 to 2018, comparing the ABA data to census data.[16] As the line declines, the number of lawyers is growing faster than the population.

In 1930, there was one lawyer for every 885 Americans. In 1970, there was one for every 627 Americans. In 2018, there was one lawyer for every 244 Americans. But 2018 was the first year since the 1990s when the number of lawyers did not grow faster than the US population. The last sustained period where the growth in the number of lawyers matched overall population growth was from 1958 to 1968. America now has more lawyers than any other country (depending on how you count India's lawyers) and more lawyers per capita than any country except Israel.[17]

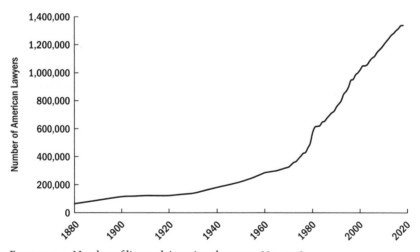

FIGURE 2.1. Number of licensed American lawyers, 1880–2018.

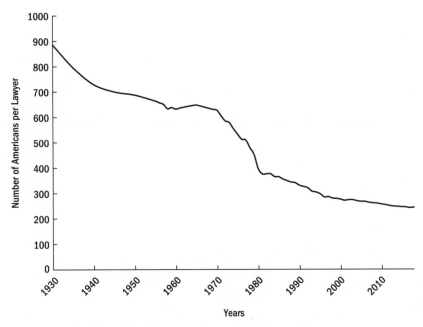

FIGURE 2.2. Number of Americans per lawyer, 1930–2018.

THE GROWTH IN LAWYERS MADE SENSE BETWEEN 1950 AND 1990; AFTER 1990, LESS SO

Not all of this growth was irrational or necessarily bad. The market for legal services in the United States grew substantially between 1960 and 2000. Figure 2.3 is the inflation-adjusted personal consumption expenditures (PCE) for US legal services from 1959 to 2018.[18] PCE is a Bureau of Economic Analysis measure of total expenditures by individuals in defined categories of goods or services. When it goes down, individuals are spending less in an area than they used to.

The growth from 1960 to 1990 is particularly marked. At the same time that the profession was increasing in size, expenditures on legal services were driving the growth. The period from 1960 through 1990 was something of an economic miracle. The profession grew in size,

FIGURE 2.3. Real personal consumption expenditures for legal services, 1959–2018.

earnings, and income. The rising tide floated all boats, and lawyers of all stripes benefitted.[19]

The collapse from 2003 to 2013, however, shows the struggles lawyers have faced recently. If you want to feel better about the recent trend, note that PCE reached a bottom in 2013, with a slight upward trajectory since. In 2013 Americans spent less on legal services than any year since 1987. Overall, the post-1990 story has been mixed. The profession continued to grow in size, but revenue growth was basically flat. If you consider the inflation-adjusted gross domestic product (GDP) for legal services, 2014 was the worst year since 1997. Nor was law's slide solely the result of the recession. By 2013 and 2014, the economy as a whole was bouncing back while law continued its worst slide in decades. Overall GDP rose steadily rise from 2009 forward. Legal services GDP kept declining through 2014 and still has not fully recovered.

THERE ARE A LOT OF AMERICANS WITH JDs WHO DO NOT WORK AS LAWYERS

Unconvinced? Consider the employment results for law school graduates since the 1990s. Every year since 1985, the National Association for Law Placement (NALP) has gathered placement data for graduates of American law schools. In a helpful and transparent move, NALP recently published two different longitudinal sets of data. The first set simply lists the percentage of known graduates of American law schools who have been able to find work requiring a JD from 1985 to 2016.[20] Note the word "known." Every year there are some law graduates that NALP has no employment information on. More on those folks in a minute.

Figure 2.4 is the NALP data from 1985 to 2017 expressed as the percentage of law grads unable to find work requiring a JD nine to ten months after graduation (the figure changed to ten months after graduation in 2014). As the bars go up, the results are worse. The first thing to note is that employment rates before 1991 were much stronger than in any year afterward. Second, every year from 2010 to 2015 is worse

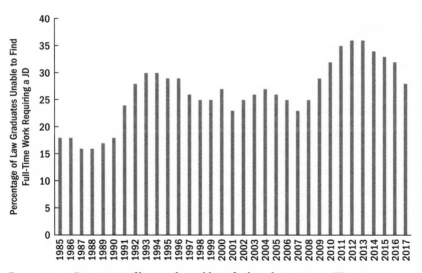

FIGURE 2.4. Percentage of law grads unable to find work requiring a JD, 1985–2017.

than any of the previous twenty-five years. The post-recession hiring market has indeed been rough. Third, the graduating classes of 2014 and 2015 showed improvement expressed as percentages. Those graduating classes were smaller though, so the absolute number of jobs requiring bar passage actually fell in those years.[21] The years 2016 and 2017 presented unmitigated good news: the percentage finding work as a lawyer and the total number of those jobs increased. These were the first years both of those numbers increased since 2007. This book went to press before NALP released its 2018 report, but the ABA's 2018 data suggests another year of improvement in this percentage. Last, even though the numbers have been especially bad recently, employment has been weak since the 1990s. As Marc Gans has aptly noted, the problem of law graduate underemployment and unemployment is not new.[22]

But figure 2.4 only includes *known* graduates from law schools. Given that there is an unknown group every year, what would employment results look like if we lumped the unknown folks in with the known grads who could not find work as a lawyer? Not so good.

But first, two caveats:

1. The percentage of unknown graduates comes from a different dataset that only runs from the present back to 1994. So, figure 2.5 does not include the more robust placement results from 1985 to 1993.
2. The percentage of unknown graduates starts at a relative high point in 1994, when almost 20 percent of the class was "unknown," and steadily declines over the years, reaching a low point in 2017 when NALP had data on almost all graduates.[23] Thus, in 2017, it is very likely that almost all of the unknown graduates did not have full-time employment as lawyers. Law schools make every effort to unearth every last employed graduate for at least three reasons. The first is that employment (and especially full-time, continuous legal employment), is a significant component of the *U.S. News* rankings, so schools desperately want their numbers to look better, not worse.[24] Second, as chapters 6 and 7 explain, the Department of Education

and ABA are paying increasing attention to employment outcomes in accreditation, so schools have an existential concern with these results. Last, websites like Law School Transparency and *The Last Gen X American* have spent a lot of energy gathering and disseminating sometimes-embarrassing school-specific outcomes, and there is nothing like sunshine to focus attention on a problem. Other evidence of law school desperation on this front? A random audit of ten law schools in 2016 found that five of them had some level of irregularities in their employment data.[25] So if anything, the number of fully employed law students is likely to be fudged higher than lower.

But as figure 2.5 shifts backward in time, a skeptical reader may begin to doubt the supposition that all or virtually all of the unknown graduates did not have legal employment. In the 1990s and early 2000s it is apparent that law schools did not try as hard to unearth every employed law graduate, so it may well be that some portion of the 1994 unknown graduates did, in fact, have jobs requiring a JD.

With those caveats in mind, we see in figure 2.5 that our post-recession slump is just part of a twenty-year story of employment struggles for law graduates. Figure 2.5 shows the percentages of law graduates unable to find work that requires a JD plus the percentage of unknown graduates, counted at nine or ten months after graduation.

I present a number of caveats with this data because if you combine the graduates whom we know were unemployed or underemployed with the unknown category, the results for law schools since 1994 look pretty terrible. The three best years for employment were 2000, 2007, and 2008, and the *only* year where this measure of underemployment was below 30 percent was 2007. Looking at all of the data from 1994 to 2017, it appears that more than a third of law school graduates were unable to find full-time work as a lawyer in the period immediately after graduation.

Things have calmed down since the 2011–13 period, when the results were the worst since the mid-1990s, but the situation is still relatively grim: every year from 2010 to 2016, 35 percent or more of American law graduates

What about those who don't intend to be lawyers?

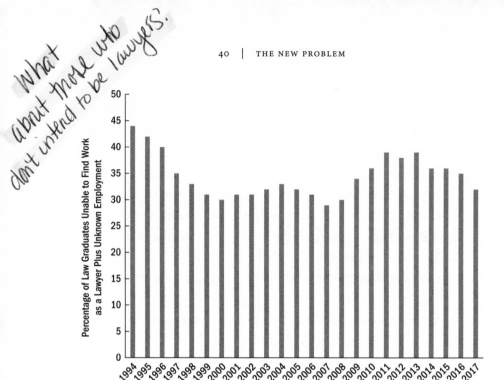

FIGURE 2.5. Percentage of law grads unable to find work requiring a JD plus unknown employment result, 1994–2017.

failed to find full-time work as a lawyer nine to ten months after graduation. The year 2017 was slightly cheerier but hardly offsets the last decade.

The results above are also expressed as percentages, not in absolute numbers. Because recent graduating classes have been much smaller, the raw number of jobs has shrunk considerably. Just looking at the raw numbers, 2017 was the worst hiring year in the last twenty. The high point for these jobs was in 2007, when more than 31,000 law graduates gained employment as a lawyer. In 2017, that number had fallen to 23,906, which was the lowest total number of legal jobs for graduates since 1995. The overall downward trend in hiring since 2007, and the more recent slide from 2013, belies optimism over a bounce back in the market.

The situation for full-time jobs working in law firms was equally bad. The year 2007 was the peak year, with 20,611 graduates finding work at a law firm. That number had fallen to 16,390 by 2017, again the worst number of law firm jobs since the mid-1990s.

BigLaw hiring (as opposed to all law firms) has been worse since 2008, but is not as drastic as overall law firm hiring.[26] Nevertheless, the prognostications for BigLaw going forward are pretty mixed. If you are particularly interested in this topic, two 2017 reports, one by Hildebrandt Consulting/Citi Private Bank and another by Altman Weil consulting capture the current market pretty well.[27] BigLaw has certainly "recovered" since 2008, if by recovered you mean "pulled out of a death spiral." But the days of go-go growth are clearly behind us, and both reports are packed with discouraging information about an "oversupply of lawyers" and "decreasing demand for services."[28] Between technological shifts, increasing demands for efficiency from corporate legal offices, and resistance to change, potential law students are wise to worry about the top end of the market going forward.

The NALP data actually looks better than the American Bar Association (ABA) data over the same period. In 2011 the ABA changed the way that law schools reported the employment results of their graduates.[29] The bad news is that the changes make it hard to draw any conclusions from the ABA data before 2011 (which is why we start with the NALP data that go back to the 1990s). The good news is that the ABA reporting is mandatory and linked to accreditation, so much less likely to be fudged or "misreported" than the NALP data. Unsurprisingly, the ABA data also looks worse than the NALP data. Here are the percentages of graduates who had full-time, long-term employment in jobs that required a JD nine months after graduation:

Year	Percentage of grads employed in FTLT, JD required
2011	55%
2012	56%
2013	57%
2014	60%
2015	59%
2016	62%
2017	66%

There is good news and bad news in the data as well. The good news is the 2017 result, which is a massive improvement over 2016, let alone 2011. Across most measures, law schools are seeing better numbers in 2017–18, with none stronger than the 2017 employment result. The bad news is that the ABA's number started at such a low baseline. In four of these seven years, less than 60 percent of law grads had full-time jobs as lawyers nine months after graduation! And the high-water mark is 2017's result, where a third of law graduates ended up in a suboptimal employment situation. We do not have the data from before 2011, but if 2017 is the best law schools can do, much work remains.

DO SHRINKING CLASSES MEAN BETTER EMPLOYMENT OUTCOMES?

In 2014, *Slate*'s Jordan Weissmann wrote a column entitled "Now Is a Great Time to Apply to Law School." The central theme was that smaller classes would make finding work after graduation a relative cinch, even if hiring stayed flat going forward.[30] Steven Freedman made a similar point in 2014 in a series of blog posts at *The Faculty Lounge* entitled "Enroll Today!"[31]

The problem is that hiring out of law school appears stubbornly consistent regardless of the size of the graduating class: roughly a third of all graduates will not be able to find work as a lawyer. As of yet, the trend seems structural, and an understanding of law firm hiring suggests why. Law firms largely hire based on law school GPA and associated class rank.[32] At almost every law school that is not named Yale, Harvard, or Stanford, there is a group of students in the lower percentiles of the class that really struggle to find work. So, shrinking the number of graduates does not really address the "bottom half of the class" employment problem. There is always a bottom half of the class no matter how small the class is.

In defense of Weissmann and Freedman, note that law graduate hiring does seem weirdly inflexible so far. The available evidence suggests that the market for legal services has improved over the last three or four years, or at least stabilized. But then shouldn't entry-level hiring have improved or stayed the same? The answer is no. It appears that even in an improving market there is a large chunk of law graduates whom employers will not hire, even if the total number of available applicants shrinks. It may be that these employers are just leaving these positions unfilled until they can find a more suitable applicant next year. Or maybe they are hiring lateral and other underemployed candidates before the less attractive law graduates. Whatever the cause, law graduate underemployment appears to be here to stay, regardless of the size of the graduating classes.

BUT MAYBE NONLAWYERS ARE HAPPY/HAPPIER?

Remember to read these underemployment graphs against the tuition and debt graphs presented later in chapter 5. When law school was cheaper, it was much easier to argue that "you can do anything with a law degree" or that "it's inherently valuable to learn to think like a lawyer." When the average debt load for a law graduate is above $130,000, it is not hard to imagine that graduates who get jobs they might have been qualified for without a JD will not be very happy.

But maybe that supposition is wrong. Maybe the JD holders who are not working as lawyers are perfectly happy with their choice. Most readers of this book will know a law school graduate who is flourishing outside of law. For example, Barack Obama and Jerry Springer are not working full time as lawyers, and they seem pretty chipper about it. More run-of-the-mill examples abound. Anecdotally, I have had multiple students who graduated, passed the bar, and then happily chose to do something other than practice law for a variety of valid reasons.

There is also evidence that nonlawyer JD holders do pretty well financially. Michael Simkovic and Frank McIntyre have controversially claimed that a law degree boosts lifetime earnings by as much as a million dollars, including for JD holders who do not work as lawyers.[33] One large study of law graduates who failed to pass the bar found that over time their earnings did come close to their classmates who were working as lawyers.[34]

Nevertheless, the available data suggests that JD holders who are not working as lawyers are not particularly happy about it. The best longitudinal information on law graduates is the American Bar Foundation's outstanding "After the JD" study, which surveyed the same sample of law school graduates three times after graduation: three years out (After the JD I), seven years out (After the JD II), and finally at twelve years out (After the JD III).[35] In both the After the JD II and After the JD III studies, the lawyers who were the *least* satisfied with their employment were working in jobs that did not require a JD.[36] These same graduates were also the least likely to be pleased with their decision to go to law school, and their satisfaction declined in each of the three surveys.[37] The percentage of graduates in these jobs also grew between the first and the third survey, suggesting that the disappointing job placement results nine to ten months after graduation do not ameliorate over time.[38]

But perhaps this was only a postgraduation problem. Maybe after more people passed the bar or had time to network they eventually ended up with full-time jobs requiring bar passage. The available data suggests that roughly "one-third to one-half of U.S. residents with law degrees do not work as lawyers."[39]

Marc Gans published an in-depth study that compared an estimated number of Americans with a JD against three counts of American lawyers: the ABA's count of every licensed lawyer in America, the Census Bureau's count of every American who told census takers she or he was a lawyer, and the Bureau of Labor Statistics' Occupation Outlook Handbook (OOH) count of lawyers, drawn from businesses and other market studies.[40] The takeaway is that the gap between the number of JD holders and Americans working as lawyers is not limited to only nine months after graduation. To the contrary, these data confirm that a third or more of JD holders are not working as lawyers.

THE NEW PROBLEM | 45

Gans's data is interesting because as of the mid-1970s, there was not a noticeable gap between the estimated number of Americans with JDs and the various counts of lawyers, suggesting nearly full legal employment for JD holders. From the 1970s forward, the gap between the number of JD holders and lawyers has grown pretty continuously. If the 2016 OOH estimates are correct, the gap between the number of law school graduates and Americans working full time as a lawyer has reached over 700,000 people and only 54 percent of working-age law grads are working as a lawyer.

A comparison between doctors and lawyers is also instructive. In 2016, if you compare the number of licensed lawyers (the ABA count) with the OOH count, roughly 36 percent of licensed lawyers did not work full time as a lawyer. By comparison, in 2014, the gap was only about 23 percent in medicine.[41] The supposition that anyone who has an MD, is licensed, and wants to work as a doctor *can* work as a doctor is supported by the available data. Some even project a *shortage* of doctors going forward.[42]

BUT WAIT, I THOUGHT THE PROBLEMS STARTED IN 2008? AMERICA'S TWO LEGAL PROFESSIONS

So, if it is true that some portion of law grads have struggled since the 1990s, why did the "trouble with law school" narrative (and the resulting collapse/decline in applications) start after 2008? This is because the private practice of law in America is divided into two almost completely separate market segments. On the high end, we have BigLaw, where lawyers work in large firms primarily serving corporations and very wealthy individuals. This is the legal market that has traditionally been best covered by the media, most depicted in popular culture, and best understood by law professors.[43] Because this market *boomed* from the 1980s until the Great Recession, most everyone had the impression that all was well.[44]

From time immemorial, however, the majority of American lawyers in private practice have worked as solo practitioners or members of small firms serving the consumer market for legal services.[45] Those lawyers have not done as well.

Evidence for the "two professions" theory abounds, but the widening gulf between BigLaw and everyone else is still worth establishing. Start with the IRS data on the provision of legal services. Every year from 1967 forward, the Internal Revenue Service has gathered, anonymized, and released two different sets of tax returns from people who provide legal services: solo practitioners and partners.

Here are a few caveats before figure 2.6 presents the income data on these two different categories. First, the IRS category of "Legal Services" contains a small amount of nonlawyer businesses (title companies and the like). Second, neither category contains lawyers working in incorporated business entities, which may depress earnings reported for both, because some successful lawyers have chosen to form LLCs or PLLCs rather than remain in partnerships or sole proprietorships. Third, the partnership category also contains small partnerships with few or no employees that look a lot more like solo practices than corporate law firms. This means the partnership data does not include some BigLaw lawyers who work in professional corporations but does include some small partnerships, so the average earnings in this category may run low. Likewise, both categories include some lawyers who are working part time, so earnings may be slightly depressed.

Because of these caveats, some have challenged the usefulness of this data, especially for understanding the earnings of solo practitioners.[46] Nevertheless, I consider the IRS data easily the best available data for comparisons between law firm partners and solo practitioners. It is longitudinal and annual since 1967 as well as the only national data set that clearly separates out these two different types of lawyers. It is also sworn and subject to perjury, so it is all the more likely to be accurate.

Figure 2.6 shows just how much the earnings of these two cohorts of lawyers have divided over the years.

The solid line represents partner earnings; the dotted line, solo practitioner earnings. The dashed line represents solo practitioner earnings,

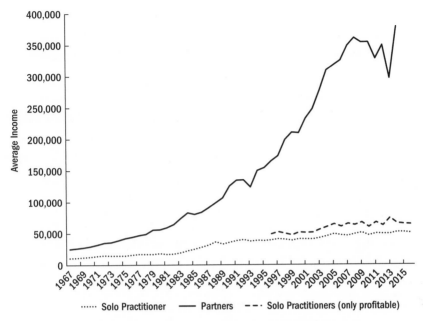

FIGURE 2.6. IRS income data, average earnings by lawyer type, 1967–2016.

counting *only* practices with net income (so eliminating any lawyers who lost money in their practice). Using either estimate of solo practitioner earnings, figure 2.6 shows several important trends.

In 1967, partner and solo practitioner earnings were much more similar than they are today. Partners earned roughly 2.5 as much as solo practitioners. In 2014, partners earned six or seven times as much. If you use the 2014 AmLaw 100 calculation of "profits per partner" ($1.55 million was the average partner payout at the 100 biggest law firms in America), the earnings are almost sixteen times as much. This means that in 1967 you could talk about the "private practice of law" or "the earnings of lawyers" as a unified whole and make sense. That has not been true for a long time. Likewise, if you went to law school in the 1950s or early 60s hoping to be a law firm partner and wound up working as a solo practitioner, you earned less than expected, but not *radically* less.

Second, the post-2008 period has been much worse for partners than solo practitioners, although the 2014 data should cheer optimists. Between 2008 and 2013, partner earnings declined by 25 percent, although they gained it all back in 2014. Over the same period solo practitioner earnings were basically flat.

Last, the earnings in figure 2.6 are not adjusted for inflation. Look how relatively flat the two solo practitioner earnings lines are. When you see a relatively flat earnings line not adjusted for inflation, you can guess that earnings were in fact down. That is certainly true for solo practitioners, who lost roughly a third of their earning power between 1967 and 2016.

The NALP starting salary curves show the same trend. The normal salary distribution is a bell curve, with most earners in the middle and a diminishing amount on the high end and the low end.[47] In a functioning market the more expensive providers earn more because of higher perceived value. The lower-end producers are just starting out or have less perceived value. The bell curve occurs so often in natural and human phenomena that it is often called the "normal distribution."[48] Business school starting salaries, for example, tend to resemble a bell curve.[49]

Starting salaries for law school grads, by comparison, look quite different. Figure 2.7 shows the NALP starting salary chart from 2017.[50] Law grad salaries are "bimodal" rather than a bell curve. This means there are two distinct peaks and that few graduates actually earn the mean salary. The graph also only displays the *reported* salaries (19,719), rather than all the salaries of the 34,922 graduates of ABA-accredited law schools in 2017. Because of how NALP gathers salary data, it is very unlikely that the uncounted salaries are in the $180,000 range, so the missing salaries should not be added to the high-end, $180,000 spike. Instead, assume that there are another 15,000 salaries in the lower-end salary hump clustered around $45,000. This is why NALP publishes a lower "adjusted mean" salary.

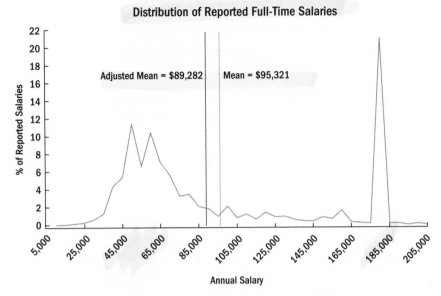

FIGURE 2.7. Starting salaries for law graduates, 2017. Source: NALP.

Note: Graph is based on 19,719 salaries reported for full-time jobs lasting a year or more—a few salaries above $205,000 are excluded from the graph for clarity, but not from the percentage calculations. The left-hand peaks of the graph reflect salaries of $40,000 to $70,000, which collectively accounted for just over half of reported salaries. The right-hand peak shows that salaries of $180,000 accounted for 21% of reported salaries. However, more complete salary coverage for jobs at large firms heightens this peak and diminishes the left-hand peaks, and as a result the unadjusted mean overstates the average starting salary by an estimated 6.8%. Nonetheless, as both the unadjusted arithmetic mean and the adjusted mean show, relatively few salaries are close to either mean. For purposes of this graph, all reported salaries were rounded to the nearest $5,000. However, the mean is based on salaries as reported and the adjusted mean reflects a weighting of those salaries.

Bimodal salary distributions are pretty unusual. When I asked a labor economist for a market that resembled law, she responded, "Hmm. Maybe professional baseball?"

The division between these two professions masked the struggles of many lawyers pre-recession. Because BigLaw was booming, many assumed all was well because many law professors, journalists, and most importantly, law school applicants thought that BigLaw *was* the entire market for lawyers. While the general public was unaware that some law grads were struggling, law schools and career services offices were certainly aware. The problem was informally referred to as a "bottom half of the class problem," meaning that schools have long been aware that students with below average GPAs have had a hard time finding full-time work as a lawyer, especially outside the top fourteen schools or so. Over time applicants and everyone else grew wiser, to the detriment of law school bottom lines.

ISN'T A LAW DEGREE WORTH ONE MILLION DOLLARS?

In 2013, Seton Hall law professor Michael Simkovic and Rutgers Business School professor Frank McIntyre released "The Economic Value of a Law Degree," which estimates the lifetime economic value of a law degree to be one million dollars.[51] Nature abhors a vacuum, and Simkovic has become the most vocal and vociferous defender of the economic advantages of a law degree. Along with the "million-dollar law degree" study, Simkovic has released further work exploring which college majors receive the largest earnings boost from law school,[52] and a series of blog posts and feuds with everyone from the *New York Times*[53] to *Above the Law*[54] to me.[55]

Simkovic has also taken some pretty big leaps from his original study, including arguing that the negative news coverage of law schools has cost the prospective law students who have not gone to law school "tens of thousands or even hundreds of thousands of dollars. The total economic harm across all prospective law students could easily be in the low billions of dollars."[56] Reread the above claim and let it sink in. Simkovic does not think that the recent downturn in law school applications is an understandable market correction. Instead, Simkovic posits that we are living through an economic disaster because of our missing JD holders.

The original study used Census SIPP data that identifies "law degree holders," rather than just practicing lawyers. This is helpful, since the IRS data (and other census data) tends to be sorted by employment, not degree earned. Given that a third to one half of all JD holders do not work as lawyers, the SIPP data is excellent for measuring the earnings of JD holders, rather than considering just working lawyers. The methodology of the study seems sound, and if past performance guaranteed future success, maybe it is a tragedy that more people are not going to law school.

There are, however, very good reasons to believe that the study does not predict such a rosy future for current students. Heaps of human effort and many pixels have been devoted to this issue. Paul Campos, *Above the Law*, Brian Tamanaha, Matt Leichter, and Steven Harper have all taken turns critiquing Simkovic's work.[57] I will not summarize that lengthy debate here, except to cover some of my own concerns. First, law school is much more expensive now than it used to be. That affects the value of the degree. Second, there are many more JD holders now than there used to be, especially given the swollen classes of 2007–2011. Simkovic's data spans a whole generation of law degree holders, including individuals who graduated law school thirty to forty years ago, when there were both fewer schools and fewer students, and thus less competition. Third, it may be correct that JD holders who fail the bar or do not work as lawyers eventually see a salary boost, but it comes at a price, as noted above. JD holders who are not working as lawyers are not particularly happy about it. Studies show the same for individuals who fail the bar and never pass: their earning potential eventually rebounds, but they remain scarred by the experience.[58] Finally, Simkovic has little to say about the technological challenges facing future lawyers. The next chapter covers that topic.

If you are unconvinced and think the preceding section has unfairly represented lawyer earning potential, that is fine. For our purposes the main point is that most Americans think a JD is worth less than it used to be, and that has affected law school applications and attendance. On this point, Simkovic and everyone else basically agree.

FUTURE SHOCK

WILL COMPUTERS REPLACE LAWYERS?

I have the good fortune to serve as the chair of the admissions committee at the University of Tennessee College of Law. The main work is reading admissions files, but as part of my role I also speak frequently with people, young and old, who are considering going to law school. Five years ago, I spent a lot of time talking about the job market, but in the last few years I've been inundated with questions about artificial intelligence (AI). Potential law students are worried about it, often asking whether there will even be lawyer jobs in the future.

It is, honestly, a somewhat puzzling concern for several reasons. First, student worries over job placement seem to have settled down, although the job market has not actually improved that much. Again, this may be because BigLaw has shown at least some signs of life, or because the media covering these issues moved on from a tired story (legal employment stinks!) to a sexier one (the robots are coming!). Regardless, the employment market is a long-standing issue and still provides a real reason not to attend law school, whereas AI is a much more speculative one.

Second, why AI? Existing and relatively well-established technologies, such as document review/e-discovery programs or the online legal services offered by LegalZoom or Rocket Lawyer, are already displacing lawyers and seem likelier to continue to do so than some more futuristic version of AI, at least in the near term. But for now, those technologies seem incremental and small bore, while AI offers a sexier worry: an existential-level threat rather than a gradual one.

Humans love to worry about this type of risk. Consider the people who refuse to swim in the ocean out of fear of sharks but drink all day on the beach and then drive home. I promise you that one of those behaviors is much more dangerous than the other, and yet our brains prioritize high salience and terrifying risks over more common ones every day.[1] Examples abound. People fear spiders and snakes more than falling, yet falling is much more dangerous. People fear cancer more than heart disease, even though heart disease is more common and more easily avoided.

Anyone with even a passing familiarity with science-fiction movies or novels will recognize that humans have a particular fascination with the threat posed by super-intelligent computers. From *2001: A Space Odyssey* through *The Matrix*, *The Terminator*, and even Pixar's *Wall-E* and *The Incredibles*, this theme has captured the public imagination. Naturally, lawyers and law students cannot help but picture a brilliant computer taking their job—it's been among our greatest fears for years.

AI EXPLODES ON THE SCENE

Lawyers have shown substantial interest in the topic. The *ABA Journal* featured legal AI on its cover in April 2016 and again in June 2017.[2] AI and computerization are now regular subjects of discussion in continuing legal education, law school, and bar association programs.

As with other "law schools/lawyers are doomed" stories, legal AI has crossed over into the popular imagination. Consider the following 2017 headlines: "Rise of the Robolawyers," the *Atlantic*; "Lawyers Could Be Replaced by Artificial Intelligence," *CNBC*; "Artificial Intelligence Closes In on the Work of Junior Lawyers," the *Financial Times*; and "Why Artificial Intelligence Might Replace Your Lawyer," Ozy.com.[3] The Ozy.com piece concludes, "So, young students who dream of becoming a lawyer—there is no longer a predictable career path to follow. Perhaps it's best to ditch law school for now and first get a degree in computer science."[4]

A 2017 Bloomberg story about JP Morgan's use of legal computeriza-tion is instructive.[5] The article described how JP Morgan had created a computer program called "Contract Intelligence or COIN" that took over the job of reviewing approximately 12,000 new wholesale contracts per year. JP Morgan claimed the program replaced "360,000 hours" of staff time between lawyers and loan officers. Because of the large volume of repetitive contracts, COIN was able to learn to spot problems in the paperwork more accurately and quickly than individual humans.

On the one hand, wow! Even in the likely event that JP Morgan is grossly overstating the amount of time lawyers spent on this task in the past (it seems probable that loan officers or paralegals would take the first and only cut at reviewing this sort of paperwork), letting a com-puter do all of that work does suggest that computers are likely taking jobs from humans, whether lawyer jobs or otherwise. Further, the article suggests that COIN is actually better than humans at the task.

On the other hand, the article oversells the program substantially and conflates teaching a computer to do a repetitive task (such as reviewing 12,000 relatively similar contracts) with teaching a computer to do all legal work. Routine contract review of the sort now delegated to COIN has not been done by lawyers for years, if ever, because an intelligent and literate adult without a law degree can check to see that a form contract is signed in all the right places and that the variable entries are correct. As a parallel example, consider real estate closings. In states that do not require lawyers to attend such closings, a real estate or title insurance agent usually handles the formalities, because actual legal expertise is rarely required.

It should also not be surprising that computers are at least as good as humans at reviewing these documents. Programs like COIN that comb through reams of documents for repeated problems or themes can focus on what computers excel at: applying a set of rules to a large mass of data/documents. Humans tend to get tired or bored by these tasks and thus make mistakes. Ironically, a single human might gain sig-nificant expertise by reviewing all 12,000 of these contracts personally, but that same human would grow so bored and surly that the error rate might overwhelm the growth in expertise. A computer, however, has the advantage of examining all of the documents with no exhaustion. To paraphrase *The Terminator*, these machines do not eat, or sleep, or feel pity, or remorse, or fear. They just quietly and quickly review form contracts for anomalies.

These sorts of programs use humans to guide the computers, and at first the computers are often relatively bad at the task. But over time as the humans point out mistakes, programmers can tweak the algorithms to the point that the computers are better than humans at catching routine errors. Computers are theoretically not as good at catching strange or "out of sample"–type errors, but as the computer assimilates feedback and gains experience, even those sorts of issues should grow less common.

The JP Morgan article thus shows two related themes perfectly. On the one hand, computers are currently very good, and sometimes better than humans, at handling repetitive, rules-based tasks like reviewing form contracts. This is already displacing some lower-level lawyers. On the other hand, it is a big leap from repetitive, rules-based tasks to more complicated and contextual tasks, where humans still seem very necessary. Marc Andreessen famously noted, "The spread of computers and the internet will put jobs in two categories: people who tell computers what to do, and people who are told by computers what to do."[6] Some (many?) law jobs are demonstrably vulnerable to replacement by machines. It is already happening. That said, other law jobs are obviously in the preferable "telling machines what to look for or do" category, and that seems likely to be the case for the foreseeable future.

AI DEFINED

Before we address the specifics, it is worth noting that despite the ubiquity of the term "artificial intelligence," there is not an accepted scientific definition for AI.[7] The "artificial" part is easy enough. We all know that means *nonhuman*. The "intelligence" part is harder to pin down though, as there is little consensus on what intelligence, human or otherwise, really consists of. One working definition of AI is a computer's ability "to perform tasks that normally require human intelligence."[8] This description is helpful because it avoids philosophical niceties about the nature of intelligence and focuses instead on *functional* intelligence, in other words, places where computers can reliably replace human efforts.

This definition may seem overbroad to some readers, however, as it includes a mass of existing computer applications in law and elsewhere in the definition of "AI." COIN or other document review programs are obvious legal examples. More generally, run-of-the-mill programs like Google Maps clearly fit this definition. Humans used to spend significant time examining maps and considering the best routes from here to there. I, for one, counted on this as a friendly and neutral topic of conversation when visiting with distant family or friends. If conversation lagged, I would ask, "I took I-81 to Route 7 to get here. Is that the fastest way?" A lively debate inevitably ensued. Sadly, I have rarely had that conversation since the advent of Google Maps. Why bother? We have machines to definitively answer that sort of question now.

There is a technology truism that before a computer can handle a task, we consider that task an example of artificial intelligence. Once that task is automated, we call it programming.

RULES-BASED VERSUS DATA-DRIVEN VERSUS TRUE AI

If you use the broad functional definition of AI (computers handling tasks that once required human intelligence), you can see three categories of legal AI: rules-based programs, data-driven programs, and the science-fiction future of "true AI." These three categories proceed from the simplest programs to the most advanced. Predictably, the simplest of them, the rules-based field, is farthest along.

The American law professor who has been hustling the hardest in this space is Chicago-Kent's Daniel Katz.[9] He is the first law professor to apply these three categories to law, and if you're looking for a quick and pithy overview of the state of AI and the law, Katz has a continuously updated version of his slideshow on the topic on his blog, *Computational Legal Studies*.[10]

RULES-BASED AI

Rules-based programs use decision trees and set rules to guide a computer through a legal task. If you have used the interactive document production programs on LegalZoom, Rocket Lawyer, or A2J Author, you have used a rules-based legal program. Tax-preparation programs like Turbo Tax work in the same way. The computer asks the user a series of questions and uses the answers to populate a legal or tax form at the end, as well as to decide what questions to ask next.

Take LegalZoom's will-writing program. It starts with some introductory information about wills and then asks the user to answer some preliminary questions: Are you married? Do you have minor children? Adult children? Grandchildren? A pet? A home or other real estate?

You then enter your name, address, and county of residence. The program uses your answers to guide what questions to ask next based on what you have already written and the local, governing law. The process continues from here, with some humorously specific questions such as, "Do you want to disinherit a child (optional)?" Each answer leads to another question and also populates a portion of the eventual will documents.

LegalZoom, Rocket Lawyer, and A2J Author have worked very, very hard on these "smart documents." If you haven't taken these programs for a spin, you absolutely should, just to see how sophisticated they are. That said, as a matter of programming or technology, these programs are remarkably simple. The decision-tree- or branching-logic-style programming of "If the answer to question A is yes, then ask question A.1; if the answer is no, then skip to question B" has been the norm since the 1970s.

While the programming is easy, the real challenge is to reduce complicated or fuzzy legal areas into rules-based areas. Programmers work with lawyers to "storyboard" each of these programs, thinking carefully about what questions are and are not necessary, how to ask them in a simple yet precise fashion, and what level of detail and nuance is too much. These challenges are compounded by the need to draft the text in plain language so that an average reader can understand. Further, because the program must use strict rules, accommodating legal or personal nuance is challenging.

Drafting baseline questions such as "are you married" is easy. Drafting questions to help the machine decide whether the user would be better served by a living trust rather than a traditional will is harder. As the complexity grows, drafting becomes exponentially more challenging. The most prevalent critique of LegalZoom and its kin is that its questions and documents lack the necessary nuance to correctly address complex legal issues. A simple will is likely to be something the program can handle reliably well, but more complicated documents for trusts or tax shelters may arguably encounter problems.[11] That said, there are almost no examples of injured consumers suing LegalZoom to date, so the arguments for consumer harm may be overstated.[12]

These do-it-yourself online legal services are now well established. If you visit the LegalZoom or Rocket Lawyer sites, you can see hundreds of forms matching almost any kind of legal document a small business or individual might need. As of yet, these forms have not reached the most complicated areas of law, such as mergers or a complicated civil complaint, but they could get there eventually. The main barrier to expanding their reach is legal complexity. This is, as we'll discuss below, great news for lawyers, as the law seems unlikely to get simpler anytime soon.

DATA-DRIVEN AI

The next category is what Katz calls "data-driven AI." You are probably already familiar with the term "big data," and data-driven legal AI is a subspecies of that general area. Because of the exponential growth in computing power and inexpensive data storage, companies can gather more data than ever before and can set algorithms loose on the data to find helpful patterns. A stand-out example is the *New York Times* story of how Target figured out that a young woman was pregnant before her father did, based solely on her buying habits in her first months of pregnancy.[13] Basically, Target reverse-engineered the buying habits of pregnant women by looking backward at the purchases of women who later signed up for baby registries at Target. Algorithms identified common patterns of purchases (such as onesies or ice cream), and Target's program created a likelihood of pregnancy scale. At the point where your purchases began to closely resemble those of other pregnant women, Target sent you a bunch of coupons for diapers, baby furniture, and formula. This type of sorting only became available because of Target's mass data collection and the ability of computers to work through a staggering and unimaginable volume of information: individual sales of every Target customer over a period of years. In the *Times* article, a pregnant teenager received the coupons, and her father, who did not yet know she was pregnant, found them and complained vociferously to Target, wondering why they were encouraging his teenage daughter to become pregnant. A few weeks later, after a heart-to-heart with his daughter, he apologized to Target—their algorithm had known more than he had.

Document or contract review works on the same basic premise. A computer program examines a massive database (all of a company or division's emails or contracts, for example) and then uses algorithms and human guidance to find responsive documents for discovery or noncompliant documents for contract review or due diligence. These document programs are among the earliest and most successful applications of data-driven programming to the field of law.

For example, a typical eDiscovery program starts with a human lawyer looking over a small number of documents and telling the program the key terms to look for, which documents are useful and which are irrelevant, and which ones may be privileged from discovery. Then the program uses that guidance to process a larger subset of the documents. The human assesses these results and then "teaches" the computer by indicating which legitimate candidates the computer failed to spot and which irrelevant documents the computer erroneously flagged. It is this iterative process that allows the computer to improve. On its first time through the documents, the computer is not much better than a simple "search and retrieve" process for certain terms or names. But as the computer learns which documents it failed to categorize correctly, it can start to recognize what to look for from the documents themselves, rather than by following a set of inflexible human rules created ahead of time. This process can go through multiple iterations, depending on how challenging the project is and how important absolute accuracy is.

This computer learning process is the key distinction between rules-based and data-driven programming. It is also the reason that data-driven programming has so much more disruptive potential for the field of law than rules-based programming. Rules-based programming is inevitably limited to the human insight, time, and effort required to program the rules in the first place. These programs also tend inevitably to be inflexible and pitched to the lowest common denominator. Data-driven programs, by contrast, can acquire nuance over time through a combination of human guidance and mining the existing data for patterns humans might not find.

At least for eDiscovery, these programs work quite well. Both the *Atlantic* and the *Wall Street Journal* have highlighted the advantages in accuracy and cost of using computers to do large-scale discovery work.[14] The programmers claim that these programs are cheaper *and* more accurate than humans.[15] Again, like the COIN program described above, it makes sense that over time computers would be at least as good as humans at document review for litigation. Having spent some unfortunate days digging through boxes of corporate documents in my previous life in BigLaw, I can report that while the body was willing, the mind and spirit were weak. I often got bored and made mistakes.

Due diligence is harder to mechanize, because rather than looking for a mass of compliant documents with common features (say, emails to or from Ben Barton discussing AI and the law), due diligence searches a company's data for weird or noncompliant documents that signal the existence of something undisclosed and potentially harmful (such as a future legal liability or some kind of underlying fraud).[16] As you can imagine, telling an algorithm "look for something weird or scary" in databases is much harder to organize than "look for a mass of similar documents." The difference between these two tasks is a helpful reminder that there are some (many?) legal tasks that it will be hard to teach a computer to handle. For now, repeated tasks with clear answers are already easily handled by a computer. Tasks that require more context or insight, and that are less clearly defined, remain a struggle for machines.

TRUE AI

True AI (or "advanced AI" if you prefer) is the science-fiction version of AI, where a computer can do the highest levels of legal work, incorporating natural language skills, a nuanced understanding of the interplay between different sources of law (such as statutes, regulations, or case law), and a feel for the human aspects of a deal or dispute. Or in popular parlance, true AI involves the science-fiction future of chatty and super-intelligent computers like HAL in the movie *2001* or Data on *Star Trek*.

You may be familiar with the "Turing test" for computers, named for British AI pioneer (and World War II code-breaker) Alan Turing. In a seminal 1950 paper entitled "Computer Machinery and Intelligence," Turing proposed a test where a neutral third-party evaluator listened to a conversation between a computer and a human and could not tell the difference between them.[17] The legal version is a computer that can handle all sorts of legal work indistinguishably from a human lawyer. When we use the term "AI" and suggest that machines may put lawyers out of business altogether, this is what we often picture in our minds.

As the *New York Times* recently noted, this future is far in the distance and may never come.[18] For now, the optimal use of AI, from chess to baseball scouting to law, is a combination of data-driven programming and human experience and expertise.[19] As machines get better at more menial legal tasks, it is true that humans may be pressed into only higher-level, in-person work such as court appearances or negotiating and counseling, as well as individualized drafting, advising, or strategizing, but this does not mean that humans are going to be cut out of the process entirely anytime soon.

To the contrary, I warn my students that if and when computers are capable of the highest level of legal work, we will probably have much bigger problems than keeping our jobs for at least two reasons. First, if computers can handle that level of legal work, what will they not be able to handle? That version of the future suggests massive joblessness, an issue much bigger than reformatting law schools into programming schools.[20]

Second, in every science-fiction story of AI run amok, the computers have a moment where they figure out that the humans are, in fact, the problem, regardless of the problem. Given a desire to fix any particular issue, free-flowing AI naturally (and logically) decides to eliminate/enslave us. If we assume this is a real possibility, what possible task could be more likely to convince computers that humans are irrational and useless than dealing with humans and legal work? Anyone who has spent any time at all advising clients in contentious litigations or bruising transactional work (let alone a nasty divorce) will know that if we assign computers the task of ironing out these issues, they will determine that humans are the problem much sooner than we'd hope. If I were writing the sci-fi version of the "true AI" legal future, the first scene would be the computer trying to mediate a dispute (whether a divorce or an acrimonious failed business deal) by explaining the economic irrationality of continuing to fight, followed by the humans angrily declaring, "It's the principle of the matter!" In the next scene, AI-driven kill-bots would murder those same irrational, litigious humans, sparking the Great AI War.

THE SCHOLARLY DEBATE OVER AI AND LAW

With these three categories in mind, we can now weigh whether AI will truly pose a threat to lawyers and law schools in the near or even medium-term future. There is a lively scholarly debate on this issue. British futurist Richard Susskind is the leader in the field, writing books on the topic since 1988, including 2010's ominously titled *The End of Lawyers?*[21] His last two books, *Tomorrow's Lawyers* and *The Future of the Professions*, are his two best, and if you are interested in this topic I highly recommend them. Susskind's early work sometimes felt bogged down in technical details, but recently he's whittled it down to crisp, clear, and persuasive think pieces.[22] They're also relatively short, which helps.

Despite the relative cheer of the title *Tomorrow's Lawyers*, Susskind sees a rather dire future for the bread-and-butter work of the majority of lawyers in private practice:

> As for much smaller firms with very few partners, aside from those which also offer a genuinely specialist or personal service that some market is prepared to pay for, I find it hard to imagine how these businesses will survive in the long run. . . . One person who formally reviewed my publication proposal for this book said that they hoped that I would pay more attention than in the past to general purpose small firms. I am afraid that I was not inclined to do so, because I do not see much of a future (beyond 2020) for most small firms in liberalized regimes.[23]

Well, alrighty then! Susskind puts the timeframe on this future as "beyond 2020," which probably seemed far away in 2013. But 2020 is almost here now, and as of yet, his imagined scenario seems pretty unlikely.

John McGinnis and Russell Pearce are American law professors who take a similarly dim view of the future for lawyers vis-à-vis artificial intelligence. Their 2014 law review article, "The Great Disruption," details the current progress in computerization and law and concludes that "the future of the journeyman lawyer is insecure."[24]

Daniel Katz is more copacetic than Susskind, Pearce, and McGinnis, predicting a future where lawyers, computers, and crowdsourcing work together to improve legal prediction and the practice of law.[25] Katz sees lawyers and machines working together, not machines replacing humans wholesale.

For an opposing view, consider the work of Dana Remus and Frank Levy.[26] Remus was a law professor at the University of North Carolina (UNC) at Chapel Hill and Levy a professor at the Massachusetts Institute of Technology (MIT). Remus and Levy take a more skeptical look at the state of the art and conclude that while computers will continue to make headway in areas like document review or eDiscovery, they will struggle in less rule-bound and more fluid areas such as legal analysis. Since the great majority of legal work involves uncertainty in the facts or the law, Remus and Levy predict that AI will stall roughly where it is now, handling simple and repetitive tasks but making little progress into the heart of legal work.

UPSHOT

As with many academic disputes, these opposing sides are actually closer together than they might at first appear. Excluding Susskind's particularly aggressive prediction of extinction for many (most?) lawyers, even the pro-AI forces recognize that for the foreseeable future a combination of machine intelligence and human intelligence will be optimal.

THE GOOD NEWS FOR LAWYERS AND LAW SCHOOLS

If the AI question is an existential one, will today's and tomorrow's law graduates have work as lawyers in the coming years? The answer appears to be yes for the foreseeable future. There are a number of legal tasks that will remain primarily human driven for a long time. These include higher-level strategizing, drafting, and legal analysis, as well as in-court appearances and person-to-person negotiating. Unless and until judges and other humans prefer to talk to robots, humans will still be paid (and paid well) to handle most in-person tasks.

Likewise, the seemingly relentless advance of technology cuts both ways for lawyers. Better technology also allows for greater legal complexity. Historical examples include the typewriter and then word processing. The exponential growth in citable case law, statutes, and regulations are all related to these new technologies, each of which made memorializing law easier. When regulations, court opinions, and statutes had to be handwritten, they tended to be shorter. Consider our Constitution or the original Judiciary Act. Same with Supreme Court opinions. The typewriter made length easier, and the word processor basically eliminated almost all barriers. New technologies will likewise allow for greater flexibility and nuance in law, and by "flexibility and nuance" I mean overweening complexity. The explosive growth in all of these overlapping areas and sources of law makes establishing a cohesive understanding of what the "controlling law" is in any given circumstance ever harder. Bad news for the country? Maybe. Awesome news for lawyer paychecks? Obviously.

The same is true for law schools. For years, law schools have focused on gray areas and on creating complexity and uncertainty out of any area of law, resisting simple answers.[27] This has always been an excellent strategy for creating work for lawyers, but it will be especially relevant when we begin battling machines for our jobs. This growth in complexity may be terrible for the country, and I have argued that exact point, but it does make lawyer jobs safer than other jobs that better lend themselves to clear answers.[28]

Similarly, we have gone through a long series of technology-driven upheavals from the Industrial Revolution forward, and at every step we have freed humans from physically harder, less meaningful tasks to devote themselves to what most would agree are better jobs.[29] The transition may take a while, and the initially displaced rarely see the benefits, but for the last 150 years or so we have seen a story of overall progress, despite Luddites predicting mass joblessness and ruin. When humans left subsistence farming to live and work in cities, there was hardship, but specialization emerged. When factories mechanized the production of clothes and shoes, cobblers and tailors lost their jobs, but it freed up humans for even more specialization. The growth in the number of lawyers is one example of how the Industrial Revolution created new jobs.

Optimists can look at this history and predict more of the same this time. If computers replace low-level, relatively rote legal work, that will free up resources for the higher-level work, while also lowering prices and offering legal services to the masses. There will be more work for lawyers, and that work will be more interesting, while the access-to-justice crisis will be simultaneously ameliorated. I argued for a version of this happy future in my book *Glass Half Full: The Decline and Rebirth of the Legal Profession*.[30]

THE BAD NEWS

Nevertheless, the general rule that capitalist economies replace jobs lost to technology with better jobs is not an ironclad law of physics. At some point, we may hit a brave new world where technology tips over the calculation and humans suddenly find themselves with little useful work to do. Could this happen to lawyers? Is there a future where the number of humans doing legal work is very small and machines handle almost everything else?

One scary data point is an outstanding 2017 *New York Times Magazine* article that outlines how Google is using the most advanced type of AI to improve Google Translate.[31] The article is the best kind of long-form journalism: impeccably sourced work covering a topic you would likely have otherwise missed and filled with insights reaching far beyond the immediate subject area.

Basically, Google Translate used to be a much more rules-based form of AI, attempting to train a computer to do literal word-for-word translations from one language to another. Anyone who used Google Translate a few years ago knows that this approach resulted in some awkward translations. I spent the academic year 2014–15 teaching comparative law on a Fulbright Award at the University of Ljubljana, in Slovenia, and I can attest to the hilarity of various translations. For example, we rented a lovely home in Ljubljana for the year, and at one point we received what turned out to be an advertisement for a local chimney sweep that included a quote from a Slovenian law requiring regular chimney inspections. The advertisement looked very official, and when we plugged it into the old version of Google Translate we were convinced that the chimney sweep was coming to arrest us sooner rather than later. A friendly colleague set us straight, but it was a vivid reminder of the importance of context and nuance in translations.

To fix this problem, Google decided to pour resources into Google Translate and to abandon the more rules-based approach. In its place, the team created a massive database that used probability theory and repeated efforts to translate entire sentences and phrases colloquially, using a very advanced version of the data-driven learning process described above.

It took time for the computer to "learn," and there was a tremendous amount of coding and human teaching involved, but the end result was a breathtaking success. Google Translate between major languages like Japanese and English is now markedly improved. The article includes several examples of Google Translate successfully translating poetry between languages in ways that closely resemble translations done by specialized human translators.

Teaching a machine to accurately and fluently translate from one language to another, especially considering all the irrational and very human details involved in communication, is a remarkable feat. It should also frighten lawyers, because while translation does not involve the exact same skill set that legal analysis does, it strikes me as more related to lawyering than other AI examples, such as the self-driving car, because both law and translation require close analysis and understanding of uniquely human language skills.

Fortunately for lawyers, the Google Translate story suggests it is not easy to teach machines these things. Google dedicated most of its best AI minds to work on this project for a significant period of time. It will be a while before anyone finds the time, expertise, or money to do the same for law. That said, the Google Translate story suggests that if and when it happens, it may be more possible to mechanize law than we would imagine.

SO, WHAT SHOULD LAW SCHOOLS DO?

This is the million-dollar question, isn't it? Sadly, there is no simple answer, because the long-term future is so unclear. One thing is obvious: it is critical that all law students and new lawyers embrace technology and think carefully about the areas of their practice that can be mechanized, so that individual lawyers can focus on the difficult (and more lucrative) stuff. Most law schools are actively bad at this, either doing nothing to promote technological competence or actively resisting it. Counter-examples such as Stanford Law School's CodeEx project or the large and innovative Chicago-Kent computerization program exist, but these exceptions prove the rule.

Should law schools become coding factories? In my opinion, no. The technology is moving so fast and the expertise of all but a tiny handful of law professors is so shallow that trying to work on the nuts and bolts of computerization would almost assuredly be a fool's errand.

But that does not mean we should ignore technology altogether. To the contrary, law schools should absolutely be working on the lawyerly part of computerization: the creation of processes and the "storyboarding" of legal issues into rules-based or data-driven programs that make simpler activities cheaper. When lawyers and law professors discuss technological advances, they tend to speak hostilely or passively, imagining a future being pressed upon us. But we have agency in these changes, and the sooner we work to shape and improve them the better off we will all be—the profession and the public at large.

◆ 4 ◆

BOOM TO BUST FOR LAW SCHOOLS

Chapters 1, 2, and 3 lay out a series of challenges facing law schools, some of relatively recent vintage and some long-standing. This chapter describes three different eras for law schools. In the first era, which ran roughly from the 1960s through the 1990s, law schools grew in number, size, tuition, and revenue. This growth was at its peak in the 1970s and was largely rational: the market for legal services was exploding, and law schools went along for the ride.

The next era, from the 1990s until 2010, featured still more growth for law schools, except that the employment market, especially the main street/solo practitioner portion, was saturated. This meant that law schools continued their relentless expansion and tuition hikes despite limited evidence that the market needed more lawyers. Floated by press reports of rising salaries and employment in BigLaw, and by television shows such as *L.A. Law* and *Ally McBeal* and books such as *The Firm*, law schools of all stripes implied that working at a large corporate law firm was typical for law school graduates.

This was false. The percentage of lawyers working in BigLaw has never reached 50 percent of the lawyers in private practice, let alone a majority of all lawyers. To the contrary, the great majority of American lawyers have always worked in government, nonprofits, small firms, or in solo practice, where earnings are much lower. Plus, roughly a third of American law grads do not work as lawyers at all, making BigLaw salaries especially inapplicable.

Law schools and their placement offices knew all of this, but the public did not, so students kept rolling in and law schools kept expanding and charging more. Law schools grew continuously: more schools teaching more students, who were paying higher tuition and borrowing more money. If there are stretches in this book where you feel bad for law schools and their predicament, remember this unwarranted period of expansion.

As of 2009 or so, law schools might have thought that growth on all fronts would continue forever. After all, law schools had basically seen uninterrupted growth for the last fifty years. And yet, to paraphrase economist Herb Stein, if something cannot go on forever, it won't.

This truism leads us to our last era: the post-2010 collapse. Law schools have seen a decline in every possible category, leading some to the brink of bankruptcy or even closure. We have seen a turnaround in applications with the Trump Bump, so it appears the worst is behind us. How far we climb out of the valley, however, remains to be seen.

THE BOOM YEARS: MORE SCHOOLS, MORE STUDENTS, HIGHER TUITION, EXPLODING DEBT

Figure 4.1 shows the number of American Bar Association (ABA)–accredited schools in America from 1964 to 2019. This count of accredited law schools does not include the closed Charlotte School of Law but does include Whittier, Arizona Summit, and Valparaiso since they were still operating in 2019. It also reflects the mergers of Rutgers Camden and Rutgers Newark and William Mitchell and Hamline. Even with those mergers, the 2019 accreditations of Lincoln Memorial and Concordia brought the count of fully ABA-accredited law schools to an all-time high of 203. But wait, there's more! University of North Texas at Dallas is provisionally accredited and still hoping for full accreditation.[1]

The steepest growth occurred between 1968 and 1982, when America added thirty-six ABA-accredited law schools (26 percent growth). That period of growth was probably defensible. The market for legal services grew substantially over this same period. The growth after 1990,

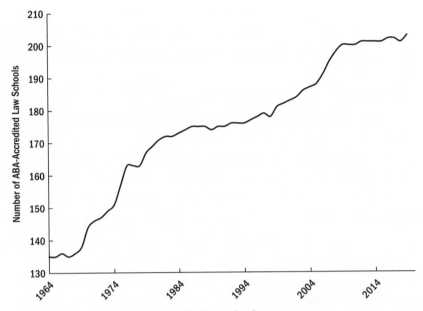

FIGURE 4.1. Number of ABA-accredited law schools, 1964–2019.

however, is more problematic. America added another twenty-eight law schools (16 percent growth) over the same period in which the market for legal services stalled.

SIDE NOTE: WHY WE ARE STILL ADDING LAW SCHOOLS IN 2019

Wait, I thought that the market for law schools was so bad that the relevant question was whether more schools would close. Why are we still adding law schools? Humans are a puzzling species and can be quite stubborn with their preconceptions. Along with the provisionally accredited UNT Dallas, there are discussions about opening new law schools all over the country. Lawmakers and university officials still remain convinced that a law school can work in their locality, regardless of the national trends.

For example, the Appalachian School of Law was founded in 1994 partially as an economic development project in Grundy, Virginia, in rural Appalachia.[2] The school may well have served that purpose before this decade, but recent history has been unkind. The entering class of 2016 consisted of 38 students, down from 146 in 2011, and the full-time faculty has shrunk from 16 to 8. The school is now rumored to be leaving Grundy for greener pastures.[3]

Nevertheless, other rural areas are still pushing for law schools as an engine of economic development and prestige. In the Rio Grande Valley in Texas, the state legislative delegation voted unanimously for a bill to create a new state law school near Brownsville. Figure 4.2 is a picture from the local paper (the *Monitor*) of the legislators celebrating their vote.[4]

Similarly, existing universities often look to add a law school as part of an attempted prestige boost. Two different Tennessee universities

FIGURE 4.2. Texas lawmakers from the Rio Grande Valley celebrating a vote for a new law school at the University of Texas at Brownsville, November 2016.

created brand-new law schools in the last ten years, Belmont University and Lincoln Memorial University, partially to raise their academic profile and expand their professional graduate programs. Other universities such as Western Michigan, University of Illinois Chicago, and Texas A&M have absorbed existing, struggling law schools. Western Michigan's Cooley Law School is even opening a new Kalamazoo branch.

When it first looked as if the Charlotte School of Law might close in January 2017, the University of North Carolina at Charlotte immediately resurrected the idea of replacing it with a new, public law school in that city.[5] University of Washington, Tacoma, by contrast, has slowed down its plans for a new law school because of "trends in law school applications and available jobs."[6] Yet the delay is just from 2019 to 2021 for now, not a permanent scuttling.

In short, regardless of the available data, many universities and localities remain convinced that having a law school is a net positive. Presumably they also think that the current situation is cyclical, or not an issue in their region. Even if a "Trump Bump" brings applications and attendance back, unless there is a radical change in employment outcomes, it will be a long time before there is a need for a new ABA-accredited law school.

MORE SCHOOLS MEANS MORE STUDENTS

Along with the growth in the number of law schools, there were more students and graduates. Figure 4.3 shows first-year enrollment at ABA law schools from 1948 to 2018. The peak year was 2011. In that year, 52,488 students enrolled in ABA-accredited law schools. The biggest boom years were from 1969 to 1982, when first-year law student (1L) enrollment grew from 23,652 to 42,521 (80 percent increase). Enrollment bounced around from 1982 until 1999 or so, and then climbed again from 2000 forward. Law school 1L enrollment grew by 22 percent between 2000 and 2011, despite worsening job placement, and continued through the worst economic downturn since the Great Depression.

FIGURE 4.3. First-year law student enrollment, 1948–2018.

The growth was not solely due to new law schools; many existing law schools expanded their classes as well. Again, the pre-1990 increase was defensible; the later classes, less so.

HIGHER TUITION AND MORE DEBT

As more law schools were admitting more students, tuition (and debt loads) spiked as well. Figure 4.4 shows average tuition at ABA-accredited law schools, separating private from public out-of-state and public in-state. The darker black lines show the actual tuition, and the slower rising gray lines show what the tuition would have been if law schools had just tracked inflation since 1985. This chart was inspired by Law School Transparency's online, interactive Tuition Tracker.[7] If law school was the same price as it was in 1985 in inflation-adjusted dollars, in-state tuition in 2018 would average $4,713, nonresident tuition would average $11,098, and private tuition would average $17,681. Over the same period that employment results weakened for a significant segment of law grads, tuition ran ahead of inflation almost every year.[8]

Higher tuition means more debt. It is true, as discussed below, that many law students are now negotiating discounts off the sticker price. Yet these discounts have not slowed the overall rise in indebtedness. Figure 4.5 shows just how much student debt load has increased since 2002. Note that the data comes from two different sources. Through 2013 the data comes directly from the ABA and thus reflects every accredited law school. After 2013 the ABA stopped releasing this data, so the remaining years come from the excellent website Law School Transparency. Between 2002 and 2013, average indebtedness rose 100 percent for public law schools and 83 percent for private schools. The growth is especially marked during the Great Recession and the "lawcession" that followed. The recent trend is slightly better, and 2017 shows a dual

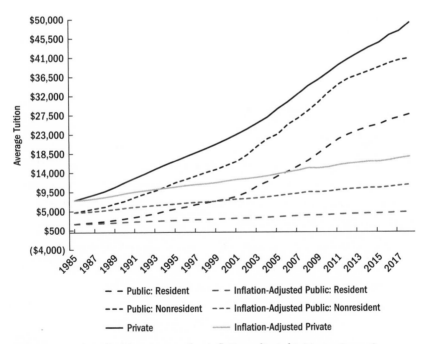

FIGURE 4.4. Actual tuition compared to inflation-adjusted tuition, 1985–2018.

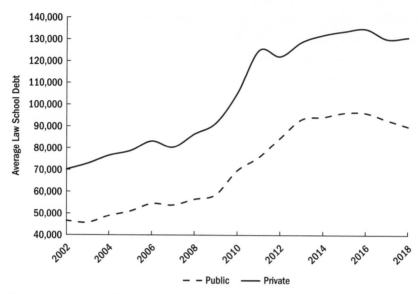

FIGURE 4.5. Average law school debt, 2002–2018 (multiple sources).

decline for the first time since 2007. That said, average indebtedness remained jaw-droppingly high in comparison to even fifteen years ago.

WHERE DID ALL THAT MONEY GO?

What did law schools spend the money on? The money went toward a
combination of things, but three areas stand out. Many law schools built
very nice new facilities.[9] In fact, if you are a law student or a recent law
grad, ask yourself, "Did my law school either build, renovate, or expand
since 2000?" I'll bet the answer is yes.

Law schools also reduced their student-faculty ratio. In 1979 there
was an average of 26 students for every law school faculty member. By
2014 there were just 13.6 students per professor.

Law schools have also expanded the size of their administrative staff.[10]
Brian Tamanaha's book *Failing Law Schools* has a particularly damning
chapter entitled "Teaching Load Down, Salary Up" that details how the

shrinking student-faculty ratio and the addition of administrative staff allowed professors to teach less and do less administrative work, while their salaries and perks continued to rise.[11] There is certainly an argument to be made that these expenditures have improved student experiences in law schools, so some of the debt and tuition increases may be defensible. Nevertheless, it is also notable that law schools remain stubbornly similar to each other and to their past practices. Even the most ardent defenders of law schools would be hard pressed to argue that law schools are twice or three times better than they were in 1985, even though tuition has increased that much.

CANARIES IN A COAL MINE

When the Great Recession began in 2008, there was an expectation that law schools would actually benefit. The October 2009 sitting of the LSAT was the largest on record.[12] And yet the seeds of the collapse were already in place. We start with the rise of the law school "scamblogs."[13] These blogs were founded on the idea that the cost of attending law school in time, tuition, and debt was too high for many (most?) incoming law students. They pointed out poor employment results. They harped on cost and debt. They pointed out what they felt were hypocritical and self-serving statements by the Association of American Law Schools (AALS), the ABA, and various law schools. And eventually they went from the shadows to the main stage, with USA Today, the New York Times, Slate, and others covering them.[14] Scamblogs embodied the homily, "First they ignore you, then they laugh at you, then they fight you, then you win."[15]

These blogs ranged in quality and tone, with *Third Tier Reality* the flagship for the low road, featuring pictures of toilets covered in fecal matter and vomit and scathing reviews of various law schools.[16] On the higher end, *Law School Transparency* and *The Law School Tuition Bubble* offer thoughtful and original research by recent law graduates.[17] I have relied extensively on both in researching this book.

The most famous scamblog was probably Colorado law professor Paul Campos's *Inside the Law School Scam*.[18] At first the website was anonymous, and Campos pulled no punches. He argued that law school is a scam that exists mostly to bilk its students. He laid the blame squarely on law professors. He described the bulk of his colleagues as overpaid, lazy, uninformed, and bad teachers. For a time, there was intense curiosity as to who exactly was writing the blog.[19] Campos unmasked himself in August 2011 and went on to publish a 2012 book entitled *Don't Go to Law School (Unless)*.[20]

The year 2012 was a banner year for the topic, with Brian Tamanaha publishing the tamer, but comparatively more devastating, *Failing Law Schools*.[21] *Failing Law Schools* was more powerful because of both the messenger and the tone of the message. Tamanaha is a legal academic's academic and hardly a flamethrower. The book was well researched, well argued, and lacking in any ad hominem or overboard attacks, making it harder to dismiss.

And yet, the full scope of the damage to law schools was unclear at first. In 2011, for example, Tamanaha argued there was no real crisis in law schools other than the undercovered problems of debt and employment results: "Thousands upon thousands of law graduates have debt far above what their salaries can bear. Meanwhile, law schools are doing fine, thank you."[22]

There was also a spate of high-profile lawsuits against various law schools in 2011 and 2012 for allegedly faking their employment data. These cases eventually died at summary judgment and even at trial, and as of yet no law school has lost.[23] Nevertheless, "winning" these cases came at a significant cost to public relations. For example, even the courts that granted summary judgment have generally not disputed that the underlying employment information was misleading but rather held that law school applicants are savvy customers who should have known better.[24] These lawsuits generated quite a bit of publicity, with coverage in the *L.A. Times*,[25] the *Wall Street Journal*,[26] and elsewhere. *New York Magazine* ran a particularly lengthy and unflattering piece that featured a picture of a birdcage lined with a New York Law School diploma covered in bird feces.[27]

This is all added to the steady stream of stories detailing the pitiful state of the job market for law grads.[28] For years, law school appeared to be a safe bet for a cushy life, almost regardless of price. In the internet era, narratives reverse quickly, however, and now potential applicants face a gauntlet of news stories, blog posts, and YouTube videos encouraging them not to go to law school.[29]

If you are a reader of this book and have not done a YouTube search for "don't go to law school," you really should. Readers born before 1982 will be duly impressed by the sharp critiques of law schools in hallowed news sources such as the *Wall Street Journal* or the *New York Times*. Millennials and younger Americans likely prefer YouTube, and those critiques are much cruder and crueler.[30]

AND THE LEVEE BREAKS: APPLICANTS AND MATRICULANTS

With the drumbeat of bad news, we finally saw a change in the market. Law schools went from a relative high point around 2010 to their nadir just five years later. Figure 4.6 shows four different correlated numbers. The top line is the number of LSAT takers from 2000 to 2017. The other three lines show the number of applicants, the number of admittees, and finally 1L enrollment.[31] The 2009–10 period was the all-time high point for LSAT administrations at 171,514. From this high point the numbers collapsed to 101,689 just five years later in 2014–15. This was the lowest number of LSAT takers since at least 1988. Even with the rebound in 2015–18, we are in the worst stretch since 1996–2000. The recent uptick from 2015–18 looks promising, and 2017–18 looks even better. LSAT administrations grew 18 percent in 2017–18 alone, despite some law schools choosing to accept the GRE, as discussed in chapter 5. The LSAT boom has been attributed to the Trump Bump, as news stories of heroic lawyers rushing to airports to battle the travel ban and other stories from the "resistance" make law school cool again. It is too early

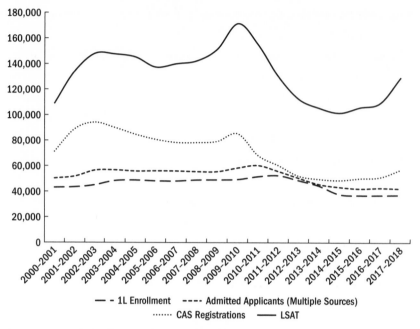

FIGURE 4.6. LSAT takers, applicants, admittees, and 1L enrollment, 2000–2018.

to proclaim a 2001–2003-style boomlet in LSATs, but law schools are certainly encouraged.

But from 2010 to 2015, fewer LSAT takers meant fewer applicants. The dotted line in Figure 4.6 shows the number of applicants who signed up for the Credential Assembly Service (CAS) from 2000 to 2018.[32] Every ABA-accredited school requires the CAS, so it is a good proxy for applicants.[33] Like the LSAT administrations, CAS registrations have improved steadily since 2014 and look to be picking up steam. CAS registrations also show the depths of the 2013–15 stretch. From 2013 to 2015, fewer people *applied* to law schools than *entered* law schools as 1Ls in fall 2011.

Fewer applicants mean fewer students. The drop from 2011 to 2015 was as precipitous as it looks (although again, it appears we may have reached the floor). After miniscule growth in matriculation from 2015 to 2017, fall 2018 finally showed some signs of life. In 2015, 37,058 new matriculants entered ABA-accredited JD programs. In 2017 that number had "risen" to 37,320. In 2018 there were 38,390 new matriculants, so enrollment was up roughly 3%. It is thus too early to know how the Trump Bump will affect actual enrollment going forward, but that will be the acid test for whether law schools can exhale or not. Regardless, in a market that basically collapsed between 2011 and 2015, small growth from 2015 to 2018 was welcome news indeed.

The last time that fewer students entered American law schools than in 2017 was *1974*. How many law schools were there in 1974? One hundred and fifty-one. So, these same 37,320 students were now being spread over an additional fifty-two ABA-accredited schools.

The post-2014 growth in the number of people taking the LSAT, the growth in CAS applications, and the bottoming out in matriculation suggests better times ahead, right? It turns out that as of 2018–19 the returns are mixed. The LSAT suggests optimism. As figure 4.6 reflects, the number of students taking the LSAT rose by 7.5 percent from 2014 to 2017 and even more in the first Trump Bump year of 2017–18.[34] If you just considered LSAT administrations, the bounce back over the period of 2015–18 would look like the start of the bounce back from the last collapse in 1996–2001. Just compare the two low points in figure 4.6. If that version of the story is right, law schools will be dancing when 2019–2023 resembles 2001–2006.

The number of matriculants, however, tells a different story. Figure 4.6 shows several important trends. The first is that the number of LSAT takers, CAS applications, and matriculants are correlated, but the LSAT is more volatile than CAS applications. The number of matriculants moves the least. Second, the LSAT boost from 2014 to 2018 has not translated into a concurrent rise in matriculants. It does look like attendance has stabilized but thus far not improved that much. The gap between the LSAT and attendance suggests that while more prospective law students are serious enough to take the LSAT (a significant investment in time and hassle), those LSAT takers have not yet translated into matriculants, likely because those students have a more jaundiced view

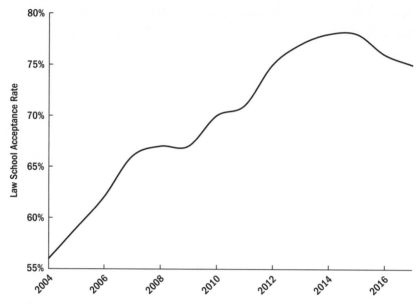

FIGURE 4.7. Law school acceptance rate, 2004–2017.

of the value of attending law school. Again, fall 2019 will tell us a lot about the actual Trump Bump's effects.

Third, look at how much closer the number of CAS applicants and law school matriculants grew from 2010 forward. Anecdotally, we have thought that anyone who applies to law school today will get into law school and can attend if they like, and figure 4.6 certainly shows a decline in selectivity. Figure 4.7 shows the acceptance rate for law schools from 2000 to 2017 as measured by AccessLex, a pro–law school research group. Look at how many more applicants are now accepted to at least one law school. In 2004, 56 percent of applicants were admitted to law school. Since 2011, slightly more than 75 percent have been admitted every year.

In a related trend, the students who test the best, as measured by high LSAT scores, have been choosing not to apply to law school.[35] The 2018–19 trend was slightly rosier with these applicants. Students with lower LSAT scores did, however, apply in increased numbers, probably because they had a better chance of being admitted than ever before. Paul Caron of the *TaxProf Blog* analyzed the data and concluded that the proportion of law school applicants with scores above 160 shrunk by 35 percent between 2010 and 2017. The percentage of applicants with LSATs below 150, however, rose by 146 percent. This trend suggests that even if applications have reached a floor, the flight of the most attractive students (at least as measured by the LSAT) continues unabated.

So where have all of these students gone? It seems too glib to say that they're all going to business school, but . . . they're all going to business school. The AALS gathered data on first-time matriculants at four different types of graduate programs over the period 2006–14: medical school, public administration, law school, and business school. Figure 4.8 shows the results, and the growth of the MBA at the expense of the JD. The MBA is now the most popular master's degree in the US, passing

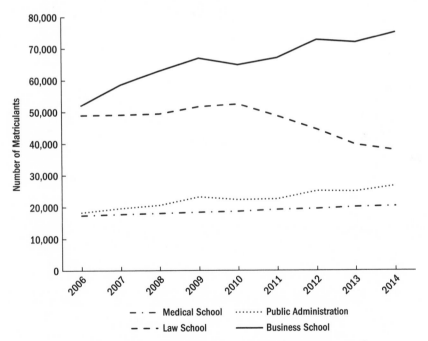

FIGURE 4.8. Matriculation at medical, business, public administration, and law schools, 2006–2014.

the master of education in 2011.[36] Predictably, business schools are now taking their turn in the barrel, with a decrease in enrollment and applications in 2017–2018.[37] Nevertheless, the MBA has maintained its dominance over the JD.

Fewer applicants and fewer students also mean more competition over the students in the pool. This is especially so given that many law schools have attempted to keep the LSAT and GPA averages for their entering class roughly the same, either in an effort to maintain the overall quality of their entering classes or to rise in the *U.S. News* law school rankings, or both.[38]

As a result, there has been a precipitous decline in the percentage of students paying full freight. Figure 4.9 shows the percentages of students receiving a discount broken out in four different categories of law schools: private, public, private stand-alone, and the top fifteen (T15) schools. Figure 4.9 is inspired by Matt Leichter's great work on his blog *The Law School Tuition Bubble*, so go there if you want to see a different

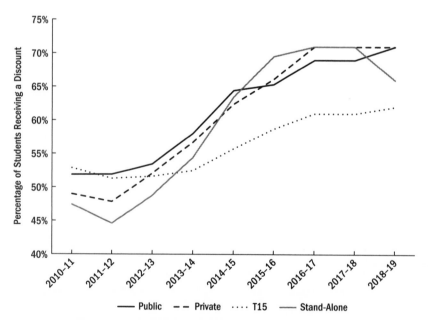

FIGURE 4.9. Discount percentage by school type, 2010–2019.

take on the data.[39] The percentage of students receiving a discount actually declined between 2010 and 2011, reflecting the relative surge in attendance. Since 2011, the bottom has fallen out though, with a full 70 percent of all law students receiving a grant or a scholarship in 2016–17.

Start by looking at 2010–11. That year the T15, the top fifteen law schools according to *U.S. News*, were the most generous, granting discounts to 53 percent of their students. Stand-alone law schools, including four for-profit law schools, were the least generous, at 47 percent. By 2017–18, the roles had completely reversed. The T15 offered discounts to 61 percent of their students, and stand-alone law schools had risen to 71 percent. Figure 4.9 makes clear that the last six years have been brutal for stand-alone law schools, and harder on private law schools of all stripes. Stand-alone schools saw some relief in 2018–19 as they showed their first decline in discounts since 2012. Yet note the overall trend for every type of school: discounts are up and revenue is down from top to bottom.

The decline has been steep recently, but discounts on full tuition have steadily grown since 1999. In 1999–2000 more than 67 percent of law students paid full price. In 2018–19 that percentage had cratered to just 29 percent. More students are receiving grants, and those grants are rising in value as well. The average grant amount for law students grew 53 percent from 2011 to 2018. The percentage of students receiving grants grew by 45 percent, all while attendance collapsed by 30 percent. Fewer students paying less is not a recipe for fiscal health. Consider just the hardest-hit law schools, the stand-alone, private law schools. In 2011, these schools gave 7,468 students roughly $95,478,380 in discounts. By 2015, they gave 7,678 students roughly $122,394,998 in discounts. But the growth in discounts only tells half the story. In 2011, roughly 9,275 students paid full tuition, for revenue of $378,856,700. Four years later in 2015, only 3,363 students paid full freight, for an estimated rough revenue of just $148,130,061. Revenue from students paying full price fell by 60 percent over a four-year period. When fewer customers pay less for your product, revenues fall precipitously.

Bernard Burk, Jerry Organ, and Emma Rasiel looked at the tuition and discounting data from 2010 to 2016 and concluded that law schools lost roughly $1.5 billion in annual revenue between 2010 and 2016.[40] $1.5 billion!

The upshot is that the years 2011–15 were unimaginably bad for law schools. There are signs of life everywhere, and the recent Trump Bump is especially promising, but we still do not know if we are on a true upswing that looks like previous robust rebounds in the mid-eighties, mid-nineties, and early in the first decade of the twenty-first century or whether the Trump Bump is a dead-cat bounce. Either way, law schools would be wise to learn some lessons from the last few years of downturn. Now we turn to a discussion of how different market segments responded to the meltdown.

♦ 5 ♦

WHY HAVEN'T MORE LAW SCHOOLS CLOSED?

PART 1: MARKET-BASED CLOSURES

Chapters 5, 6, and 7 discuss the law schools in the greatest danger of closing. The law schools under the greatest stress generally share more than one of the following characteristics: (1) they are among the lower-ranked law schools, either by *U.S. News* or another ranking system; (2) they are private law schools with limited endowments; (3) they have struggled with job placement and bar passage, especially recently; (4) tuition and debt levels tend to be high; (5) admissions standards are low and collapsing (for reasons we discuss below); (6) they have hemorrhaged faculty since 2011; and (7) they have gotten into trouble with American Bar Association (ABA) accreditors. Relatively new, for-profit law schools stand out especially, because none of them have endowments (being for-profit) and their owners are less likely to be willing to float a for-profit endeavor for very long while losing money.

We will spend a lot more time on these attributes below, but for now just assume that the law schools in the greatest danger of closing are the ones that cluster near the bottom of the market on several different measures. This should come as no surprise: when a market sees a drop of 30 percent in consumers and a concomitant wave of discounts and competition over the remaining buyers, we would expect at least some of the weaker market participants to fail and close. Again, this is just Economics 101: when expenses run above plummeting revenues for more than a few years (and the years 2011–16 were pretty uniformly bad), some businesses cannot make payroll and must close. I call this a market-based closure, meaning that the free market itself drives some (or many) law schools out of business.

The real puzzle is why *more* law schools haven't gone out of business. In 2012 the decline in applications began in earnest, and there was a spate of predictions of law school closures, including the *New York Times* describing a "death spiral" for some law schools.[1] That same year, Glenn Reynolds predicted as many as twenty-five schools would close.[2] Dean Phillip Closius listed the sixty-eight law schools he considered immune to closure (the top twenty-five and the forty-three flagship state institutions), leaving 132 on the endangered list.[3]

So why have we not seen more closures? The market for law schools is not a typical market for goods or services. To the contrary, law schools are highly regulated and massively subsidized (by federal loans and some state governments), and that combination of factors, plus the fact that law schools are very inexpensive to run when they have few full-time staff members, has kept law schools afloat.

OVERVIEW

I will discuss the strategy in detail below, but for now note the three-step playbook for law school survival at the low end of the market: (1) *Cut costs.* The largest expense category in a law school is people. So, to cut costs, you must cut people, notably full-time faculty. (2) *Boost revenue part 1.* Loosen (eliminate?) admissions standards. If there are students that are facially qualified for federal loans and admission to an ABA-accredited law school (they have taken the LSAT and completed the necessary undergraduate work) who are willing to borrow money to come, let them in, regardless of whether they are likely to succeed in law school or pass the bar. (3) *Boost revenue part 2.* Raise tuition and squeeze every drop of borrowing from the bodies that are in the building. As of yet, the government has not put a firm lid on the total amount a student can borrow other than each school's own tuition and cost of living estimations. So, encourage your students to borrow more to pay your school more.

- When you combine strategies 2 and 3, you see that strangely the *most* valuable applicants at low end law schools are the least competitive ones. Why? Because the most valuable student is one who is willing to borrow and pay the full amount of the tuition. The fewer law schools any student is admitted to, the less competition there is for the student through discounting, so paradoxically the least competitive applicants become the most valuable ones, as they are likeliest to be willing to pay full freight.

But wait, you say, I thought you just said the market was highly regulated? Won't these strategies run afoul of some (or many) of those regulations? Absolutely! Chapters 6 and 7 will discuss possible regulatory closures. When an American law school faces a choice between a market closure (shutter the doors, fire everybody, and the school ceases to exist) and the chance of a regulatory closure sometime in the future, the school will *always* take its chances with the regulators. Risking regulatory closure is dangerous but easy to swallow when the other option is closing immediately.

CUT COSTS—AND "COSTS" MEANS FULL-TIME FACULTY AND STAFF

When demand, sales, and revenue are down, businesses cut costs or run at a deficit. Outside of the top fifteen law schools or so, every law school in America has cut costs since 2011. These cuts have been especially hard on struggling law schools, because they had fewer easy places to cut. For example, many middle-class law schools have been able to cut costs without layoffs by shrinking their faculty through retirements or early retirements/buyouts (and freezing hiring), shrinking or eliminating summer research grants, cutting faculty or staff salaries, limiting faculty travel, or starving the law library. The lower-ranked schools often could not follow this playbook because they may never have offered much in the way of travel, research grants, or library funds, so cutting nonexistent expenses hardly helps. The same goes for early retirements. A bunch of the hardest-hit schools are relatively new, so waiting for new faculty to retire will not help at all.

Thus, more aggressive layoffs have ensued. The good news with these cutbacks is that law school faculties grew substantially from the 1970s through 2010. In 2010, just on the verge of the collapse, the *National Jurist* ran an (unintentionally ironic) article trumpeting the fact that law school faculties had grown 40 percent between 1998 and 2008, lowering the student-faculty ratio by almost 50 percent.[4]

This left some room for cuts after 2010. The most expensive part of running a law school is the people, notably the faculty, so any real cost-cutting requires shrinking the number of folks on the payroll.[5] Matt Leichter has done the spadework to gather the data on the size of law school faculties from 1999 to 2016.[6] Between 2010 and 2016, ABA-accredited law schools lost 1,460 full-time positions, a 16.1 percent decline. The 1,460 count is a net count. Overall, three-quarters of American law schools have been shrinking, and the loss of faculty at just those schools is 1,902 (the lower net loss reflects that some law schools have grown since 2010).

Over the same period, part-time law professors have remained steady, and administrators who teach have actually increased.[7] Thus, almost all of the burden for layoffs, buyouts, early retirements, and firings has basically come from the ranks of the full-time faculty (and the staff, although we have only anecdotal data to go on for staff).[8]

As you will recall, Glenn Reynolds predicted the closure of twenty-five law schools by now, roughly 12.5 percent of all American law schools. When I pointed out to Glenn that many fewer had closed, he said, "Law schools have shed over 16 percent of their full-time faculty since 2010. This means I was too *low* on my percentage guess; I just did not foresee that the losses would be so widely dispersed."

A list of the thirty schools that have seen the largest shrinkage in faculty size is instructive:[9]

Rank	School	Net change, 2010–16
1.	WMU Cooley	−60
2.	American	−52
3.	John Marshall (Chicago)	−48
4.	Florida Coastal	−45
5.	George Washington	−37
6.	St. Louis	−31
7.	Catholic	−29
8.	Seton Hall	−27
8.	Vermont	−27
8.	Seattle	−27
11.	Widener (Delaware)	−26
11.	New York Law School	−26
13.	McGeorge	−24
14.	Pace	−22
14.	Cleveland State	−22
16.	Santa Clara	−21
16.	DePaul	−21
16.	Hofstra	−21
19.	Nova	−20
19.	New England	−20
21.	Golden Gate	−19
21.	Texas	−19
23.	California–Berkeley	−18
23.	Stetson	−18
23.	Valparaiso	−18
23.	Suffolk	−18
23.	Western New England	−18
23.	Capital	−18
23.	Wisconsin	−18

This list is dominated by exactly the law schools you would think are in the most trouble: lower-ranked, private law schools that are highly tuition dependent, especially freestanding schools with limited endowments. In 2016 there were *five* law schools operating with fewer than ten faculty members: La Verne (nine), Lincoln Memorial (eight),

Concordia (eight), Appalachian (seven), and the soon-to-close Indiana Tech (five).[10]

There are several surprises on the list. American, Seton Hall, and Seattle are all schools I think of as long-standing, top-one-hundred-type law schools, and yet they find themselves with massive faculty cuts. The appearance of George Washington (GW), Wisconsin, Texas, and Cal-Berkeley is also pretty stunning. Berkeley and Texas consider themselves to be charter and eternal members of the top ten, and GW and Wisconsin feel the same way about the top twenty-five. This illustrates that cuts have been deepest at the lower end, but faculties have shrunk at every level of legal academia.

Nor are the cuts finished. Vermont Law School announced another wave of cuts in 2018, stripping tenure from fourteen of nineteen law professors and slashing salaries as well.[11]

BOOST REVENUE PART I: ACCEPT AND ENROLL ALL FACIALLY QUALIFIED APPLICANTS

It is not enough to just cut costs. Revenue also has to be propped up by any available means. If law schools have a simple cost calculation, they have an even easier revenue structure. The most basic input is student tuition. Sure, law schools gather some funds through endowments or other charitable giving, and public law schools may receive a state subsidy, but the great bulk of almost every law school's revenue comes from student tuition. If there are fewer students in the building and they are paying less to attend, then revenue is down.

As chapter 8 discusses, this is one of the great pressures on midlevel schools. In an effort to maintain student quality and rankings, many of these schools have shrunk the size of their classes or increased tuition discounts, or both. But some schools do not have a central university to float the law school temporarily through smaller enrollment. These schools have cut faculty and staff but also need to up revenue if they are to keep the doors open. How do they keep the seats filled? Lower admissions standards.

Start by reviewing figure 4.6 from last chapter that shows the decline in applicants and the size of 1L classes. The recent high point for applications to law school was 2003–2004, when more than 94,000 people applied to law school. Law schools enrolled a little under 49,000 new JD students that year, so roughly half of all applicants were accepted and attended law school. The other half were either rejected or decided not to go.

Between 2004 and 2015, applications shrunk by almost half. Class size, however, fell by only about a quarter. What does this mean? Applications have dropped much more steeply than enrollment. Law schools, especially law schools closer to the bottom of the food chain, became a lot less selective over the last ten years.

It also highlights the fact that applications were in decline *before* the recession of 2008 and the law school collapse after 2010, yet law school enrollments continued to grow. In 2009–10, for example, 85,400 people applied, and law schools enrolled more than 52,000 students the next fall. Law schools were enrolling a greater percentage of applicants and swelling the size of their classes to all-time highs *despite* the recession and the job placement statistics. The period from 2004 to 2010 actually marks the beginning of the "let them in if they can pay" strategy, which makes it harder to gin up much sympathy for any law school's post-2010 struggles.

There are more granular signs of virtual open enrollment at law schools. The easiest way to track declining admissions standards is to track the LSAT scores of incoming law students (LSATs work better for this analysis than undergraduate GPA because they offer a more standardized score across years, schools, and applicants).

A BRIEF DETOUR TO DEFEND DISCUSSING AND USING THE LSAT AT ALL

Before we turn to the data, here is a brief defense of discussing the LSAT. The LSAT has been criticized for having a cultural bias and for discriminating against racial minorities and women.[12] Law schools have also been criticized for a slavish, often *U.S. News*-rankings-centered, devotion to maintaining certain entering LSAT scores, regardless of other equally or more pertinent criteria, such as life experiences, undergraduate performance, military service, or racial, religious, or political diversity. These critiques are fair, and I am not here to defend any law school using the LSAT (or any standardized test) as the most important factor in admissions.

Nevertheless, there are a couple of reasons a study of law school behavior must use the LSAT as a proxy when discussing changes in incoming student quality. The first is that the LSAT has been created and scored consistently for years, offering the only constant way to compare incoming students from 2017, 2007, and 1997. Undergraduate GPAs (UGPAs) have been subject to grade inflation, and of course the mix of undergraduate institutions (and also their grading policies) make UGPA poor data for comparisons across law schools and over time.

Second, whether it is wise or not, historically law schools have heavily relied on LSAT scores in admitting students. So, if we are measuring a slide into open admissions, the LSAT is a fair measure, regardless of whether one likes or hates the test.

Most importantly, some studies have found that LSAT scores are correlated with at least two things we care about: first-year law school GPA and bar passage.[13] First-year GPA matters because most law school attrition happens during the first year. Bar passage rates matter even more, because law grads must pass the bar to practice law.

Opponents of the LSAT will now retort, "So to defend one flawed and unfair standardized test, you're going to use another *even more* flawed and unfair and partially standardized test?" Every state requires the standardized Multistate Bar Examination (MBE).[14] The bar examination is arguably even more problematic than the LSAT, because at least the LSAT is somewhat positively correlated with things we care about. Bar examiners have almost no forward-looking empirical support for their examination. Lower bar examination scores are not correlated with professional discipline or malpractice lawsuits. Higher bar examination scores are not correlated with professional success. In fact, many states keep bar examination scores secret, only telling examinees whether they passed or failed the exam. Critics, including me, have argued for years that the bar examination is primarily a tool for lawyer protectionism rather than consumer protection. I've boiled this argument down to a single question: what exactly is it that bar examination passage guarantees in terms of consumer protection? That the newly minted lawyer can memorize a lot of different types of law and then apply it to hypotheticals in an essay and multiple-choice format on a challenging, two-day examination? How often will those skills be necessary in practice? Almost never.

Does the bar examination guarantee even minimal professional competence? No. An American law student can graduate law school and pass the bar and have no idea how to draft an actual contract, how to file a simple negligence lawsuit, how to file a suppression motion in a criminal case, how to take a will through probate, or how to prosecute a divorce. And yet anyone who has passed the bar can hang out a shingle and start taking these sorts of cases immediately.

But even if the bar examination is flawed, does this mean law schools can afford to ignore it? Obviously, no. The most selfish reason is that bar examination performance is part of the accreditation process, and as failure rates rise a law school may lose accreditation. Most of the recent ABA disciplinary actions have been based at least in part on poor bar passage rates. More on this in chapter 6 and 7's discussion of regulatory risks for law schools.

But much more importantly, it is an absolute disaster to accept students into law school who have a limited chance of passing the bar exam, regardless of whether you think that exam is fair. Law students are now regularly running up nondischargeable debts of upward of $250,000 and spending three years of their lives in law school in the hopes of a rewarding career as a lawyer. If they never pass the bar, that time and money is lost for good.

Some law school fans will argue that over time their earnings will normalize and law school will still be a net benefit, but I promise you, both anecdotally and empirically, repeatedly failing the bar before finally giving up is a soul-crushing and devastating loss. There are, of course, some students who have poor incoming statistical profiles who do pass the bar, and those who have great profiles who repeatedly fail. It is also true that a focus on the LSAT *uber alles* necessarily depresses diversity in law schools as well as later on in the profession, because African Americans and Latinos score worse on the exam. That effect is clearly bad.

That said, the whole reason why law schools consider the LSAT and UGPA in admissions is to balance risk. At a certain point it is simply irresponsible to accept students who are likelier than not to fail the bar and charge them tuition. This is especially so for the students with the worst statistical profiles, who currently pay and borrow the most to attend law school.

So yes, the LSAT and the bar examination are admittedly flawed. But the bar examination is a flawed examination with immense stakes for everyone involved. Studies show that the LSAT does correlate with bar examination passage rates. As Glenn Reynolds points out, this correlation is commonsensical: both of these exams are high-stakes, multiple-choice exams that test legal reasoning. Because the bar examination matters so much, we are stuck with the LSAT also mattering. If and when a better proxy is introduced for deducing the chances that a law school admittee will pass the bar, I will happily shift over to that measure. For now, let us turn to the LSAT scores of recent admittees.

ENTERING LSAT SCORES ARE DOWN A LOT SINCE 2010

There has been a precipitous decline in incoming LSAT scores since 2010. Part of this is because the students with the best LSAT scores are choosing not to apply to law school in the first place.[15] Paul Caron used the Law School Admission Council (LSAC) data to calculate what percentage of the applicant pool has LSAT scores of 160 or above, scores of 150–159, or scores below 150. Figure 5.1 covers the percentages from

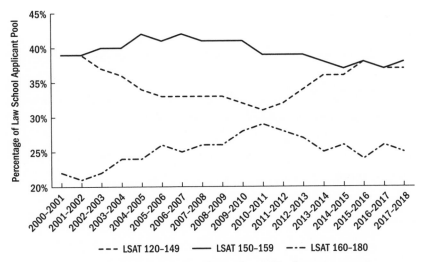

FIGURE 5.1. Percentage of law school applicants by LSAT cohort, 2000–2018.

2000–2018. I love this chart. First, it shows how the mix in applicants is affected by the overall number of applicants. In the last twenty years there have only been four times when the sub-150 LSAT group was the most prevalent among all applicants: 1997–99 and 2014–16. What do those periods have in common? They are the low points in a valley for applications. Basically, in the last twenty years when applications overall have fallen, it has affected applications from higher LSAT scorers more than the lower group. Relatedly, the Trump Bump has seen a larger gain on the high end of LSATs than the low end. Figure 5.1 suggests that the applicants with the highest scores are most sensitive to perceptions about law schools. When applications are up and law school is hot, those students are more likely to apply. As law school cools, the best and middle LSAT scorers are less likely to apply. When we reach a floor in applications, the below-150 group becomes the most likely group to apply. This makes strategic sense, because when overall applications are down the students with lower LSATs are more likely to be admitted.

Second, look at how strong 2010–11 was! We hit a peak in applications and applications by students with the highest LSATs. There were a lot more applications to law school, and the number of applicants with LSATs of 160 or above hit a twenty-five-year high.

Third, look at the fall from 2010 to 2015. The raw number of applicants with 160 or higher on the LSAT fell by almost half over just five years. By 2017, the bottom group had jumped up to almost 35 percent and the highest group had fallen to 26 percent.

If LSATs are not your bag, Keith Lee has gathered evidence of a significant decline in applications from America's top universities (Ivy League schools plus Stanford) since 2010.[16] The trend seems to have hit bottom in 2017, but overall applications are still down significantly since 2010. The early returns from the Trump Bump are more promising. As of April 2018, applications from students with LSATs of 160 or above were up 21 percent over 2017.[17]

When the applicant pool shrinks *and* has worse statistical profiles, the admitted group of students naturally looks worse. If one looks at the twenty-fifth percentile of entering LSAT scores from 2010 until 2017, they are uniformly down. A whopping 183 law schools (out of 204 ABA-accredited or provisionally accredited schools) saw entering LSATs at the twenty-fifth percentile fall between 2010 and 2017.[18]

The decline has been particularly marked (and disturbing) in terms of admissions of students with the lowest LSAT scores. Figure 5.2 shows how the makeup of incoming classes changed between 2011 and 2017. These charts were inspired by Jerry Organ's older work on LSATs from the Legal Whiteboard.[19] Figure 5.2 shows the number of ABA-accredited law schools with twenty-fifth-percentile LSAT scores in certain bands: under 145, 145–149, 150–154, 155–159, 160–164, 165–169, and above 170. In 2011, only nine schools admitted classes with a twenty-fifth-percentile LSAT score of below 145. By 2014, thirty schools did, a 233 percent increase. In 2011, the number of schools admitting classes with a twenty-fifth-percentile LSAT score of 160 or above was thirty-six. In 2014, it was twenty-five, a 30 percent decline. The numbers have improved since 2014, but mostly as schools moved from the below-145 category into the better, but still worrisome, 145–149 group. In 2016, the

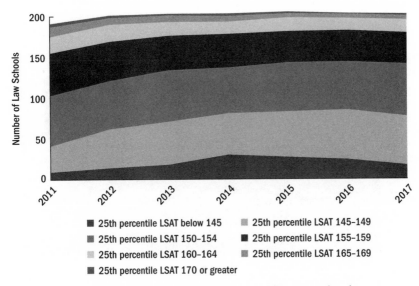

FIGURE 5.2. Number of law schools by LSAT twenty-fifth-percentile cohort.

145–149 range briefly passed the 150–154 range as the most prevalent type of school, a dubious peak.[20]

In 2010, there were only nine ABA-accredited law schools where a majority of entering students had LSAT scores below 150. In 2015, there were thirty-seven such schools.[21] According to Law School Transparency, four out of five law school applicants in 2015 were admitted to at least one law school, confirming the shift to nearly open admissions at the bottom of the market.[22]

If you look at the undergraduate GPA (UGPA) of incoming law school classes, you can see the same drift toward open admissions. Figure 5.3 shows how the makeup of incoming classes changed between 2011 and 2017. Each shows the number of ABA-accredited law schools with twenty-fifth percentile UGPAs in certain bands: below 2.7, 2.7–2.8, 2.9–3.0, 3.1–3.2, 3.3–3.4, 3.5–3.6, and 3.7 or above. From 2011 to 2015, you can see continuous growth in the three lowest UGPA categories. The lowest category, below 2.7, hits a peak in 2016 with eighteen schools, roughly 9 percent of American law schools. As elsewhere, 2017 shows improvement.

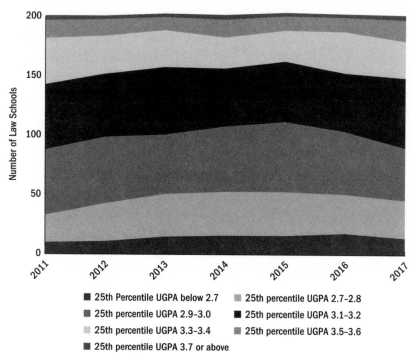

FIGURE 5.3. Number of law schools by UGPA twenty-fifth percentile.

DIVERSITY?

Is there good news from the trend toward open enrollment? Minority students tend to have lower LSAT scores,[23] so minority law school enrollment is at an all-time high, even in a time of lower enrollment. Figure 5.4 shows the number of minority enrollees in ABA schools from 1972 through 2017 as vertical bars, as well as a line showing the percentage of minority students in law schools. Because enrollment has shrunk overall, you may be discouraged by the post-2012 decline in minority enrollment. Expressed as a percentage of total enrollment, however, figure 5.4 tells a heartening story of continued and basically uninterrupted progress on this front.

Given the legal profession and law schools' long and woeful record on diversity, we may have finally found some good news! The ABA and the Association of American Law Schools (AALS) have made minority enrollment a priority since the 1970s, and the last five years appear to be a giant leap forward in that regard. In fact, if you were to choose a single defense for the cohort of law schools that have basically moved to open admissions, it would be that they are boosting minority enrollment. The for-profit law school holding company Infilaw has said exactly that about its law schools, claiming they were founded to "bring more blacks and Hispanics into the practice of law."[24] Florida Coastal's 2018 lawsuit against the ABA similarly alleged that enforcement of the ABA standards on admissions constituted "an attack on diversity."[25]

Unfortunately, there are several data points that suggest these gains have come at a significant cost for these students. Consider debt levels. Deborah Merritt has studied the numbers and come to an upsetting conclusion: in recent years minority JD students are carrying a much higher level of debt than their white counterparts.[26] This effect has accelerated significantly over the last ten years, at the same time that minority enrollment has spiked. On a granular level, the data suggests that the minority students that are borrowing the most are

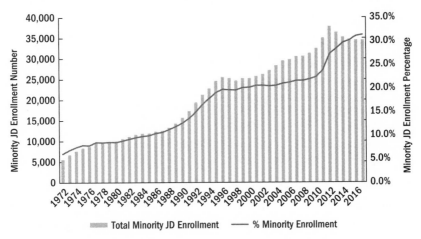

FIGURE 5.4. Total minority JD enrollment by number and percentage, 1972–2017.

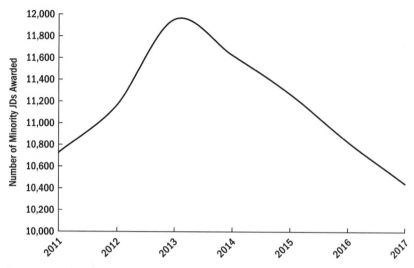

FIGURE 5.5. Total minority JDs awarded.

the students with the lowest entering credentials. Thus, we are admitting more minority students but burying them with a disproportionate share of debt.

And that's not even the worst news. Students with the lowest entering credentials are, not surprisingly, also the students who are most likely to struggle in law school and most likely to fail the bar.[27] Compare figure 5.5, which shows total minority JDs awarded from 2011 to 2017, with figure 5.4, showing total minority enrollment. Minority enrollment grew significantly between 2006 and 2012, suggesting that graduation numbers should have increased through 2015. Unfortunately, despite the growth in overall enrollment, figure 5.5 establishes that the number of minority JDs has actually declined since 2013, which is terrible news for the additional minority enrollees from 2014 to 2016. When you combine the cost in nondischargeable debt with the questionable results, your enthusiasm for the growth in minority enrollment is likely to sour. If law schools are letting in more minority students who are able to pass the bar and find gainful employment, that is indeed a reason for cheer. On the other hand, if law schools are letting in students, minority or otherwise, unlikely to succeed in law school, only to saddle them with a load of student debt and the psychic damage of never passing the bar exam, I am considerably less enthusiastic.

A large driver of this phenomenon is that law schools are distributing the great majority of their financial aid chasing students with higher LSATs and UGPAs, rather than on the basis of need.[28] Charitably, this is to build the "best" class possible. Uncharitably, it is just another way that the rankings game is perverting law school management. Generally speaking, the students with higher LSATs and UGPAs are more likely to be white and affluent.[29] This suggests that the minority students who are now being admitted when they might have been denied in the past may actually be subsidizing wealthy nonminority students, a particularly perverse result.

Again, I am not here to question the motives of the great bulk of the critics of the LSAT or the bar examination, or those who argue that the news of falling LSAT scores is good if this results in greater diversity in law schools or in the profession. But it is fair to question the motives of the schools that are accepting entire classes of students who would have been rejected just seven years ago—classes that have, as a whole, a very low chance of eventually passing the bar. These schools are charging these same students, whose profiles suggest the highest likelihood of bad results (either failing out after a year or two of law school or graduating but failing the bar), the most they possibly can, all subsidized by non-dischargeable government loans. When bar passage and other measurables inevitably crater (we cover the collapse in bar passage in chapter 6), these schools hide behind a diversity rationale, as if they are doing these students or the profession any favors.

BOOST REVENUE PART 2: GET THE GRE PARTY STARTED

ABA Standard 503 requires each law school applicant to take a "valid and reliable admission test."[30] This has been a controversial accreditation factor for years. In 2011, the ABA considered dropping it altogether.[31] In 2015, the ABA granted waivers to some law schools to allow them to accept a portion of their class without the LSAT.[32] In May 2018, the ABA Section of Legal Education and Admissions to the Bar voted to eliminate it altogether.[33] The section withdrew the proposal in August 2018, after significant outcry, so the Standard 503 requirement of a valid and reliable admissions test survives for now.[34]

Why the sudden interest in eliminating Standard 503? The possibility of using the Graduate Record Examinations (GRE) as an admissions test. Standard 503 does not actually require the LSAT by name, but interpretation 503-1 requires a law school using any other test for admissions to "demonstrate that such other test is . . . valid and reliable."[35] In January 2016, Wake Forest, Arizona, and Hawaii decided to try to demonstrate the validity of the GRE as a measure for law school entry by running a study comparing incoming LSAT and GRE scores and student success at each school.[36] A month later Arizona announced that it was ready to begin accepting the GRE as an admissions test. Arizona argued they had conducted a study that demonstrated that the GRE is a valid and reliable alternative to the LSAT.[37]

The news received a mixed reception. Many assumed that Arizona was mostly interested in gaming the rankings, by taking students with lower GRE scores who had not taken the LSAT or who would have done worse on the LSAT.[38] Alternatively, this was viewed as a relatively cynical ploy to boost applications and overall admissions by opening up a whole new group of potential law students.[39]

LSAC (the company behind the LSAT) was not amused and initially threatened Arizona with sanctions for abandoning the test. One hundred forty-nine law school deans signed a letter objecting to LSAC's actions, and LSAC backed off.[40]

At that point, it looked as if there might be some slow movement toward the GRE, but the future was hardly clear. As of February 2017, no other school had joined Arizona—not even its original compatriots Wake Forest and Hawaii. On March 8, 2017, that changed in a big way.

Without any advance warning, Harvard Law School announced that it would accept the GRE as well as the LSAT.[41] Harvard argued that the change would "diversify" its applicant pool: "Accepting the GRE should help the school draw more students with science and technology backgrounds, which are sorely needed in the legal profession, and applicants who already have graduate degrees," as well as international students.[42]

Harvard's decision sent shockwaves through law school admissions offices and made the rapid acceptance of the GRE much more likely. By May 2018, eighteen other law schools had joined Harvard and Arizona.[43] By May 2019, the total number had swollen to forty, even *after* the ABA declined to eliminate the LSAT requirement in Standard 503.[44] As of spring 2019, the ABA has not explicitly approved using the GRE as a replacement for the LSAT, so there is a risk that the ABA might find some or all of these schools out of compliance with accreditation standards somewhere down the road. As such, the rapid adoption of the GRE as an admissions test is quite remarkable and shows the power of the Harvard brand name to change law school behavior. Three top-fifteen law schools (Cornell, Penn, and Virginia) announced in 2018 they would also accept the Graduate Management Admission Test (GMAT; the business school admissions test).

Regardless of how the ABA will eventually handle the GRE (or the GMAT), how could the GRE revolution help struggling law schools? It can help by potentially boosting applications and matriculation. First, students think the GRE is easier than the LSAT. Here's a representative description of the two tests from the website LawSchooli: "I could mince words here, but instead I'm going to take a firm line on this. The LSAT is a harder test than the GRE. The LSAT is like the Ferrari of standardized, whereas the GRE is more like a Hyundai."[45] The Quora answer to the question "Which is harder, the GRE or the LSAT?" begins, "It is generally said the LSAT is the hardest of tests."[46] Regardless of whether the GRE is actually easier, it is a shame to invite potential law students to waste time trying out both exams, or add any more fuel to the "law schools are desperate to admit anyone" fire.

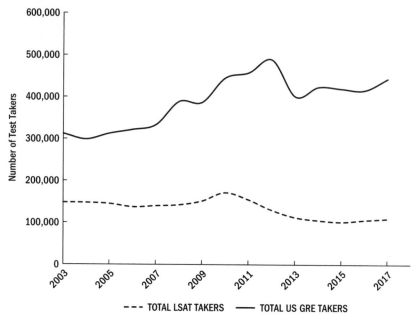

FIGURE 5.6. Number of LSAT and US GRE takers, 2003–17.

The GRE also opens a vast new target audience for law school admissions. Figure 5.6 shows that many more students take the GRE than the LSAT. In 2017 four times more people took the GRE than the LSAT. If law schools could convince even 10 or 20 percent of the GRE takers to take a flier on applying for admission, the potential for new enrollees is staggering.

Third, the advantage of taking the GRE may prove especially large at the low end, because law schools may admit uncompetitive students with lower GPAs or GRE scores who cannot gain admission to other types of graduate programs. Some law schools are currently admitting students with very low LSATs just to fill seats. They will be more than happy to do the same with low GRE scores. Further, the first low-end law school to accept the GRE will have the early adopter advantage. In January 2018, John Marshall Law School (Chicago) announced plans to accept the GRE.[47]

Last, accepting applicants with poor GRE scores will be much more palatable in the near future than accepting those with poor LSAT scores. This is because the ABA and others are familiar with the studies that have linked lower LSAT scores and bar failure.[48] As of yet there are no similar studies for the GRE (how could there be?). Thus, a struggling school could take any college graduate with any GRE score and argue that they were a better risk to pass the bar than a similar student with a low LSAT score. This is not a permanent fix (none of these patches are), but it would kick the can down the road a bit, allowing time for the market for law schools to further improve.

BOOST REVENUE PART 3: EXPAND NONACCREDITED PROGRAMS

There are two natural brakes on open admissions. The first is the absolute number of applicants, which is down by about a third since 2010. Law schools can't let applicants in if they don't ever apply. This is what makes the move to accept the GRE suspect. The second is the regulatory and rankings risk of watering down admissions standards.

What if there were a way of letting in paying customers whom regulators and the purveyors of law school rankings barely noticed? Enter the nonaccredited law school programs. The ABA does not accredit non-JD law programs, although as part of its JD accreditation process, schools must seek "acquiescence" before offering a non-JD program.[49] In order to attain acquiescence, a school must establish that the non-JD program will not negatively affect the JD program.[50] If you are thinking that this sounds like a pretty low bar, you're understanding the situation perfectly. As long as a master of laws (LLM) or another non-JD program does not harm the ABA-accredited portion of the program, it is fine with the ABA. These programs may be covered by regional accrediting bodies or other internal quality controls, but they are essentially excepted from the rigorous ABA accreditation process.

The difference in regulatory structure means that many law schools are now operating in two completely different markets. The

ABA-accredited JD market is highly regulated. The non-JD market is the Wild, Wild West. As a quick illustration, compare the availability of online JD programs with online LLM programs. There are no fully on-line JD programs at ABA-accredited law schools. Mitchell Hamline and Syracuse offer hybrid JD programs, where some classes are online, but students are required to take classes in person as well.[51]

Likewise, various non-ABA-accredited law schools in California, such as Concord or Cal Southern, offer wholly online JD degrees, but those schools are not ABA accredited and thus offer limited opportu-nities to take the bar examination.[52] They also appear to be offering a pretty raw deal, according to their 2017 mandated disclosures: Concord Law School cost $57,402 in tuition, and 3 percent of its students com-pleted the program on time.[53] Cal Southern cost $33,000 and shared an extremely high attrition rate with Concord.[54]

By comparison, there are a bevy of online LLM programs, including several by very well-known institutions such as New York University (NYU), Northwestern, and Washington University in St. Louis.[55] Unlike the online JD, all types of law schools, from the most to the least presti-gious, offer online LLMs.[56]

The online programs are just the tip of the iceberg, as there are many more in-person non-JD programs. The ABA categorizes non-JD pro-grams under one of three different names: academic master's degrees for nonlawyers (juris master), post-JD law degrees for foreign lawyers (LLMs), and academic-based doctorate-level degrees (JSD).[57] There are also LLM programs for law school grads, such as tax or intellectual property specializations. Recently the University of Arizona created yet another category—an undergraduate major in law. The program has been a runaway success in terms of enrollment and presumably revenue. Whether it is a good deal for the students remains to be seen. Arizona's success virtually guarantees imitators though, so prepare for a wave of undergraduate students attending law schools virtually or in person.

Because these programs are not accredited, we have very limited infor-mation about them. For example, the ABA counts the number of students

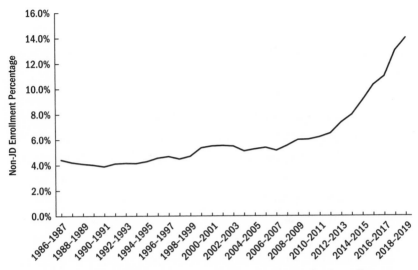

FIGURE 5.7. Non-JD enrollment as a percentage of overall law school enrollment, 1986–2019.

at ABA-accredited law schools who are enrolled in "non-JD" programs, but not what kind of program it is, how much students pay, whether the program is online or in-person, and so forth.[58] If you are interested in these programs, Hanover Research published a lengthy study of non-JD programs in 2013 that covers their nature and their explosive growth.[59]

Non-JD master's programs are proliferating. The ABA reportedly "acquiesced" in as many as twenty-five or thirty new programs just in 2015.[60] Likewise, the percentage of non-JD students in ABA-accredited law schools has skyrocketed. Derek Muller used the ABA's data to detail the rise of the non-JD student.[61] Figure 5.7 shows that between 1986 and 2009 the percentage of non-JD students bounced around between 4 and 6 percent, before spiking up to 14 percent in 2018–19. Consider the growth in online non-JD programs. In 2013, only twenty-five schools offered an online non-JD program. In 2017, fifty did. In 2014, there were 1,590 students in non-JD online programs at ABA-accredited law schools. There were 4,558 in 2017, 186 percent growth over three years.

If you are interested in the current state of non-JD programs, consider reading an amazingly acerbic internal evaluation of the University of Florida's in-person Tax LLM Program that leaked in 2016.[62] The takeaway? As currently structured, the Florida program, one of the oldest tax LLM programs in the country, is a money loser and a bad investment of resources. In response to the suggestion that possibly hiring more faculty might help boost demand for the program, the letter states, "The belief that hiring more tax faculty to man podiums is the answer to the demand problem is like hiring more sailors to man the Titanic once it has hit the iceberg."[63] Florida's challenging experience with trying to run a prestigious, in-person LLM program shows why schools have drifted to an online model, where overhead can be lower and the potential student population larger.

Foreign LLM programs (programs for foreign lawyers to gain an LLM and possibly become US lawyers) have been around for years and have long been a cash cow for law schools. Carole Silver estimated that LLM programs brought in between $130 and $160 million in 2009, before these programs expanded post-recession.[64] LLM tuition tends to run higher than typical JD tuition, and foreign students often pay full freight, so these programs can be quite lucrative.[65]

The effect of the Trump administration on foreign LLM applications and attendance is not yet clear, but early press reports suggest that his immigration rhetoric and policies may drive both down.[66] Moreover, the value proposition of foreign student LLM programs is unclear. Derek Muller has looked at the bar passage rate in California and New York for LLM holders from foreign countries and found that it floats around 30 percent and (like other bar passage rates) has declined since 2012.[67]

If you crave a different, sunnier, take on LLM programs for foreign lawyers, Michael Simkovic has argued that they are "probably" a benefit to international students, if not through bar passage in the US than in a return to the home jurisdiction with better knowledge of American law.[68] Generally speaking, the success of LLM programs does provide some good news about US legal education. If I told you about a product that was good enough that people from all over the world traveled to the

US and paid a premium to receive it, you would probably infer that the product is a pretty strong one. Obviously, this is not a perfect analogy, but still, if you're looking for support for our current model, the popularity of our LLM programs internationally is a helpful data point.

BOOST REVENUE PART 4: RAISE THE STICKER PRICE AND BRING IN THE LOANS

If you are seeking a single factor that explains why few law schools have closed in very challenging market conditions, consider that, despite a collapse in demand, law schools have raised prices and asked their customers to borrow more than ever to attend. Pause for a second to consider this move, and ask yourself whether the Great Recession led to Ford or GM raising the prices of their vehicles or homeowners asking more for their houses? Of course not, because in a depressed market prices go down, all else being equal.

But all else is not equal in the market for law schools. Recall figures 4.4 and 4.5 from the last chapter showing the incredible run-up in law school tuition and student indebtedness. Private law school tuition rose by almost 30 percent between 2008 and 2015. Debt went up by more than 50 percent. The continuing rise in tuition and debt is not equal across all law schools, however. It is concentrated at the high end and the low end of law schools. If you want to see a puzzling list, consider the 2016 ranking of the top twenty law schools for student debt:

	Law School	2016 Avg. Student Debt	2018 U.S. News Rank
1.	Thomas Jefferson	182,411	rank not published
2.	Whittier	179,056	rank not published
3.	San Francisco	167,671	rank not published
4.	New York University	167,646	6
5.	Georgetown	166,027	15
6.	American	164,194	86
7.	Golden Gate	161,809	rank not published

	Law School	2016 Avg. Student Debt	2018 *U.S. News* Rank
8.	Columbia	159,769	5
9.	John Marshall (Chicago)	158,888	rank not published
10.	Florida Coastal	158,878	rank not published
11.	Cornell	158,128	13
12.	New York Law School	157,568	112
13.	Pennsylvania	156,725	7
14.	Virginia	155,177	8
15.	Northwestern	154,923	10
16.	Pepperdine	154,475	72
17.	Elon	153,347	rank not published
18.	Harvard	153,172	3
19.	Ave Maria	152,476	rank not published
20.	Detroit Mercy	152,000	rank not published

Almost half of the schools are listed "rank not published," which means they are in the bottom quartile of ranked law schools. Another 40 percent are among the top fourteen law schools. Only two midlevel law schools (American and New York Law School) are on this list. How is it possible that lower-ranked law schools that are in danger of closing are charging more than healthier and higher-ranked schools? In what other industry would the top and the bottom of the market cost the most?

While these two different types of school predominate in the debt rankings, they actually do so for very different reasons. Top schools appear on this list because they can charge what they like and expect their students to borrow whatever it takes, based on the promise of a top-flight, and potentially very remunerative, legal career. See chapter 9 for more on whether that assumption makes sense outside of Yale, Harvard, and Stanford, and on the pernicious effects of having the top schools lead the way in tuition and debt.

The lowest-ranked schools also assume they can charge whatever they like for a very different reason: they are letting in the very last applicants in America who want to go to law school, those with very low UGPAs and LSAT scores. These students are unable to benefit from the discounting and competition over more qualified applicants. If they get into law school, they borrow enough to pay what is asked.

Wait, what? In a horrible market for postgraduate employment, and after a post-2010 collapse in applications and enrollment, the sticker price *and* the actual cost of attending the lowest-performing law schools has continued to rise—and faster than inflation! Why? The simplest answer is that the remaining law students are not paying for law school out of pocket. The federal government is. To explain, we need a short primer on federal student loans.

Before World War II, the federal government had very little to do with higher education. The federal involvement in higher education started with the G.I. Bill after World War II. The US government offered education grants in an effort to make homecoming for veterans easier. The educational benefits proved extremely successful and popular, so Congress added subsidized student loans for education for all Americans with the Perkins Loan Program in 1958 and the Stafford Loan Program in 1965.[69] Student loans were seen as a vehicle for increasing social mobility and educational opportunity.[70]

These loans were capped, however, and passed through some long periods without any upward adjustment. For example, the main Stafford Loan cap stayed at an annual limit of $18,500 (despite inflation) from 1992 to 2005.[71] The Stafford Loan was the main federal loan program for law students, so federal loans for law school were essentially capped at $18,500 over this period. Law students could borrow more from private lenders if they needed to (and many did) but under less favorable terms.[72]

Because there were two different types of loans (government-provided and private) and one was clearly a worse deal than the other, the Stafford Loan cap acted as a natural break on borrowing. When I attended Michigan Law School in the mid-1990s, I experienced this effect firsthand. Out-of-state tuition for my first year (1993–94) was $19,576, so roughly $1,000 over the Stafford Loan cap.[73] I had worked for two years after graduating college, so I had a small amount of savings that could cover the rest of the tuition. That meant between the full Stafford Loan and savings I could pay for law school tuition. I was thrilled! Unfortunately, there was the remaining issue of books, food, and shelter. I had heard good things about those items, so I needed to find a way to pay for them.

The financial aid folks explained that I could borrow for those as well, but I would need to do so from a private institution, not directly from the government, since I had already reached the government's cap. The private loan terms were worse, the paperwork was scarier, and if I avoided that road I could put a natural limit on the total amount I would borrow. It also sounded as if some lenders might want my parents to co-sign, which raised the stakes substantially. So, I limited my expenses and worked my way through law school. I still graduated with a substantial amount of debt (I borrowed the maximum Stafford package every year) but never took on any additional loans and graduated with much less debt than many of my classmates.

As tuition outstripped inflation (and not just at law schools) and the Stafford Loan amounts remained capped, more and more students faced my problem. Congress attempted to fix the problem with the Higher Education Reconciliation Act of 2005.[74] The act raised the Stafford limit slightly but radically changed the nature of graduate school loans.[75] Congress created Grad Plus loans, which came on top of Stafford Loans and allowed students to borrow the entire amount of the cost of the graduate school education (including living expenses and books) directly from the US government. It also applied the federal government's income-based repayment and loan forgiveness programs to all federal graduate school debt.

Congress thought there were few better ways to improve the country and the lives of its citizens than to encourage students of all income levels to go to graduate school. Based on the available information, this was absolutely correct. For time immemorial, the lifetime value of a graduate school education has greatly outstripped its cost on average. Moreover, student loans for graduate school historically had a very low default rate.

Congress could encourage more people to go to graduate sch[...] they would improve their lives and earnings potential, and th[...] government back their loans over time, running the entire pr[...] profit, or at least breakeven. What could go wrong?

We are still living with this system today. In 2018 if you went to the official Department of Education Grad Plus Loans page and read through the frequently asked questions, you would come to "How much can I borrow?"[76] The answer? "The maximum PLUS loan amount you can borrow is the cost of attendance (determined by the school) minus any other financial assistance received." Let's unpack this answer. You can borrow as much as you would like from the government for law school, capped only by *the law school itself.* Law schools do not have purely unfettered discretion (more on that later), but they apparently do have discretion to raise tuition faster than inflation every year and to allow for a generous living stipend.

If you visit any ABA-accredited law school's website and click through to tuition or cost of attendance, you will find their calculations of the maximum amount a student can borrow. For example, a Thomas Jefferson Law School student could borrow $77,450 for the school year 2016–17.[77] That figure was $89,342 per year for NYU and $88,600 for Harvard.[78]

At this point it should be clear why the federal loan structure has allowed for the price to rise in a down market. Students aren't paying for it; the government is. So, this explains the "how" of the debt explosion but not the why. Shouldn't law students (who are all full-grown adults and graduates of college) know better? And in a related vein, if law students are willing to borrow the money, what's the problem here? Maybe this is just an opportunity for prospective law students to learn the meaning of "caveat emptor" in advance of law school.

First, law schools have not been fully transparent over the years on the value of a law degree, fudging employment results by reporting the percentage of graduates with *any job* rather than just the graduates with legal jobs. This is the central claim of the various lawsuits filed against some law schools.[79] Students thus might think that borrowing $200K to earn $180K per year seems fair enough, which may be true under Harvard's employment statistics. I promise you that the vast majority of graduates from lower-ranked schools do not earn $180K upon graduation.

And the problem was not simply misleading students with selective presentation of otherwise accurate data. Even after the lawsuits and the ABA significantly tightening the reporting requirements for employment, more aggressive fudging may still be a problem. A 2016 random ABA audit of the employment figures at ten law schools found problems with five of them.[80] As Paul Caron pithily noted, that's a 50 percent failure rate.[81]

Many potential law students remain unclear on what exactly law grads earn or do. Some of this is based on excitable coverage of the recent raise in the starting salary for first-year associates in some large law firms from $160,000 a year to $180,000 a year.[82] Some of it is the continuing prevalence of good-looking, wealthy lawyers handling very interesting cases (often in trials!) in television shows like *Suits*, *The Good Wife*, and *Franklin and Bash*.

Second, many of these students may be relying on the currently generous income-based repayment program (IBR) or the loan forgiveness plan for public service. Philip Schrag has done an excellent job of detailing how these programs work. He explains how the programs help a hypothetical law student named "Sarah" who borrows $120,000 to pay for law school at an interest rate of 7.25 percent and then takes a job paying $63,000.[83] Schrag admits that Sarah would have a hard time paying off her debt based on her income. Yet, thanks to IBR and possibly loan forgiveness, Schrag is confident that Sarah will pay off relatively little of her loan:

> By electing [IBR] Sarah could limit her annual payment to 15 percent of her discretionary income, defined as her adjusted gross income minus 150 percent of the poverty level for a family of her family's size. Even if Sarah

has no other family members, this formula would reduce her monthly repayment to $578 in the first year of repayment, about 11 percent of her actual income. Furthermore, the law that created IBR forgives any remaining debt after 25 years of repayment. If Sarah received 3 percent annual raises (and continued to have no other family members), in her 25th year she would pay $1,175 monthly, still only 11 percent of her income, and the remainder of her debt would be forgiven. If she were married with two children, her initial payments would be $355 per month, and her final payments would be $722 per month, 6.8 percent of her income.

The terms of repayment under the 2007 legislation are more generous for those who are fortunate and self-sacrificing enough to do long-term public service. If, after graduating, Sarah spends 120 months working for a government entity or any non-profit organization described in Section 501(c)(3) of the Internal Revenue Code, she would have to repay at the IBR rate only for those 120 months. Under the federal Public Service Loan Forgiveness program (PSLF), forgiveness of the remaining balance would take place at the end of that ten-year period, and (unlike forgiveness for those who do not do public service) cancellation of the remaining debt would be tax-exempt.[84]

Schrag is not alone in touting the benefits of these programs. The ABA Section of Legal Education has a special website dedicated to informing students about these programs, and law schools certainly make enrollees aware of them.[85]

So maybe the problem is solved? Hardly. The full bill for these programs is just starting to come due, and there is no guarantee that Congress will continue the program for future or even current participants. In 2017, the Government Accountability Office (GAO) released a lengthy report presenting revised estimates for the cost of IBR.[86] Unsurprisingly, Congress has radically underestimated the cost of IBR, and as much as $137 billion in federal loans will eventually be forgiven or discharged.[87] Figure 5.8 shows the GAO's analysis of student loan debt from 1995 to 2017.[88] You might be confused by the $29 billion in figure 5.8 that will be

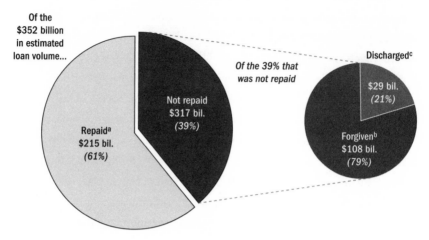

FIGURE 5.8. GAO analysis of student loan debt, 1995–2017. Source: GAO analysis of estimated income-driven repayment plan cash flow data provided by US Department of Education.

"discharged." Student loan debt is generally nondischargeable in bankruptcy, so how is that figure possible?[89] The GAO notes that the "discharged" debt comes from "loan principal that . . . will be discharged due to death or disability."[90] If you want a statistic that encapsulates the student loan crisis, consider how many people will die with substantial balances left on their loans.

Almost 40 percent of the current federal loan balance will not be repaid, to the tune of $137 billion. Does that sound like a program that a Republican Congress that is generally hostile to higher education might want to reconsider? The first Trump budget proposed eliminating the public service loan forgiveness program altogether. It also proposed raising the income-based percentage to 12.5 percent and extending the period to thirty years.[91] A similar bill passed the House of Representatives in 2017.[92] The bill would cap all federal lending for graduate school at $28,500 and would eliminate public service loan forgiveness.[93] If either of those provisions became law, it would radically change the finances of law schools.

Moreover, the early returns have shown that actually following the rules and properly gaining a full loan forgiveness is much harder than advertised. Of the 28,000 borrowers who filed for loan forgiveness in 2017, just 289 were approved because of confusion about which plan to join and how to apply. The Department of Education expects to iron out this snafu, but still, the first impressions are not promising.

It is true that many law students, especially some of the law students that do not have the highest entering credentials, are relatively innumerate. As with much received wisdom, there is truth in the old saw that students attend law school rather than business school or medical school because they hate math. Likewise, some law schools offer conditional "scholarships" that require students to earn a certain GPA during law school to keep the support.[94] Some of these springing scholarships were set at GPA levels well above the average GPA in the school, guaranteeing that some (or many) of the scholarship recipients would be asked to pay full freight for the second and third years of law school.

It is also true that the loan amounts are now so large that many law students simply glaze over when the figures are presented. There are (possibly apocryphal) stories of tribal languages where the words for numbers go "one, two, three, four, many."[95] These societies do not need numbers for large amounts because the difference between fifteen or twenty animals or berries is well captured by the word "many." Further precision is unnecessary. This is my exact theory on law school debt. For the students who have just graduated college and have never worked a long-term job, the difference between borrowing $80,000 or $200,000 is hard to quantify. Both sums of money are unimaginably large and will take forever to pay back, if they will ever be paid back at all. This effect is worsened by what behavioral economists call "hyperbolic discounting." Humans naturally overvalue current benefits (such as attending law school) while devaluing future costs (such as paying off student loans for the rest of their lives).[96]

Last, when assessing motivations for human actions, it is often an error to assume ignorance or irrationality is the main explanation. That is true here too. Many of the students who are borrowing full freight from the government to attend a lower-tier law school are first-generation college graduates who come from modest and even impoverished backgrounds. Behavioral economists have started to realize that individuals from impoverished backgrounds have a different taste for risk: favoring longer shots and disfavoring some behaviors, such as saving, that seem obvious and rational to wealthier communities.[97] This trend helps explain the prevalence of lotteries, payday loans, and layaway stores in poorer communities. Not all of these purchases are irrational when the actual circumstances of being poor (where long-term planning often seems more detrimental than helpful) are taken into account. To a person who grew up in community where much worse and riskier borrowing such as payday loans or layaway are an everyday feature, the risk of borrowing heavily for law school tuition for the chance, even a relatively remote chance, to leap into the upper middle class seems like quite a rational risk.

Congress certainly had the best intentions in allowing students to borrow the full cost of a graduate school education. A graduate degree has long been associated with higher earnings, and the Grad Plus program did encourage more students to attend graduate schools, including some who might have been put off by the prior borrowing schemes.[98] But, at least at law schools, the help has come with a significant downside: mountains of debt.

PLUS A LITTLE (UNWITTING) HELP FROM OUR FRIENDS

If you assume it's true (because it is true) that some law schools are now admitting pretty much any even facially qualified applicant, the current number of matriculants (somewhere around 38,000 each year from 2013 to 2017) is pretty close to the maximum number of law students we can scrape together. This raises another puzzle. Even with law schools hustling hard on the strategies above, some or many law schools at the bottom of the food chain should be completely empty of students. If every law school from Yale down had kept their class sizes the same in 2017 as they were in 2011, there would be 14,000 fewer students to enter the law schools near the bottom, and we might see some actual market closures. There are roughly a third fewer law students than there used to be, but rather than there being a third fewer law schools, law schools from the top to the bottom have shrunk in concert, sharing the pain roughly equally and allowing the lower-ranked law schools to survive. Why?

Ah, yes, the *U.S. News* obsession. One of the best sections in Brian Tamanaha's prescient and still excellent book *Failing Law Schools* details American law schools' obsession with and mania over the *U.S. News* rankings.[99] That obsession (and its many downsides) is now well chronicled. Wendy Espeland and Michael Sauder, two sociologists, wrote an excellent recent book entitled *Engines of Anxiety* on the topic.[100] The book is packed with data and anecdotes that lay out in painful detail the way that rankings stand in for money as the main battleground in legal academia. One of the feeblest predictions in my own 2015 book, *Glass Half Full*, was that in the wake of an existential crisis, the iron grip of rankings on law schools would lessen and we would see a return to some sanity.[101] Hardly.

If anything, the rankings have grown *more* powerful. The vast majority of law schools have worked very, very hard to maintain or even improve their numbers by admitting smaller classes, partially in a salutary desire to maintain the "quality" of the student body, but largely to maintain or improve in the rankings.

Consider just the schools at the very top of the food chain. Figure 5.9 shows that *fifteen* of the top twenty-one law schools experienced a decline in applications between 2011 and 2016, with most experiencing drops of 10 percent or greater.[102] These schools thus faced something of a prisoner's dilemma. If they all worked in concert and accepted the same number of students in 2016 as they did in 2011, they would have slightly lower "quality" classes, but they would have the same cash flow as they did in 2011. More likely than not the rankings would be relatively unaffected, as everyone would just have a slightly less qualified (by the numbers) entering class, roughly canceling each other out ratings wise.

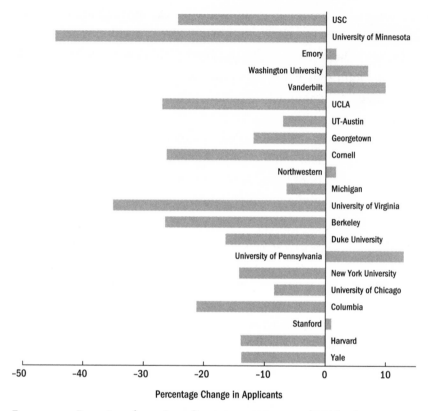

FIGURE 5.9. Percentage change in applicants to top twenty-one law schools, 2011–2016.

But if any one or two schools defected and shrank their class to improve or maintain their numbers, they might take a sudden leap up in the rankings vis-à-vis the others. This worry about defections meant that almost everyone shrank their classes out of fear that everyone else would shrink their classes. Figure 5.10 shows this result in practice. Rather than face a possible rankings loss, fifteen of the top twenty-one schools shrank class sizes, with many shrinking by more than 10 percent.

Looking at figure 5.10, there is one clear outlier in class size: Berkeley. Did they suffer the lash of a rankings drop? The jury is still out, but for now the answer is a qualified no. In 2011, Berkeley was ranked seventh.[103] Between 2012 and 2017, Berkeley bounced between seven and nine. In 2017, Berkeley fell to twelfth, but they bounced back to ninth in 2019.[104] Berkeley seemed especially poised for trouble: remember that they are also one of the schools that have cut the size of their faculty the most since 2011.

Yet veteran students of these rankings know that the top fourteen law schools not named Yale, Harvard, or Stanford bounce around quite a bit, often moving up or down by as many as three slots, while maintaining a rough equilibrium over time. As of yet, there is limited evidence of a clear rankings plus or minus depending on class size.

Nor are shrinking class sizes limited to the top law schools. Between 2011 and 2016, roughly 80 percent of ABA-accredited law schools shrunk

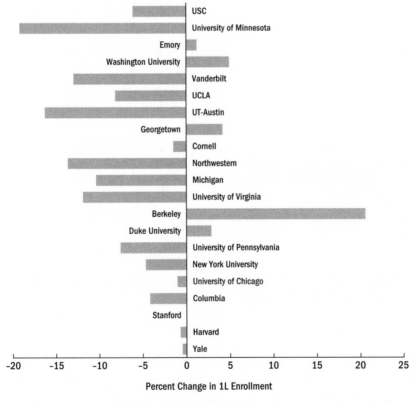

Percent Change in 1L Enrollment

FIGURE 5.10. Percent change in first-year class size for top twenty-one law schools, 2011–2017.

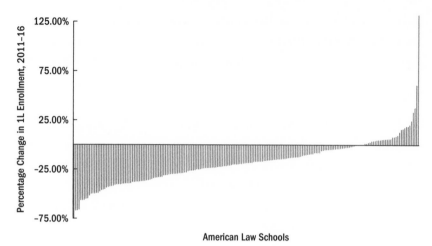

FIGURE 5.11. 1L enrollment percentage decline or increase, 2011–2016.

the size of their entering classes. Figure 5.11 shows the percentage of the decrease or increase in entering class size between 2011 and 2016, with the largest percentage decline on the left (Appalachian) and the largest percentage increases (Irvine and La Verne) on the far right. As you can see, the declines greatly outnumber the increases, so the vast majority of schools have chosen to shrink the size of their classes. The median law school shrunk by 19 percent over this period.

This choice has been a massive boon and gift to the law schools that are struggling, because law schools from the top to the bottom have shared the pain of smaller incoming classes rather than simply sticking the least competitive law schools with empty buildings. In this way, every law school that shrank its class size has subsidized the lowest-ranked law schools, an unwitting life raft.

TRUMP BUMP!

In early 2017, just weeks into his presidency, Donald Trump announced a travel ban on citizens of several Muslim countries. The ban itself was not particularly clear (did it apply to green card holders? Visa holders?

Everyone from those countries?) and also caused a massive uproar among opponents of President Trump. Lawyers went to airports all over the country to help stranded travelers and challenge the ban.[105] Lawyers likewise battled later versions of the ban in court, as well as a bevy of other Trump administration actions that were unpopular on the left. For the first time in a while, lawyers were seen as heroes, at least by some Americans.[106]

Lo and behold, fast-forward by a year to 2018 and law schools all over the country experienced a "Trump Bump" in interest. LSAT administrations jumped up 18 percent in 2017–18.[107] Applications rose as well, albeit by less: 2017–18 applications were up 8 percent.[108] As per usual, the rubber hits the road with matriculants, who grew more slowly, so it is still too soon to say. Nevertheless, the Trump Bump raised the hopes of law schools all over the country.

One reason to believe that the Trump Bump may be the start of a return to greener pastures is that previous declines in law school applications and attendance have tended to hit a two- or three-year bottom (very much like the 2014–17 period where these number stabilized and rose slightly) and then bounced back to historical norms or even new heights. If history is our guide, the Trump Bump may well mean the beginning of a new bounce back. The scuttlebutt among deans and admissions officers in 2018–19 certainly reflects this optimism.

That said, the underlying cost versus value calculation for a law school degree has not improved substantially. Neither the Trump Bump nor an improving economy has changed postgraduate employment that much, and law school continues to be very expensive measured by either tuition or debt levels. When a product suddenly grows more popular despite little change in the product itself, it may not be wise to expect the popularity to simply grow. After all, as *Above the Law* noted, Trump will not be president forever, but your student debt might last that long. Likewise, the number of law school graduates who get to stick it to the man by driving to airports on the weekend to fight travel bans will remain, sadly for all lawyers, relatively low, regardless of an enthusiastic resistance to Trump.

UPSHOT

On the one hand, the collapse in applications from 2009 to 2015 was a perfect storm of bad publicity and bad luck, as the bill for years of educational and job placement decisions seemingly came due all at once. And yet, there has been another perfect storm of *good* luck that has kept almost all law schools afloat, despite cratering application and matriculation numbers. Schools have cut costs and maintained revenue flow by hook or by crook. They've loosened admissions and radically shrunk their faculty and staff. They've benefitted from a somewhat irrational rankings race among their brethren. And just when it looked as if things were stabilizing, they received the great boon of a Trump victory and a resulting Trump Bump in applications.

WILL THE GOOD LUCK CONTINUE PAST 2019? THREE QUESTIONS REMAIN.

First, is the Trump Bump real? Did we reach bottom in 2015 and are now simply experiencing the natural reversion to the mean of a greater number of applications? Or is this a dead-cat bounce? If it is the latter, we should see more closures, as we are past the point of easily cutting costs or increasing revenue. Past experience and the Trump Bump suggest that law schools are back, but nothing about the last decade suggests we are in typical times for law schools.

Second, will other law schools continue to keep their class sizes smaller? All over America, law school deans are having unpleasant conversations with their central administrators. We'll cover this question in greater detail in chapter 8, but note for now that a temporary period where law schools shrink their class sizes to improve their rankings is one thing. A permanent shrinkage and the resulting permanent loss of revenue is quite another. If the current shrinkage is the new normal, some central administrators will want to see lowered costs through layoffs or pay cuts, or a return to previous class sizes, or both. If enough law schools grow back to their 2010 size, that could still substantially harm the law schools lower on the food chain. Likewise, the Trump Bump will be of little use to the hardest-hit law schools if the top and middle-class law schools grow their classes to absorb all of those students.

Third, will taking these extreme steps in terms of cost-cutting and open admissions endanger accreditation? Chapters 6 and 7 cover that very real risk.

WHY HAVEN'T MORE LAW SCHOOLS CLOSED?

PART 2: ABA ACCREDITATION

I have to admit that after describing the long list of savvy moves and good luck that have kept America's most endangered law schools open for business, I have a grudging, but not insignificant, measure of admiration for their management. While they haven't exactly turned lemons into lemonade, they have managed to keep their lemon trees alive, which is an achievement in a once-in-a-lifetime drought.

Yet today's solutions are sometimes tomorrow's problems, and the phrase "out of the frying pan and into the fire" is one that must worry these schools. These schools are not out of the woods yet, not by a long shot. That is because the strategies that have kept them from the jaws of a market-based closure have actually opened up the strong possibility of what I call a regulatory closure: either disaccreditation by the American Bar Association (ABA) or the loss of federal loans from the Department of Education (DOE), or both. This chapter discusses the dangers presented by the ABA, and the next chapter covers the DOE. Both of these regulatory bodies present risks to a good number of law schools.

A STRUCTURAL OVERVIEW OF THE REGULATION OF LAW SCHOOLS

The majority of American law schools are overseen by their accrediting body, the ABA. The ABA is the main body that writes the standards governing the operation and maintenance of law schools. The ABA is the body that sends out inspection teams and decides whether a new law school can become accredited and whether existing law schools remain accredited.

Befitting an organization run by lawyers, the ABA accreditation process is quite complex. The 2016–17 Standards and Rules of Procedures is over 140 pages long, including prefaces and appendixes.[1] The standards and procedures are too involved for detailed coverage here, but a few general points should suffice.

First, there are a lot of standards and a lot of different ways that a school can violate them. There are standards requiring faculty governance.[2] There are standards barring discrimination and compelling diversity efforts.[3] There are standards governing the size, responsibilities, and qualifications of the full-time faculty.[4] There are even standards mandating some of the contents of the law library.[5]

Along with the standards themselves, there are a series of complex procedures for accreditation.[6] There are procedures for becoming provisionally accredited, and then another set of procedures for becoming fully accredited. There is a set of procedures for the inspection and reaccreditation of already accredited law schools. There is also a process for sanctioning or disaccrediting a law school.

ABA accreditation is critically important for two and a half reasons. The first and main reason ABA accreditation matters is that the vast majority of states require graduation from an ABA-accredited law school to sit for the bar exam and become a licensed lawyer.[7] Some states, such as California or Tennessee, allow students to graduate from a non-ABA-accredited law school, but only if the state itself has approved the school.[8] Others states, such as California, Virginia, and Washington, still allow apprenticeship to stand in for law school.[9] Remember that Kim Kardashian is trying to become a lawyer under California's apprenticeship track, potentially making her the most famous self-trained lawyer since Abraham Lincoln.

But these non-ABA-accredited routes into legal practice come with a crippling downside: it is nearly impossible to transfer bar admission from one state to another unless you have graduated from an ABA-accredited law school. As a functional matter, this means that the ABA has a near stranglehold over law school regulation.

The second reason ABA accreditation matters is that students at non-accredited institutions of higher education cannot receive either federal grants or loans. If you know anything about the financing of American higher education, you will know that the inability to receive federal funds is very, very close to a death sentence. We will discuss the DOE role more in the next chapter, but just know that law schools have to be ABA accredited (or accredited by another DOE-approved accrediting body) to have access to federal student loans.

The "and a half" reason that ABA accreditation matters is all of the other benefits of reputation, quality, and prestige that come with accreditation and association with the ABA. ABA accreditation itself was created to drive "diploma mill" law schools out of the market. Given the recent outcomes for many ABA-accredited law schools, whether measured by bar passage or employment figures, this reputational effect has been watered down substantially.

Ultimately, the ABA is the gatekeeper that decides whether an American law school has access to federal loans and can offer an opportunity to join the bar in all fifty states. Those powers come from two different sources: the DOE and state supreme courts. Traditionally, neither of these bodies has been particularly vigorous in oversight. We'll discuss the DOE below, but first a word on state supreme courts.

In every state in the union, state supreme courts, not state legislatures, control the regulation of lawyers, often under a claimed constitutional "inherent authority" over the area.[10] Legislatures remain involved of course, but state supreme courts are the final authority because of their inherent authority over lawyer regulation. I promise I will not bore you with a full explanation of the history and case law underlying this structure, but we should note a few of its salient features: (1) Unlike every other American profession, lawyers are regulated by the judicial branch rather than the legislative one. (2) Because the power and role of state supreme courts is a matter of state constitutional law, changing this structure would require a constitutional amendment in most states, making any change virtually impossible. This means that even in states with elected judiciaries, there is very little in the way of voter oversight over lawyer regulation. Few voters even know that state supreme courts handle it. (3) State supreme courts are pretty busy with their day jobs, so they are even more prone than legislatures to delegate regulatory authority. (4) As a result, lawyer regulation is often delegated back to bar associations, especially the ABA. (5) If you're guessing that means lawyer regulation, including the regulation of law schools, is typically congenial to the regulated entity, in this case law schools and their faculties, you would be correct.

It is an exaggeration to say that state supreme courts have allowed the ABA to regulate law schools mostly for the benefit of the people who run law schools, that is, their faculties. But it's not much of an exaggeration. One of the main points of Brian Tamanaha's *Failing Law Schools* is exactly this one: if you examine any particular aspect of law school regulation and ask, "How does this serve the interests of the faculty?" an answer should be readily available. Just consider all of the various faculty-friendly regulations that require faculty governance of law schools, such as a large full-time faculty devoted to both scholarship and teaching. How these regulations serve the students or the public at large is often a harder question to answer.

This helps explain a central puzzle of ABA regulation: if the accreditation process is so detailed and complex, why is it so ineffective? In other words, why haven't more lower-performing schools been disaccredited? The system is not set up to protect vulnerable students or to safeguard federal loan dollars; it's set up to benefit faculties and law schools themselves. The threat of disaccreditation has been used historically by law schools to squeeze additional funds or new buildings or other perks out of larger universities, not as an actual cudgel against the lowest-performing schools.

The ABA Section of Legal Education and Admissions to the Bar has long been criticized as a classic example of regulatory capture. Two decades ago, Emory Law professor George Shepherd wrote two very persuasive law review articles excoriating the ABA for using the accreditation process to keep lower-cost and innovative competitors out of the market and using the reaccreditation process to enrich law faculties at the expense of their students.[11] The capture theory also explains why the ABA would work hard to keep new competitors *out* but also hustle to keep existing schools *in*. Law school accreditation has been like the legal profession: very hard and expensive to get into (the accreditation process guarantees that) and then very hard to get kicked out of.

The ABA has denied accreditation to start-up law schools. It has taken away provisional accreditation. It has even put fully accredited law schools on probation. But before Arizona Summit in 2018, the ABA has *never* even attempted to disaccredit a fully accredited law school.[12] The ABA has certainly played a role in the recent wave of closures, but none of those closures came after disaccreditation.

Please do not conclude that I am accusing the ABA and law faculties of conscious collusion or an explicit conspiracy to stick it to students and the public. On the contrary, that sort of scheme would have been easily spotted and defeated. What happened over the years with the ABA was much more insidious. The folks at the ABA have a sincere desire to see better law schools push out better lawyers. Theoretically that goal would benefit everyone: the students, the profession, and the public. And who would better know how to ensure that law schools were excellent than the distinguished faculty at those schools?

Most law professors graduated from a top law school, so their vision of an excellent law school was pretty narrow. For years, America's best law schools have featured large, well-compensated faculties that spent a significant amount of their time on scholarship and taught limited class hours. As these have been the hallmarks of excellence, law schools and the ABA sought to reproduce them at every law school, regardless of whether it makes sense to run the University of Tennessee the way you run Harvard or Stanford, let alone the Thomas Jefferson School of Law.

THINGS HAVE NEVER BEEN GREAT AND THEN THEY GOT WORSE:
THE THREAT OF ANTITRUST

You do not need to be an antitrust expert to spot the danger in the ABA/ law faculty team-up. It looks an awful lot like the ABA is a trade organization working to keep out competitors and to raise monopoly prices and profits for those inside the organization. This connection becomes even more explicit when you consider the many examples of the ABA and the Association of American Law Schools (AALS), which is an actual trade organization, working together on accreditation issues.

The Antitrust Division of the Department of Justice (DOJ) went so far as to sue the ABA in the 1990s under exactly this theory. The story starts in 1993, when the ABA denied accreditation to the Massachusetts School of Law at Andover (MSL). MSL sued the ABA under antitrust and other grounds.[13]

The ABA eventually won the case at summary judgment.[14] The district court held that the ABA was immune from suit under the state action doctrine.[15] The state action doctrine basically says that the government and those who operate under a government delegation of authority cannot be liable under the antitrust rules, because the government is allowed to act anticompetitively when it chooses to. Since the ABA operates under a grant of authority from state supreme courts, it is exempt. The ABA has repeatedly won similar lawsuits under the state action doctrine.[16]

Despite this victory, the MSL lawsuit proved very costly to the ABA. The lawsuit jarred loose a DOJ investigation, and two years later the DOJ brought its own antitrust suit.[17] This raised the stakes for the ABA considerably. The ABA is used to being sued if it refuses to accredit a new law school, and they have yet to lose one of those lawsuits. But a lawsuit brought by a new, and allegedly substandard, law school is quite a different animal than one brought by the DOJ. Any American judge is very likely to be susceptible to the ABA's arguments that a denial of accreditation was deserved and served as a hedge against new diploma mills. American judges tend to come from elite backgrounds, including studying at the best law schools, so they are naturally sympathetic to the ABA on this front. When the plaintiff is the US government, however, the balance shifts considerably.

Unsurprisingly, the ABA settled the DOJ case relatively quickly. The resulting consent decree agreed to several changes in the accreditation process.[18] Here are highlights from the settlement: The ABA agreed to stop "fixing faculty salaries," and to consider revising standards mandating low "student to faculty ratios [and] teaching loads." It also required the ABA to "open up the ABA accreditation process so that it is no longer controlled by legal faculty who benefit from requiring better pay and working conditions." Alrighty then!

The settlement did have some notable effects, but it hardly ended the ABA's role in protecting law school faculties and budgets. Ten years after the signing of the decree, the ABA ended up admitting to repeated violations, resulting in a 2006 agreement where the ABA paid $185,000 in fees and costs to the DOJ.[19] Nevertheless, the DOJ terminated the investigation and the case in 2006.[20] The ABA breathed a provisional sigh of relief. It had won the MSL case and settled the DOJ case, but it was hardly in the clear.

The ABA knows better than most that the DOJ rarely brings a lawsuit they think they might lose, so it could hardly rest easy and assume that the state action doctrine would continue to operate as a foolproof defense on all fronts. The risk of further DOJ action or other lawsuits lingered. The ABA made some changes to its standards to eliminate some of the most obviously anticompetitive and pro-faculty standards, but the biggest change came in the attitude of the regulators. The ABA became much more skittish about denying accreditation or pushing too hard on existing law schools. Consider the pace of accreditation. The ABA approved eight new law schools in the 1980s and another eight law schools in the 1990s—sixteen in twenty years.[21] The ABA then approved sixteen just in the years 2000–2008.[22]

You can also see the change in the revolving door between the ABA and start-up law schools. Starting in the 2000s, a new strategy for gaining law school accreditation was born: hire an ABA insider as dean to shepherd a fledgling law school through the accreditation process. In 2004, the *Chicago Tribune* ran an article detailing the "unseemly" links between the ABA as regulator and new start-up schools as the regulated.[23] It listed the following examples of cozy connections: (1) Ave Maria School of Law hired Bernard Dobranski as its founding dean and guide through its accreditation. Dobranski had previously served on the ABA's accreditation committee. (2) John Marshall Law School (Atlanta) hired Jack Ryan as dean, the former chair of the accreditation committee, after it struggled to gain accreditation. (3) Florida Coastal School of Law hired as dean Jack Hurt, who had been the number two staff member on the ABA's accreditation team. (4) After Hurt guided Florida Coastal to accreditation, he took over as dean of Barry Law School. (5) The online-only Concord Law School hired Barry Currier, who had previously served as the number two staff member at the ABA, as dean to replace Hurt. Each of these law schools, with the exception of Concord, eventually gained accreditation.

Nor has the revolving door stopped. Currier left Concord to take over as the top staff member on the ABA accreditation team.[24] His deputy managing director is William Adams, who served as dean at Western State College of Law when they gained accreditation.[25]

Basically, ever since the early 2000s, the leadership of the ABA's Section of Legal Education and Admissions to the Bar has reflected the post-DOJ investigation priority of avoiding further antitrust troubles and loosening accreditation. As *Above the Law* has noted, if the ABA were interested in really cracking down on law schools through the accreditation process, Currier would not be in charge.[26] Nor would Adams. Currier and Adams's primary experience and qualifications come from guiding schools through the accreditation process, not denying them.

A recent change in the reach of the state action doctrine has also militated looser ABA enforcement out of fear of antitrust liability. In

2015, the Supreme Court denied the state action antitrust exemption to a state-appointed dental board because "a controlling number of decision-makers" on the board were "active market participants in the occupation the board regulates," and the board was not actively supervised by the state in *North Carolina State Dental Board v. FTC*.[27] Sound familiar? If *Dental Board* does not describe the ABA section exactly, it comes quite close. Sure, federal courts will likely be more accommodating to state supreme courts than a dental board, and maybe state supreme courts can present better evidence of active supervision, but still, the applicability of *North Carolina State Dental Board* to the ABA is an open, and frankly somewhat terrifying, question. Deborah Rhode and I wrote a 2017 article about the topic arguing that the ABA (and many state bar associations) might well be denied a state action exemption under the case.[28] This means that all of these regulatory bodies are stepping especially lightly these days.

No one wants to see a head-to-head confrontation between federal antitrust law and state supreme court control of lawyer regulation. If such a disagreement got out of hand, we could see a constitutional battle between state supreme courts' claim of inherent authority to govern the legal profession, the Tenth Amendment's reservation of powers to the states, and federal law's power to overrule state law, including state constitutional law. The last thing the ABA wants is to hang their own state supreme courts out to dry in a battle with federal regulators. The ABA and state supreme courts are collectively happiest when everything is quiet on the regulation front. Discord and lawsuits bring unwelcome attention, distracting state supreme court justices from their "A" job of deciding cases.

BETWEEN A ROCK AND A HARD PLACE: THE DOE STEPS IN FOR THE DOJ

Given these trends, one might expect the post-consent-decree ABA to be loose on accreditation, and there is evidence that is what happened until 2016. Unfortunately for the ABA, its efforts to please one portion of the federal government brought it into potential conflict with another, even more powerful agency, the Department of Education (DOE). I have studied the regulation of lawyers for years, and prior to 2016 I was only vaguely aware of the DOE's role in the regulation of law schools. This is mostly because historically the DOE's role in accreditation was *pro forma*, and it has only recently begun to flex its muscles.

Recall chapter 5's discussion of the G.I. Bill. For the first time, the federal government provided grants and federally guaranteed loans to individuals to attend college or graduate school.[29] Consequently, there was a new concern over the quality of higher education, because the DOE did not want to disperse funds to poor-quality, or even fraudulent, institutions or programs.[30]

In response, the DOE teamed up with private accreditation agencies. These agencies did the accrediting, and the DOE oversaw the accreditors.[31] If a school was not accredited by a DOE-approved accreditor, the DOE would not allow the school to receive federal funds. Note the similarity in structure to the credit rating agencies that were partially to blame for the financial crisis of 2008.[32] The schools seeking accreditation are the ones who pay for the existence of the accrediting agency. The government, in turn, relies on these private-sector, third-party accreditors as a measure of safety. A problem may arise because the incentives for the accreditor are skewed—they naturally serve their paying customer, not the government.

One way to defend against this risk is for the government to review the accreditors themselves. The DOE reviews accrediting bodies through a process called "recognition."[33] At least once every five years the National Advisory Committee on Institutional Quality and Integrity (NACIQI) reviews each accrediting body for compliance with DOE and statutory requirements.

The work of the NACIQI has been relatively low profile, and the DOE has rarely sanctioned or barred an accrediting agent during the recognition process.[34] Nevertheless, in response to sharp criticism of for-profit institutions during the Obama administration, the DOE announced an intention to tighten up the recognition process.[35]

Accreditation decisions are absolutely critical in higher education. Because the federal government now supplies the vast majority of educational loans in higher education, it is not an exaggeration to say that the accreditation decision is a life-or-death matter for most institutions. The increasing importance of accreditation makes the DOE recognition process critical. A DOE denial of an accrediting agency, especially a large one, could have seismic market effects. If the DOE decides an accrediting agency fails its standards, the agency itself will likely lose its participating schools (read, paying clients), because those schools need to be accredited by a DOE-approved accreditor to receive federal loans.

The ABA was among the first accreditation bodies to be approved by the DOE and has been the only recognized national agency accrediting law schools since 1952.[36] The ABA's recognition process through the NACIQI has grown increasingly rocky over the years, however. In 2006, for example, the NACIQI raised several issues of transparency and consistency but recommended continuing to allow the ABA to run accreditation.[37]

In 2011, the NACIQI gave the ABA something of a tongue-lashing, noting that they were out of compliance with DOE regulations in seventeen different ways, including failing to consider student-default rates or job placement in accreditation.[38] This resulted in some unpleasant attention from Congress.[39] But again, these critiques came at the same time that the ABA was operating under the shadow of possible antitrust enforcement, so it continued to run a relatively loose ship.

By 2016, the NACIQI had run out of patience. The committee noted multiple problems with the ABA accreditation process and recommended a one-year suspension of the power to accredit law schools for the ABA.[40] You read that right: the main DOE body in charge of determining who can accredit law schools wanted to suspend the ABA. The NACIQI noted some well-worn problems: law schools publishing misleading job statistics, law schools enrolling high-risk students who are unlikely to graduate or pass the bar, and sky-high debt loads.[41] The DOE eventually decided not to follow the NACIQI recommendation and declined to suspend the ABA, but the entire process certainly sent a stern and frightening message to the ABA: tighten up accreditation or face the possibility of losing accreditation power altogether.[42]

The ABA tried to downplay the dispute as mostly an issue of small, technical problems.[43] Nevertheless, it is hardly a coincidence that around the same time the NACIQI was taking a harsher look at ABA accreditation, the ABA awoke from somnolescence and took a series of actions against underperforming law schools. The headline news was the decision to try to strip Arizona Summit of accreditation in June 2018.[44] The ABA also found ten different law schools out of compliance between 2016 and 2018: Appalachian School of Law, Ave Maria School of Law, Charlotte School of Law (more in chapter 7), Cooley Law School, Florida Coastal School of Law, Golden Gate Law School, Atlanta's John Marshall Law School, North Carolina Central, Thomas Jefferson School of Law, Thurgood Marshall School of Law, the University of Puerto Rico, and Valparaiso University Law School.[45] Some of the schools on this list have gotten off of probation (Cooley and North Carolina Central, for example). Others seem to expect to follow Arizona Summit. Thomas Jefferson, for example, recently took the unusual step of gaining California State accreditation, presumably as a hedge against losing ABA accreditation.

The ABA also tightened up on provisionally accredited law schools. The ABA denied full accreditation to the University of North Texas–Dallas College of Law, although it remains provisionally accredited.[46] It also sanctioned the Duncan School of Law at Lincoln Memorial University for loose admissions, although the school was eventually fully accredited in 2019.[47]

The main point here is that the ABA has found itself whipsawed between two different branches of the federal government. At the beginning of the 2000s, the ABA operated under a DOJ-based understanding that it should take it slow or face possible antitrust enforcement. But the

DOE has presented an equal and opposite force recently, especially after the ABA's close call with the NACIQI in 2016.

It is also worth remembering that the ABA regulators read the same newspapers and websites that other lawyers do, so they are acutely aware that law schools have been buried under negative press for the last six or seven years. They are also likely receiving calls from state supreme court justices and others asking, "Why the hell is bar passage collapsing? What are y'all doing over there?"

In response, the ABA has suddenly lurched its disaccreditation machine into gear. The first move came in 2009 as the ABA decided to shift its accreditation standards from what they call *input measures*, such as the size and compensation of the faculty or the number of books in the law library, to *outcome measures*.[48] Bar passage is an obvious outcome measure, but accreditors were also hoping to reach broader concerns such as "knowledge, skills, and ethics." The ABA added new accreditation standards requiring more careful attention to experiential learning, student assessment, and explicit learning outcomes for every class and program.[49] These changes have, in fact, required some soul searching and a massive amount of work for associate deans at law schools all over the country. Whether these new requirements will have a meaningful impact going forward is a harder question.

KITTEN'S GOT CLAWS? BAR PASSAGE SUGGESTS YES!

If the ABA had only adjusted their input measures, struggling law schools would have had little to worry about. These schools have become quite expert in facial compliance with the ABA's many and varied regulations. This is why the change to outcome measures is potentially so seismic. If the ABA criticizes a law school for underfunding their law library or for using too many adjunct professors, the school can rightly claim that the ABA is prioritizing form over function. Prosecuting input standards is also much more likely to implicate antitrust concerns than outcome measures.

FIGURE 6.1. Mean multistate bar exam scores, 1974–2018.

The ultimate outcome measure is bar passage. Bar passage rates have fallen since 2008. Figure 6.1 shows the February and July scaled Multi-state Bar Examination (MBE) scores stretching from 1974 to 2018. The scaled multistate scores are helpful because the MBE is a standardized test that theoretically has been graded consistently over time, while the overall pass rate in most states include written components that change more over time or may be graded subjectively.[50] The year 2018 proved to be a rough one. The July scores were the worst since 1984, and the February scores were the worst since at least 1974. The scores on the February exam are always lower than the July scores, because the February bar sitting includes a higher percentage of test takers who have failed at least once.[51] Recently there is a weird syncopation between the July and February scores. July started its collapse in 2012, hitting a low point in 2015 before temporarily bouncing back in 2016 and 2017 before cratering again in 2018. The July 2017 MBE score was just a touch below the average July result since 1974, so as of 2017 the July scores looked as if

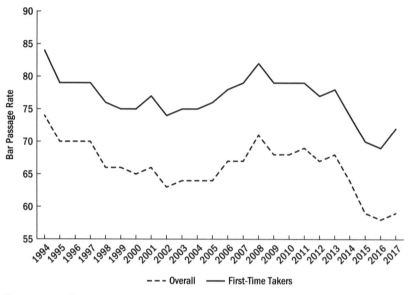

FIGURE 6.2. Bar passage rates, 1994–2017.

they were returning to normal, undercutting the "open admissions are harming bar passage" trope.

The July 2018 scores and the February scores tell a different story. One explanation for the acute collapse in February scores is that following bad July years in 2014 and 2015, the percentage of repeat takers has been up for the February MBE.[52] Repeat takers do worse than first-time takers. That said, the February scores since 2015 are positively apocalyptic. February 2017 was the lowest score on record. February 2018 beat that low point handily. Derek Muller, who has done yeoman's duty with this data on his blog *Excess of Democracy*, reports that the February 2018 MBE score is the lowest in the history of aggregated MBE results.[53]

When MBE scores decline, the overall pass rate declines as well. Figure 6.2 displays the national bar passage rate from 1994 to 2017, separating first-time takers from the overall pass rate. The first thing to note is the utter collapse between 2013 and 2016. The first-time passage rates in 2015 and 2016 were below the *overall passage* rate from 2008. Second, note that

2017 showed a rally. The numbers are still down, but any improvement is a welcome sign. The national 2018 results were not released yet, but the results from individual states suggest 2017's uptick will be short lived.

California was the poster child for the collapse. The July 2017 overall passage rate was 56 percent for first-timers and 43 percent overall.[54] The first-time pass rate for graduates of California's ABA-accredited law schools was 62 percent. Breaking it out by school and over time is even more shocking. Paul Caron created a chart that shows the July 2016 pass rate and that year's *U.S. News* ranking for each ABA-accredited California law school:[55]

Bar Pass Rank (Rate)	California School	*U.S. News* Rank CA (Overall)
1 (91 percent)	Stanford	1 (2)
2 (88 percent)	USC	4 (19)
3 (84 percent)	UC-Berkeley	2 (8)
4 (82 percent)	UCLA	3 (17)
5 (81 percent)	UC-Irvine	5 (28)
6 (72 percent)	UC-Davis	6 (30)
6 (72 percent)	Loyola-L.A.	8 (65)
8 (71 percent)	San Diego	10 (74)
9 (70 percent)	Pepperdine	8 (65)
10 (66 percent)	Santa Clara	11 (129)
62 percent	**STATEWIDE AVERAGE**	
11 (61 percent)	McGeorge	13 (144)
11 (61 percent)	Cal-Western	Tier 2
13 (57 percent)	Chapman	12 (136)
14 (51 percent)	UC-Hastings	7 (50)
15 (42 percent)	Western State	Tier 2
16 (38 percent)	Southwestern	Tier 2
17 (36 percent)	San Francisco	Tier 2
18 (31 percent)	Golden Gate	Tier 2
18 (31 percent)	La Verne	Tier 2
18 (31 percent)	Thomas Jefferson	Tier 2
21 (22 percent)	Whittier	Tier 2

Several things stand out. The overall pass rate is very low, and it is low across schools. Roughly one in ten *Stanford Law* grads failed the July 2017 California bar exam. Look at poor University of California (UC)–Hastings, which is by all accounts a fine law school. A 51 percent passage rate! Hastings had struggled in recent years, posting 68 percent first-time pass rates in 2014 and 2015, but no one could have seen this collapse coming.[56]

Most of the bleeding came at the lower-ranked California schools. *Seven* different California law schools had first-time pass rates below 50 percent. If you are wondering which schools might face ABA sanctions, start with these schools. Whittier has since closed, and in 2017–18, both Thomas Jefferson and Golden Gate received notices of noncompliance from the ABA. The February 2018 results were even worse, with a 45 percent passage rate for first-time takers and a 31 percent pass rate for repeaters. July 2018 offered no respite, as the pass rate hit a sixty-seven-year low.

There are differing views on the cause of the drop. The bar examiners have quite confidently stated that the drop is mostly or completely a result of lowered-entry standards at law schools. Erica Moeser, president of the National Conference of Bar Examiners, called the decline "deceptively simple" and blamed the entering class of 2011.[57] There is empirical evidence that lower LSAT scores correlate with lower bar passage scores, and that the effect accelerates as the scores get lower.[58]

The data itself presents a more muddled picture. Figure 6.3 shows the average LSATs for students matriculating at an ABA-accredited law school from 2011 to 2017. Comparing LSAT scores to bar passage hurts the "lower admissions standards" narrative because the average entering LSAT score fell continuously from 2011 to 2016, so the upticks in July bar passage in 2016 and 2017 look strange. If loose admissions were driving the fall in bar passage, we would expect to see a downward trend stretching into at least 2020, as the relatively weaker entering classes work their way through the system. The poor 2018 results fit the "falling LSATs lead to lower MBE scores" narrative much better.

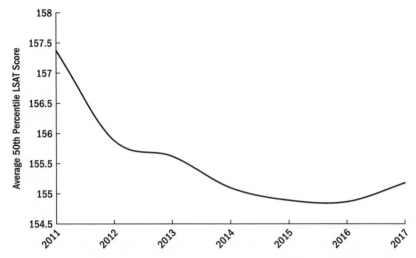

FIGURE 6.3. Average fiftieth percentile LSATs for incoming law students, 2011–17.

Others see protectionism. After all, we are suffering through a continuing down period in the market for lawyers, so bar examiners might be tempted to consciously or subconsciously grade the essay portion of the exam more harshly. UC-Hastings's dean David Faigman compared California's plummeting pass rate to other jurisdictions and blamed protectionism:

> As an aside, let me express my utter incredulity with the conduct of the Committee of Bar Examiners of the State Bar of California. The pass-rate for first-time takers of ABA accredited California law schools was 62%. In comparison, New York's bar-pass rate was 83%. The California Bar is effectively saying that 38% of graduates from ABA accredited law schools are not qualified to practice law. This is outrageous and constitutes unconscionable conduct on the part of a trade association that masquerades as a state agency.[59]

Regardless of the cause, bar passage has declined significantly since 2011, presenting a much more pressing regulatory issue for struggling law schools. Bar passage is a hard number, and other than tightening admissions or turning law school into a three-year bar review course it is a hard number to move, so there is no easy way to manipulate them back to respectability.

THE ABA REACTS

At first the ABA sought to tighten its standards on bar passage. Under the current Standard 316, a law school can meet bar passage requirements by showing that in three of the last five years, 75 percent of its graduates who took the bar eventually passed the bar, *or* that its first-time passage rate was no more than 15 percent below the average bar passage rate for ABA schools in the relevant jurisdictions.[60]

Critics argue that this standard is too easy to meet and allows possibilities for gamesmanship. For example, Standard 316's measure of eventual bar passage rates (rather than first-time rates) only requires tracking of 70 percent of the graduates who choose to take the bar, so there are two different groups of students who are missed—those who don't take the bar and up to 30 percent of those who do. Law School Transparency argues that the standard incentivizes law schools to cherry-pick the jurisdictions it reports to maximize their overall passage rate.[61]

The "first-time passage rate" portion is also a little wonky because the passage rate in a relevant state naturally includes the bar passage rate of the school involved. So as lower-ranked schools admit students who are less likely to pass the bar, they can hope that everyone's passage rate goes down in concert, allowing them to lose ground but still remain within 15 percent of the rate for the jurisdiction as a whole. As Associate dean Jay Sterling Silver puts it, "The best hope for the schools at the bottom of the LSAT and bar passage ladder is that the decline in bar passage will occur in lockstep among all the schools in their jurisdiction so they won't fall more than fifteen percent below the state average."[62] The 15 percent standard thus offers the paradoxical hope that a falling tide can raise all boats.

In 2013, the ABA's Standards Review Committee proposed a single 80 percent passage rate within two years of graduation.[63] By 2016, the proposed revision had been lowered to an eventual 75 percent passage rate within two years of graduation. In theory, this change only eliminates the first-time passage portion of the above standard, while keeping the eventual passage rate at 75 percent and giving schools two years (and four possible bar exam administrations) to cross the finish line. The change was obviously a bigger deal than that though, since deans all over the country panicked. Some law deans complained that the new standard would negatively affect diversity efforts, and others noted the logistical difficulties of compliance.[64] Others hailed the change as overdue and necessary.[65]

Nevertheless, it looked for a while as if the ABA was going to approve the higher standard. In September 2016, a month after the NACIQI's proposal to suspend ABA accreditation for a year, the ABA Accreditation Standards Review Committee met and voted to approve the new, tougher Standard 316.[66] The committee also approved a tighter standard for law school attrition. If a law school has attrition rates above 20 percent in any specific class, the school has to demonstrate its compliance with the ABA's admissions policies.[67]

Note that the proposed bar passage standard was much scarier than the attrition standard, because the bar passage number offered a crisp two-year time frame to determine compliance, and if two years passed and the overall pass rate was below 75 percent, the school was out of compliance. By comparison, the attrition standard just raises what is essentially a rebuttable presumption of noncompliance.

In October 2016, the ABA's Council of the Section of Legal Education and Admissions to the Bar passed the revised Section 316, sending it on to a vote by the ABA's House of Delegates in February 2017.[68] At this point the opposition kicked into gear. Ninety different law deans signed a letter asking for the House of Delegates to vote no, and the president of the State Bar of Michigan wrote a lengthy letter criticizing the proposal procedurally and substantively.[69] It probably also hurt that California's July 2016 bar pass rates were awful, raising fears that a 75 percent rate might close multiple schools in our most populous state.[70]

In February 2017, the House of Delegates voted down the proposed change to Standard 316, sending it back to the council for further consideration.[71] It is unclear what, if any, effect the change in presidential administration has had on the House of Delegate's rejection of the new standard, but the possibility of an antiregulation Trump administration reversing or relaxing the 2016 moves of an Obama DOE may have given the House of Delegates some comfort in rejecting the tightened standard and the council in letting it slide for now. In 2018 the council voted to send the proposal back to the House for another vote in 2019. The House of Delegates again voted it down, but in May 2019 the council approved it anyway. It will still take a few years before it hits (note the two year measuring period), but this is potentially the biggest change in ABA accreditation ever.

During the pendency of the clearer Standard 316, the ABA took a different tack. Rather than wait for approval of tighter standards, the ABA has used existing Standard 501 (which requires that law schools "only admit applicants who appear capable of satisfactorily completing its program of legal education and being admitted to the bar") to send notices of noncompliance to at least ten law schools in 2017.[72] None of these notices explicitly listed the bar passage Standard 316. Instead, the ABA seems to be using the more general admissions standards as their cudgel.

EVENTUAL PASS RATES

Part of the reason the ABA used an admissions metric rather than the bar passage numbers from Standard 316 is that we only recently have decent data on who eventually passes the bar and who does not. In fall 2017, the ABA required all law schools to collect and publish their eventual bar passage rates.[73] Before that we only had a handful of much older studies to estimate what happened to law graduates who failed the first time.

In 2018, the ABA released the first collection of the data. It turns out that 88 percent of the class of 2015 passed the bar by two years after graduation.[74] Nineteen schools fell below the two-year goal of 75 percent bar passage and thus may someday struggle to meet revised Standard 316:

School name	2-year passage rate
Arizona Summit Law School	60%
New England Law, Boston	60%
Pontifical Catholic University of P.R.	61%
Inter American University of Puerto Rico	64%
District of Columbia, University of	65%
Atlanta's John Marshall Law School	68%
Wyoming, University of	69%
Valparaiso University	69%
Western Michigan University–Cooley	70%
Syracuse University	71%
Ohio Northern University	72%
Florida Coastal School of Law	72%
Golden Gate University	72%
South Dakota, University of	73%
Howard University	73%
North Dakota, University of	73%
Barry University	74%
Whittier Law School	74%

These data also support the idea that Whittier Law School was hardly the worst law school in America when it closed. Seventeen other law schools had worse eventual bar passage numbers than Whittier.

WHY DIDN'T THE ABA ACT UNDER STANDARD 316 DIRECTLY?

The two-year bar passage rates listed above seem facially noncompliant with even the old Standard 316. Why did the ABA choose to proceed under Standard 501 and admissions rather than bar passage? It did so because the old Standard 316 offered law schools a lot of wiggle room and a lot of leash to return to compliance or to seek a variance.

First, old Standard 316's first-time bar passage rules applied to "three years of the last five years," meaning that law schools could mix and match and backfill. The better national bar results from 2011, 2012, and 2017 could be used to float recent declines.

Second, the rule only applied to "graduates who sat for the bar."[75] This made sense because there were law school graduates who chose to pursue nonlegal employment and thus never take the bar. Likewise, if students failed out of law school, it seemed unfair to count them as failing the bar, although they were functionally in a worse spot than students who graduated and failed (who at least had a completed degree). If students who never took the bar counted against bar passage, for example, a Yale Law graduate who clerked for the Supreme Court and went straight into teaching without taking the bar would have counted against Yale's bar passage rate.

Unfortunately, most law grads who skip the bar are not Yale graduates, and some law schools have been gaming both old and new Standard 316 in three different ways:

1) Failing out a lot more students. Law school GPA has a relatively high correlation with bar passage, so some schools are adjusting their curve to fail out big percentages of their students. This may eventually rub up against the new standard on student attrition (more below), but that standard has more fudge room to it than the bar passage rates. Using the "robbing Peter to pay Paul" management approach of many law schools, we would expect a school in trouble on bar passage to take their chances with attrition.

2) Pressuring students not to take the bar if the school thinks they will fail.

3) Actually paying law school graduates not to take the bar.

CHARLOTTE SCHOOL OF LAW (AND ALLEGEDLY OTHERS) PAID STUDENTS NOT TO TAKE THE BAR

According to a 2015 lawsuit, all three of the for-profit law schools owned by Infilaw (Arizona Summit, Charlotte, and Florida Coastal) were paying low-performing stipends *not* to take the bar.[76]

Wait, why would a law school, and especially a for-profit law school, *pay* law students not to take the bar? Recall that under the old Standard 316, first-time passage rate is key, so pushing lower-performing students from July to February (when the first-time passage rate is higher) alone makes sense. But the real bonus comes if these people *never* take the bar, because they will not count as "failing" a bar examination under Standard 316 at all. Six months is a long time, and studying for the bar is hard. Maybe these students will get a nonlaw job and move on. Or maybe they will give up. Or maybe they will get hit by a truck. Infilaw is likely happy with any of these results. All that matters for accreditation is that the students who are unlikely to pass do not take the exam.

But maybe this explanation is too cynical. Maybe Infilaw is looking out for the students least likely to pass by helping them take longer to study before they take the bar. A 2015 audio recording of the Charlotte School of Law dean who was in charge of student success emphatically puts that possibility to rest. The recording confirms that Charlotte was paying students not to take the exam, and that the purpose of the payments was to boost first-time passage.[77] If you have any sympathy at all for the troubles that Infilaw now faces, please listen to this recording.

The recording is allegedly from a meeting between the faculty and the administration that occurred about a week before the July 2015 bar examination. The point of the meeting is to encourage the faculty to pressure lower-performing students to take an $11,200 payoff *not* to take the bar. The administrator does not beat around the bush about why the payments are offered, stating that without the payoffs their first-time pass rate "would have been 20-something percent." The administrator is also exceptionally insulting to her own faculty and graduates, calling the graduates lazy and cursing at her own faculty while demanding that they be "coaches" and not "cheerleaders" and that they tell their students, "Get down on the f—— floor and give me forty."

The recording is remarkable on multiple fronts. First, before the recording came out, the payments to students had been unconfirmed and rumored to be around $5,000. The recording suggests they are over $11,000!

Second, before the recording it was more possible to put a positive spin on the payoffs. The recording makes it clear that the for-profit Infilaw is hardly spending the money out of the goodness of its heart.

Third, how profitable were these schools exactly? The schools were profitable enough that they could afford to pay an $11,000 stipend to multiple students to try to goose the accreditation standards. If you think that these for-profit schools are bilking the federal student loan system, the stipend looks eerily like a kickback of a small portion of the profits to a co-conspirator—just enough to wet these students' beaks.

Fourth, how bad does it have to get before law professors are recording meetings with associate deans and then leaking the recording to the media a year and a half later? The Charlotte School of Law must have been a fun place to work in those years.

Last, and most importantly, consider the poor students who signed up to go to the Charlotte School of Law. Charlotte was the largest law school in North Carolina from 2012 to 2016, and not by a small margin.[78] It also led North Carolina law schools in per student indebtedness. In 2013, 95 percent of Charlotte's graduates left the school with student debt. The average amount of debt for these students was $135,466 per student, just for law school. Most or many of these students likely had undergraduate debt as well. Seventy-three Charlotte School of Law grads took the February 2018 bar examination. Only eight passed (a 9.5 percent passage rate).[79]

Charlotte would have you believe that it is an engine for social mobility. Its 2015 report to the ABA shows that its student body was almost half minority students.[80] The report does not reflect their family backgrounds, but it seems likely that many of the students came from working-class families. Some of them were likely the first in their family to graduate college, let alone attend law school. In an alternative universe where Charlotte cared about being an engine for social mobility by charging these students less than other law schools and focusing on practical skills and bar passage, they could, in fact, have changed the lives of a bunch of deserving students. Riaz Tejani, a former law professor at a for-profit school, wrote a book called *Law Mart* chronicling his experience. He repeatedly notes that the faculty and administration at for-profit law schools were encouraged to picture their school as a mission-driven institution aimed at social mobility.[81]

In fact, almost half of the students Charlotte admitted did not graduate, with the vast majority of their attrition coming from failing out.[82] The students who did graduate passed the bar at ever lower rates. The combined July/February first-time rate in North Carolina for the school in 2015 was 45 percent. The February 2017 first-time passage rate was 25 percent.[83]

There may well be schools that are providing meaningful opportunities to students of color at a fair price and then setting most of them up for success, but the Charlotte School of Law was not among them. All of the available data suggests that the school was operating the worst kind of "public-private" partnership scam. The US government subsidizes and guarantees student loans for graduate school in an effort to allow any American access a middle-class living. Charlotte preyed on this generosity by convincing students with a low likelihood of success to sign up for a boatload of loans, which are paid directly to Charlotte. When the student fails out or eventually cannot pass the bar, Charlotte keeps the money, and the student carries the nondischargeable debt. When they struggle to pay the loans, their credit suffers, and they are blocked from other, more useful borrowing, such as for a car or a house. Arizona Summit and Florida Coastal presented similarly poor profiles in 2015–16 (poor enough that the ABA placed Arizona Summit on probation in March 2017 and started disaccreditation in 2018), so all of the Infilaw schools present poorly right now.

ATTRITION?

When the ABA House of Delegates rejected the 75 percent eventual bar passage rate in 2017, it simultaneously adopted a new interpretation to Standard 501 that presents a rebuttable presumption of noncompliance if a law school's cumulative nontransfer attrition rate rises above 20 percent for any law school class.[84] This interpretation lacks the clear bite of an eventual bar pass floor but still may do some good, depending on what the ABA means by "rebuttable presumption." Students of Title VII law and *res ipsa loquitur* know that some rebuttable presumptions are more easily rebutted than others.[85]

A 20 percent standard with teeth might make a difference. Here are the schools with attrition rates at or above 20 percent in 2017:

Law school	Total 1L attrition rate
North Carolina Central University	37.7
Thomas Jefferson School of Law	37.2
Widener-Commonwealth	32.7
Golden Gate University	30.5
Arizona Summit Law School	27.2
Florida Coastal School of Law	25.7
Southwestern Law School	24.8
California Western School of Law	24.4
Capital University	23.0
Western State College of Law	22.4
Lincoln Memorial	22.2
Atlanta's John Marshall Law School	21.9
Widener University–Delaware	21.7
Liberty University	20.3
San Francisco, University of	20.0

In 2017, fifteen different law schools hit 20 percent attrition or more, and just in the first-year class! Including second-year (2L) and third-year law student (3L) attrition would add more schools to the list. This level of attrition is a natural by-product of the ABA paying attention to declining bar passage rates. Are too many students are failing the bar? Then get them before they can take the bar, by failing them out. Many of the schools on this list have been using attrition to manage their bar passage rate, since law school GPA is the top predictor of whether someone will pass the bar. If they have to keep more of their lowest-performing students under the new attrition standard, they may meet the new 20 percent attrition rate only by hurting their bar passage rate.

SETTLE IN FOR A LONG HAUL: NOTHING MOVES FAST WITHIN THE ABA

Between attrition and bar passage, we have seen an uptick in ABA enforcement since 2017. Does that mean we may soon see our first regulatory closure? It depends on how you score the announced closure of Arizona Summit. In 2018, the ABA launched an actual disaccreditation action against Arizona Summit. At first Arizona Summit announced plans to appeal and stay in business, but it gave up the ghost in October 2018, announcing a teach-out plan and eventual closure. The ABA never actually disaccredited Arizona Summit, but still, the threat alone worked.

That said, the ABA is well aware that any attempted disaccreditation (whether Arizona Summit or otherwise) could result in a lawsuit, so its policies and procedures are explicitly designed to pass any due process challenge. That means there are layers upon layers of process and that schools who find themselves out of compliance will be given every opportunity, and sufficient time, to attempt to regain compliance.

It is beyond the scope of this article to cover every step that might be involved in permanently disaccrediting a law school, but a brief overview is instructive. Start with the time frame for detection. The ABA standards used to call for a full site inspection of accredited schools every seven years.[86] In 2018, that was stretched to ten years.[87] ABA site inspections involve quite a bit of rigmarole, and if a school is substantially or even partially out of compliance, the visits are likely to bring the problems to light. Before the actual inspection, a school must answer a lengthy questionnaire and create a self-study.[88] The visit itself lasts for days and involves a soup-to-nuts review of the entire program. If you're curious about the ins and outs, the ABA has a thirty-two-page memo describing the process in detail.[89]

If you have lived through this process at a school that is substantially in compliance, you probably remember the whole experience as a very time-consuming and annoying, but necessary and critical, work of bureaucratism. In some ways, an ABA site visit is like a good home inspection: the inspectors trek all the way out to your school, so they are going to find *something*. For instance, the last site visit at the University of Tennessee discovered a lack of compliance with the ABA's experiential learning requirements. Since we have the nation's oldest continuously operating legal clinic program, staffed by nationally renowned tenured or tenure-track faculty, as well as two different "practice-ready" concentrations (in advocacy and business), we were somewhat nonplussed by this finding. But we quickly rewrote our requirements to meet the complaint and moved on with our lives.

The process is somewhat less congenial and copacetic at schools that may be in more serious noncompliance. But since the visits now only come every ten years, there can be a significant lag between noncompliance and detection. For example, in 2016, Ave Maria School of Law faced public sanction over its admissions standards following a site visit.[90] Close observers of Ave Maria and other Florida law schools might note that Ave Maria's 2015–16 bar passage and admissions numbers were not much worse than in the past and were also not that much worse than some other Florida law schools. Why was Ave Maria nabbed in 2016 then? Most likely because of the seven-year site visit. Valparaiso and the Charlotte School of Law also noted that site visits eventually led to their ABA troubles.[91]

The visits come on a schedule, so schools have years to prep for them and get their ducks in a row. The ABA inspection process is like an Olympic drug test scheduled once every ten years and with the date known years in advance: good planning should lead to favorable results.

As required by the Department of Education, the ABA also accepts complaints about noncompliance.[92] The process is pretty formalized, and it seems unlikely to uncover many actionable violations. For example, in 2012, Law School Transparency filed a formal complaint with the ABA about allegedly false employment statistics sent out by Rutgers-Camden Law School.[93] If the allegations in the complaint are true, Rutgers-Camden certainly was in line for some sort of public censure.[94] There has been nothing but radio silence from the ABA, however.

Even when a problem is detected, there are multiple layers of appeals, especially for disaccreditation. As of 2018, the process was streamlined, so the timeframe may be shrinking for noncompliant schools. The first step for disaccreditation is now the council. Historically even in a circumstance where a law school was in substantial noncompliance, the council would likely give a school time to demonstrate compliance. Further, under the rules a law school can ask for an extension if it is struggling to fix the problem upon good cause shown.[95]

If the council recommends a serious punishment such as probation or disaccreditation, an affected school can appeal the decision to an appeals panel, which has its own set of rules and procedures and its own timeframe for decision.[96] If a law school were to lose before the appeals panel, a lawsuit relitigating the entire process (and seeking a preliminary injunction against disaccreditation) would be likely.

You might note that while the various steps and appeals involved in a theoretical disaccreditation action are clear, the amount of time involved is pretty fuzzy, except that we think it would take a while. The time is unknown because the ABA has never used many of these procedural steps. Even Arizona Summit withdrew its appeal of disaccreditation, so if we ever see an appeal to the end of the process we will all be in uncharted waters.

All of this is to say that law schools might be flouting the accreditation standards because they think they have time and many bites at the apple if they are eventually caught. And based on the process described by the ABA, it seems likely they are correct.

FINAL TAKEAWAYS ON ABA DISACCREDITATION

The ABA finds itself between a rock and a hard place. On the one hand, there is a reason that before 2018 the ABA had never disaccredited, or even really tried to disaccredit, a fully accredited law school. Disaccreditation is an extreme remedy and would be very likely to bring a lawsuit and some public outcry, and maybe political heat from state supreme courts, state legislatures, or even federal antitrust authorities. If the school has existed for a while, the alumni base, some of whom may be dues paying ABA members and prominent local or national citizens, would be very likely to object. Newer, for-profit schools like Arizona Summit appear to be easier targets for now.

Speaking cynically, the ABA has set up its accreditation standards to allow for significant wiggle room in finding concerns with a law school, giving it an extreme amount of prosecutorial discretion. In the past, the ABA was accused of threatening disaccreditation to force universities to increase funding or salaries. Given this primary use, it is unsurprising that the ABA's standards offer law schools a lot of room to fix whatever problems are found.

On the other hand, the ABA faces a significant amount of heat over lax enforcement from sources as diverse as *Above the Law* and the *New York Times*. The ABA is a membership organization largely run by and for the elite of the legal profession.[97] These lawyers are especially likely to be concerned about the future of the profession and by news stories about diploma mills, collapsing bar passage, and poor job placement numbers. Under these circumstances there is naturally some pressure to consider closing a few, or many, of the lowest-performing schools.

The ABA also faces an uncertain new future with the DOE. In its waning hours the Obama DOE signaled a clear hostility to what it considered predatory, for-profit institutions of higher education. DOE had also signaled a clear dissatisfaction with the ABA's lax oversight. They almost suspended the ABA as the nation's accreditor for law schools!

That alone may explain the recent flurry of activity. Disaccredit Arizona Summit! Sanction Ave Maria! Rewrite the standards to put a hard floor on bar passage! The effect of a laxer DOE is unclear for now. For instance, the ABA paired its tougher bar passage standard with a proposed amendment to allow for greater "distance learning" (meaning online legal education), offering a possible lifeline to struggling law schools.[98]

The remaining question is how the DOE will treat these law schools. In 2016–17, it looked as if the DOE would prove a much deadlier foe than the ABA, but so far the Trump DOE has proven much more quiescent.

WHY HAVEN'T MORE LAW SCHOOLS CLOSED?

PART 3: THE DOE

Phew! Struggling law schools have so far managed to pilot their way between Scylla and Charybdis, keeping the lights on through a series of aggressive cost-cutting and revenue-boosting measures, while at the same time maintaining American Bar Association (ABA) accreditation. From 2010 until 2016, even far-thinking strategists would have recognized only those two dangers: running out of money and losing ABA accreditation. In 2016, however, a third threat emerged. When the Department of Education (DOE) stripped the Charlotte School of Law of the ability to offer federal loans for spring semester 2017, a whole other avenue of danger opened, and one that apparently did not operate on the leisurely and forgiving pace of an ABA disaccreditation. We'll spend some time unpacking the DOE and the Charlotte School of Law below. But the story actually starts earlier, with the Obama DOE's lengthy battle against some parts of for-profit higher education.

SOME BACKGROUND ON THE OBAMA DOE AND FOR-PROFIT HIGHER ED

From 1998 until 2012, the for-profit segment of postsecondary education boomed, with more students, more profits, more campuses, and more government-backed debt.[1] Stock prices soared, and the for-profit sector tried to keep the growth coming. If you are a football fan you may remember that in 2006 the Arizona Cardinals named their sparkling new Glendale, Arizona, facility "University of Phoenix Stadium."[2] If you are like me, you asked, "Wait, what's Phoenix University? And how can it afford stadium naming rights?" Phoenix University was the flagship brand of the Apollo Group, a consortium of for-profit higher education brands/schools. At one point the Apollo Group traded at almost $90 a share and was successful enough to pay for naming rights to an NFL stadium. By 2017, Apollo traded at $10 a share and had been bought out by a private equity turnaround firm. It had also bailed on the naming rights agreement. The Cardinals' stadium is now known as "State Farm Stadium," a fitting coda to the rise and fall of the for-profit sector.[3]

There are two ways to describe the rise of the for-profit sector in the 2000s. The sunnier version argues that for-profit higher education boomed by offering innovative approaches to teaching and training, focusing on computerization, economies of scale, and new pedagogical approaches. This is certainly the story that these companies told as they grew.[4]

The harsher version argues that the growth was driven by aggressive advertising, fraudulent practices, and hoovering up federal student loans. Regulators accused these schools of misleading students about job prospects, the likelihood of graduation, the costs of attending, and the total debt load. Some schools paid recruiters bonuses depending on the number of students they enrolled, which led naturally to allegations of false promises and sharp tactics. Loan defaults ran much higher at for-profit schools than nonprofit schools.[5]

Eventually regulators started to take notice. In 2010, the US Government Accountability Office (GAO) released a scathing report alleging fraud and worse in recruiting and student loan applications at fifteen different for-profit institutions.[6] In 2012, the Senate Committee on Health, Education, Labor and Pensions released its own report excoriating for-profit higher education.[7] The picture these reports paint is not pretty. There were probably schools that were making a sincere effort to educate their students and to put veterans and first-generation college attendees on a path to upward social mobility, but this is apparently not what most schools were doing. By 2010, many for-profit schools were primarily in the business of marketing, recruiting, and pushing loans on their students/victims, with a thin veneer of classwork as a cover. The schools paid lead generators and recruiters a fortune to draw students in with false or misleading promises. Then they charged them much more tuition than comparable community colleges or state universities would have by pushing the students to borrow as much as they could from the federal government. More than half of these students failed to finish the program and get a degree. At some schools, the ratio of recruiters to career services staff was ten to one. The many students who quit or failed left the schools saddled with nondischargeable student debt that they were likely to carry with them their whole lives. Millennials sometimes describe student debt as "financial herpes," because you can never get rid of it.[8] Or maybe it's worse than herpes, because loans "carry 19 percent interest if you miss a payment" and herpes just results in temporary physical symptoms.[9]

Please allow me a one-paragraph detour to complain about one of the central disappointments of our current version of a free market. For-profit businesses in multiple sectors find it easier to hustle the state or federal government for funds rather than to try to create a freestanding, creative, and competitive product. This is why I am always frightened when I hear about a "public-private partnership" as the basis for a government service. For-profit education is a classic example. Creating a cheaper and better educational product is exceptionally hard! After years of (often justified) complaining about inefficiencies in higher education, one would hope that competition from for-profit schools would provide a jolt to the market as a whole and result in healthy and innovative competition. Not so much, actually. Rethinking and re-creating higher education would take time and effort. Creating a scam to hustle federal loans is much easier! Guess which road most for-profit providers, including the for-profit law schools, choose.

THE OBAMA DOE'S FIRST TRY: GAINFUL EMPLOYMENT RULES

By 2010, the Obama DOE had heard enough bad news about for-profit higher education and was ready to reform the market. The first step was sunshine. The combination of DOE investigations, congressional hearings, and state and federal investigations and lawsuits brought a tsunami of bad publicity and a concomitant drop in attendance and, more importantly, stock prices.[10] How much did the stocks fall? An index of for-profit higher education stocks lost 50 percent between 2009 and 2012 over the same period of time that the market as a whole rallied and doubled in value.[11]

These steps closed some of the weaker players in the market but also paradoxically placed the remaining players under even more pressure to bring in students to keep the lights on. The Obama DOE thus decided to try a more aggressive regulatory solution. In 2011, the DOE created its "Gainful Employment Rule."[12] The rule applied to for-profit higher education institutions and nondegree programs at community colleges and measured student success by various debt-to-income measures.[13] If a school failed these ratios two out of three years or came close to failing (falling within a "zone" of noncompliance) for four straight years, they would lose access to federal loans and grants.[14] The final report from the Obama DOE in 2017 showed that almost 10 percent of the programs covered by the rule were not in compliance.[15]

The Gainful Employment Rule never applied to nonprofit law schools, but just as a thought experiment, Matt Leichter did the math on what would happen if the rule were applied to law schools. His comparison of law school debt levels and reported postgraduate incomes is quite sobering.[16] According to Leichter, as many as fifty law schools might have failed the Gainful Employment Rule. We do not have to speculate about the for-profit law schools under the rule. The final Obama DOE report on gainful employment flagged all three Infilaw schools, Charlotte, Arizona Summit, and Florida Coastal, as potentially in violation.[17]

Regulatory responses present their own challenges, and for-profit schools brought a lawsuit challenging the rules; the D.C. Circuit overturned the first version in 2012.[18] Obama won reelection, and the DOE went back to the drawing board, creating a new rule that eventually passed legal muster in 2015.[19] The rule itself requires multiple years of noncompliance, so the Obama DOE was too late to use its rule to actually shutter any noncompliant schools. As of January 2017 (the last month for the Obama DOE), many schools had been found out of compliance, but none had faced the ultimate sanction of the loss of federal funds.[20]

The Trump DOE has moved to eliminate the rule. On June 30, 2017, in a classic "bury unwanted news on a Friday afternoon before a holiday weekend" move, Secretary of Education Betsy DeVos announced several weakenings and delays in enforcement of the rule, as part of her announced higher education regulatory reset.[21] A year later in August 2018, she announced the elimination of the rule altogether.[22] State attorneys general have filed various lawsuits, but like many of the legal actions against the Trump administration, winning elections seems a much likelier route to policy success.[23]

THE SECOND TRY: PPA AGREEMENTS

Because the Gainful Employment Rules took time to kick in, the Obama DOE had to look for other regulatory tools to rein in the for-profit sector. The DOE eventually found another, much more direct, route to punish malfeasance. Every higher education institution (for-profit or not) must periodically file an application to participate in the federal loans and grants program. If the DOE approves these programs, the school and the department enter into a program participation agreement (PPA). If you want to get deep in the weeds, just Google "program participation agreement template" and you can read all of the sample PPAs you care to.[24] The PPA boilerplate includes a long list of federal statutes and regulations that every institution agrees to follow. Prior to the Obama administration DOE, it seems that the PPA process was a relatively sleepy one, and that if an institution was going to face potential sanctions or a loss of access to federal loans, it would happen through the accreditation process, not the PPA process.

But every institution of higher education in America has a signed PPA on file with the DOE. These PPAs make a lot of promises and require a bunch of activities from each of these schools. The Obama DOE wondered, what if we found some of these schools out of compliance with their PPAs? Could we deny them future access to federal loans? Could we require them to post a surety bond to cover the risk of closure?

American institutions of higher education rely heavily on federal loans and grants. For-profit schools are especially dependent.[25] With stock prices, attendance, and revenue down, the DOE could use the PPA process as a sledgehammer. If the DOE found a for-profit school in violation of its PPA, it could fine the school or simply delay or suspend federal loans. Any lengthy period without federal loans was a death sentence.

The first target was the for-profit chain Corinthian Colleges. In January 2014, the DOE sent a letter to Corinthian requesting additional employment and placement information under their PPA.[26] By June, the DOE had concluded that Corinthian was not in compliance with its PPA because of false employment statistics (among other issues). It placed a three-week hold on federal loan payments to Corinthian.[27] If you are wondering how precarious for-profit finances were, or how reliant these schools are on federal loan funds, consider that a *three-week* delay almost put Corinthian out of business.[28]

In 2015, the DOE announced an almost $30 million fine because of further violations.[29] At this point Corinthian looked as if it was finished. Eventually the DOE worked out a sale that folded most of Corinthian's assets into a nonprofit status.[30] Weirdly, the buyer was one of America's biggest collection agencies on student loan defaults, the Educational Credit Management Corporation.[31] Pause for a moment to let that sink in. America's for-profit higher education sector is so misshapen that the DOE relied on a collection agency that profits from student loan defaults to buy a chain of colleges it had previously been trying to drive out of business.

ITT Technical Institute was next on the DOE hit list. The DOE again sought to punish ITT based on noncompliance with its PPA agreements. In Corinthian, the DOE argued that the schools violated the PPA by presenting false employment statistics. By contrast, the DOE argued that ITT was out of compliance with their accreditation requirements. PPA agreements require every institution to establish compliance with the requirements of their accreditor.[32] We will spend a minute unpacking this approach, since it is also the strategy the DOE used to basically shutter the Charlotte School of Law.

The DOE started by going after ITT's accreditor. The DOE sought to bar the Accrediting Council for Independent Colleges and Schools (ACICS) from accrediting schools for student loan purposes. ACICS handled the accreditation for ITT and almost all other for-profits.[33] The DOE moved against ACICS simultaneously with its attempt to delist the ABA from accrediting law schools described in chapter 6. The DOE eventually decided not to suspend the ABA, but ACICS had no such luck. In December 2016, then secretary of education John King upheld the decision to bar ACICS from accrediting schools for the DOE.[34] Affected schools had eighteen months to find a new accreditor.[35] ACICS sued the DOE to reverse the decision, and in March 2018, a federal judge ordered the DOE to reconsider the decision.[36] The DOE then reinstated ACICS "temporarily" while a longer review could be completed, and it looks for now as if ACICS will be another beneficiary of Trump's victory.[37] The for-profit sector as a whole has certainly benefited, with stock values up by as much as 35 percent.[38]

Regardless of whether ACICS survives as an accreditor, the DOE pressure had a side benefit: ACICS suddenly decided to be much tougher in accreditation, especially with ITT. In April 2016, ACICS notified ITT that two of its locations (in Indianapolis and Spokane) were in danger of losing accreditation.[39] ACICS stated dryly that ITT was under investigation by three different federal agencies and nineteen state attorney general's offices for a wide variety of possibly fraudulent behavior. It instructed ITT to appear at the August 2016 ACICS meeting to show cause why accreditation should not be suspended.[40] Note that the letter did not disaccredit the two ITT locations; it just required ITT to show cause why ACICS should not take some further action against ITT.[41]

In June 2016, two months before ITT was scheduled to appear before ACICS to defend itself and six months before ACICS (temporarily) lost its ability to accredit schools, the DOE seized upon ACICS's actions to sanction ITT. The DOE argued that ITT was currently not in compliance with its PPA. Because ACICS had found two campuses out of compliance, the DOE argued these schools were in danger of closing abruptly. Because every PPA requires compliance with a DOE accrediting body, the DOE then required ITT to increase its surety with the department from $79 million to $123 million.[42] The move was not good news for a beleaguered institution, and it immediately raised the alarm that ITT might be closing sooner rather than later.[43] ITT agreed to pay the increase in three installments and made the first $14 million payment in July 2016.[44]

ITT met with ACICS as scheduled on August 4. On August 17, ACICS determined that ITT was still not in compliance with its accreditation requirements. ACICS continued ITT's accreditation in a "show cause" status until the December ACICS meeting.[45] Given that ACICS might have suspended or disaccredited ITT, this qualified as good news of a sort, but the deathwatch remained. An *Indianapolis Star* article noted that ITT still faced two existential threats: ACICS might disaccredit ITT in December, or the DOE might disallow ACICS from accrediting schools at all.[46]

The *Star* missed a third threat though: on August 25, 2016, the DOE sent another letter to ITT noting ITT's continuing noncompliance with the ACICS accreditation standards.[47] The letter used the word "noncompliance" rather than disaccredited. This is because while ITT was in hot water as of August 2016, it was still unquestionably ACICS accredited. Regardless, the DOE raised the surety amount to $247 million and also froze federal loans or aid to any new enrollees. This was functionally a death sentence for ITT. The entire company tipped over into bankruptcy and dissolution almost immediately.[48]

THE OBAMA DOE TARGETS THE CHARLOTTE SCHOOL OF LAW

Even as the DOE was rattling the cages of for-profit institutions of higher education like Corinthian and ITT, it was similarly turning up the heat on for-profit and other poorly performing law schools. If you are familiar with the Charlotte School of Law story, the DOE's fight with ITT must have looked pretty familiar.

Like ACICS, the ABA reaction to DOE pressure was immediate. It awoke from its slumber and started finding schools out of compliance. Between August and November 2016, the ABA found the Ave Maria, Valparaiso, and Charlotte law schools out of compliance, and gave each two years to regain compliance.[49] The Charlotte School of Law faced the more serious findings of noncompliance and the scarier sounding "probationary status."[50] The ABA did not, however, suspend or attempt to disaccredit Charlotte. From 2016 until its announced demise in 2017, Charlotte remained ABA accredited.

Nevertheless, the DOE saw an opening. In the ITT case, the DOE alleged that ITT was out of compliance with its PPA agreements because it was under a "show cause" process. Even though ITT was not suspended or disaccredited, DOE treated ITT as "out of compliance."[51] Charlotte similarly faced probation, and thus should have been on alert that an ITT style reckoning was on the horizon.

Nevertheless, there were distinguishing factors between ITT and Charlotte. In its sanctions of ITT, the DOE first required a crippling surety bond and later barred only *new* students from access to federal loans. The ITT decision thus had two grounds: serious and worsening financial woes and the accreditation issue. By contrast, the Charlotte School of Law had no parallel financial difficulties, and the DOE did not require an increased surety bond.

Instead, on December 19, 2016, after the election of Donald Trump and in the last month of the Obama administration, the DOE sent a letter to Charlotte rejecting their recertification application (basically their request to renew their PPA) to dispense federal loans to their students for the spring semester of 2017.[52] This essentially cut Charlotte off from its largest source of revenue eleven days before the new year and the payment of spring semester tuition. The DOE relied exclusively on the ABA's finding that Charlotte was out of compliance with its accreditation standards and that the noncompliance was substantial and persistent.[53]

But wait, you say; I thought Charlotte was just on probation and not suspended or disaccredited? Yes, but the DOE did not rely on Charlotte's accreditation status per se. Rather, the DOE used the ABA's findings as support for the assertion that Charlotte was not meeting its accreditation requirements and refused to allow the school access to federal loans or grants.[54]

SOME THOUGHTS ON AN INCREASINGLY AGGRESSIVE OBAMA DOE TARGETING FOR-PROFIT SCHOOLS

Note the timeline of actions from Corinthian to ITT and on to Charlotte School of Law. As the last years of the Obama administration came to a close, the DOE grew increasingly aggressive. The use of the PPA agreements alone was an aggressive move. Previous DOEs had thought that the DOE's most direct tool to push back on shoddy accreditation was the National Advisory Committee on Institutional Quality and Integrity (NACIQI) process for accrediting accreditation agencies, not a direct denial of loans under a PPA.

Moreover, the PPAs do require a school to be in compliance with its accreditation standards, but it is not 100 percent clear that the "show cause" status in ITT's case or Charlotte's "probation" would be sufficient under the language of the PPA itself, given that both of those schools were still accredited and their accreditors had given them time to fix their problems.

Here's the relevant language from the DOE's letter to Charlotte School of Law:

> As a condition of eligibility to participate in Title IV programs, an institution must be accredited by an accreditor recognized by the Secretary. HEA §§ 101, 102(a)(1)(A), 102(b)(1)(D), 20 U.S.C. §§ 1001, 1002(a) (1)(A), 1002(b)(1)(D). See also 34 C.F.R. § 600.5(a)(6). In addition to that

eligibility requirement, as a separate condition of initial and continued participation, an institution must "meet the requirements established by" its accreditor. HEA § 487(a)(21), 20 U.S.C. § 1094(a)(21).[55]

Both ITT and Charlotte were likely in compliance with the first requirement of accreditation, even while under show cause or probation. Whether they fulfilled second requirement, of "meet[ing] the requirements established by its accreditor," is sketchier. But ITT and Charlotte could at least argue that until there was a final showing of noncompliance by their accreditor, they were still in compliance there as well. The DOE apparently rejected this argument.

Hopefully it is clear that I have serious doubts about the tactics and poor outcomes of many for-profit institutions of higher education. I have been particularly concerned about for-profit law schools. Former Infilaw faculty have brought lawsuits and written papers excoriating those institutions, including an entire book aptly entitled *Law Mart*. These law schools allegedly bullied their faculties, tried to ban students from transferring, paid students not to take the bar, misled applicants on their likelihood of passing the bar or getting a job, offered scholarships that were very difficult to maintain through law school, failed a significant percentage of their students out, and graduated students who could not pass the bar or get a job as a lawyer, amongst other malfeasance.[56]

I will also take a moment to say just how disappointed I have been with the for-profit law schools. Anyone who has studied the business model and educational programs of law schools knows that legal education is in *desperate* need of innovative and competitive solutions. When for-profit law schools came into the market, I actually cheered and was hopeful that they might shake things up. Could it really be impossible to offer a cheaper educational product that graduated students better prepared to pass the bar and practice law? It seemed there were a multitude of possible new approaches. Sadly, it was not to be. Infilaw created law schools that basically looked and acted like every other law school, except that their results were much worse and they were much more predatory.

I am not here to defend these institutions, and I am naturally inclined to be sympathetic to the Obama DOE's desire to run them out of business. Nevertheless, while I approve of the strategic goals, I can't help but be skeptical of the tactics, especially when it came to the Charlotte School of Law. The DOE's use of the PPA process to bar Charlotte federal loans was a stretch legally and did not seem evenly applied.

The first reason for concern is that the DOE had never done it before. The PPA process had existed for decades, and no prior DOE had used that process to abruptly deny an institution access to federal loans.

Second, the DOE treated ITT and Charlotte as if they had been disaccredited, when they were just under probation. If the accrediting agency was willing to give them time to fix their problems, why shouldn't the DOE? And if the concern was the accrediting agency's lenience or sloth, then use the NACIQI process to fix that problem, not the PPA agreements.

Third, the timing looked fishy, especially for Charlotte. If Hillary Clinton had won the 2016 election, would the DOE have attempted to shutter Charlotte on its own in the last month of a lame-duck administration? Unlikely. That is not a good look for the DOE.

Last, Charlotte was indeed a demonstrably bad actor on many (all?) measures. But it was certainly not the only law school engaged in some of these tactics or the only law school with very bad results. At a minimum, Charlotte seemed very similar in its statistical profile to the other two Infilaw schools, Florida Coastal and Arizona Summit.[57] Other ABA-accredited law schools, especially a number in California and Florida, have similarly poor bar passage rates and job placement rates, and similarly high debt burdens for their graduates.[58]

But none of those law schools were declared out of compliance by the ABA, so maybe the DOE was right to target Charlotte and let the others slide. Nevertheless, on the same day that the ABA put Charlotte on probation, it censured two other law schools, Ave Maria and Valparaiso.

If you lay the ABA's findings on Ave Maria and Valparaiso against the Charlotte findings, you can see that the Obama DOE might have chosen to deny federal loans to those two schools as well.[59] The ABA letters to both schools explicitly state that those schools are "not in compliance with Standards 501(a) and 501(b)."[60] Under the DOE's Charlotte approach, perhaps Ave Maria and Valparaiso should also have been barred from federal loans.[61] The change in the DOE approach is even clearer with Arizona Summit. The ABA moved to disaccredit Arizona Summit in 2018, a much more severe action than was taken against Charlotte. Yet the Trump DOE took no action against the school before its announced closure.

CHARLOTTE'S HOPE FOR A TRUMP BAILOUT LOOKED GOOD. WHY DID IT DIE?

But do not lose any sleep over the Obama DOE's aggression my friends. The Trump DOE was not much inclined to keep the heat on. For-profit schools of all types have enjoyed a looser regulatory approach under Trump, and law schools now seem to be entirely in the clear, at least from the DOE.

Yet Charlotte ended up closing after all. Why? In early January 2017, Charlotte and the lame-duck Obama DOE were negotiating over a "teach-out" plan and the eventual closure of the school.[62] Those talks collapsed in mid-January, and Charlotte decided to try to soldier on without loans until a Trump DOE gave them a "fairer hearing."[63] At first, the ABA was unconvinced, and it persisted in asking Charlotte to file a teach-out plan. But by March 2017, the ABA concluded that Charlotte seemed likely to survive and dropped the demand for a teach-out plan.[64]

Charlotte made it through the spring semester of 2017, but it was not pretty. The school fired two-thirds of its faculty and staff.[65] Its enrollment shrank by 62 percent.[66] Tuition was discounted, and Charlotte fronted the remaining students the money for the spring semester's tuition.[67] In the category of "world's saddest charitable efforts," the remaining faculty and staff launched a food drive for the students who had not bailed out.[68] The University of North Carolina's Board of Governors, which oversees higher education in North Carolina, and the North Carolina Attorney General launched investigations.[69]

Charlotte was not well situated to survive without federal loans: its students received $48.5 million from the federal government in grants and loans in 2015–16. Nor was Charlotte's temporary plan to act as a loan originator a long-term solution. There was the immediate cash-flow problem, of course, since today's students would not start repaying their loans until after they graduated. The much more pressing problem was that the odds that these students would ever be able to pay back upward to $200,000 in student loans with the kind of jobs available to Charlotte Law graduates (let alone the many students who fail out) were very low. Charlotte was well aware that many of its students struggle to repay their federal loans. But that's a federal government problem. If Charlotte or Infilaw took over as the lender, repayment rates suddenly become more salient.

In pinning its hopes on Trump for staying open, Charlotte took a substantial gamble. At first it was not clear what the Trump DOE would do. If Hillary Clinton had won the election, Charlotte would almost surely have closed. Clinton had repeatedly promised to continue Obama's policies and "crack down on law-breaking for-profits."[70]

But Trump presented a puzzle. On the one hand, he was (via various LLCs and shell companies) involved with Trump University, a for-profit endeavor that did not even attempt to qualify for federal loans.[71] Given that Trump University spawned a number of lawsuits alleging that it was essentially a scam, it seemed unlikely that Trump would side with the DOE against other for-profit educational institutions.[72] The Obama DOE's actions against Charlotte also hit two more sweet spots for a Trump reversal, because (1) Charlotte could claim (not without support) that the DOE's actions against Charlotte were among other last-minute, postelection and preinauguration regulatory actions meant to cement Obama-era priorities; and (2) Charlotte could claim that the Obama

DOE was overregulating the private market and it should be set free. This free market claim, of course, conveniently forgets that the entire market for higher education, for-profit or otherwise, is government supported via loans.

Nevertheless, most assumed that the Trump DOE would, in fact, be pro-for-profit higher education.[73] Stock prices in the for-profit sector surged after November 2016, suggesting that investors saw a rosier regulatory environment ahead.[74]

On the other hand, there was a chance that Trump and DeVos might have gone the other way. Trump presented a relatively generous income-based student loan repayment program during the campaign.[75] If he had decided to press that issue as a first priority, he might have become more concerned about the prevalence of defaults and the number of students borrowing to attend for-profit colleges. Trump's campaign also suggested that all universities should have some "skin in the game" on student defaults, meaning they would bear some of the cost of missed or terminated payments on student loans.[76] Following through on these promises might have led to a warmer reception for the Obama DOE's approach.[77]

There was also the broader point that many Republicans see higher education generally as a left-wing bastion at best and a political enemy at worst.[78] Trump might have decided to punish his enemies by *expanding* stringent DOE oversight. For example, if Trump decided to use the Gainful Employment Rule against all law schools (both for-profit and nonprofit), he could possibly shutter roughly a quarter of all law schools and scare the bejesus out of another hundred or so.

Instead, the Trump DOE played true to form, overturning or delaying the Obama DOE's priorities in most places.[79] Similarly, law schools not named the Charlotte School of Law appear to be back in good stead with the DOE. For example, the ABA placed Arizona Summit on probation on March 27, 2017, and moved for disaccreditation in 2018.[80] It placed Thomas Jefferson Law School on probation on November 13, 2017.[81] Those probations look remarkably similar to Charlotte School of Law's. If the Trump DOE was planning on following the Obama DOE's

Charlotte strategy, a letter suspending future law school loans would have been in the mail already. The sound of crickets chirping gives all struggling law schools a sense of DOE reprieve.

Similarly, the news for Charlotte also seemed good at first. A March 27, 2017, letter from the ABA to Charlotte mentioned that the Trump DOE had contacted Charlotte and provided a "pathway" for the law school to regain access to federal loans.[82] The money actually came through in May 2017. Charlotte used it to pay off the spring tuition it had fronted its students and to reimburse the students for their living expenses.[83]

At this point many people, including me, expected Charlotte to survive. The payment of the spring loans did not guarantee a release of loans for fall 2017, but why would the DOE release these funds at the very end of the semester (saving Charlotte's bacon) just to try to choke Charlotte out again three months later? Charlotte hired the Podesta Group lobbyist Lauren Maddox, who prepared Betsy DeVos for her confirmation hearings, to lobby for more federal loans; things looked positive.[84]

Nevertheless, the negotiations with the DOE dragged on into summer. In the meantime, Charlotte lost its North Carolina license to operate a law school. One of the stated reasons was the lack of federal loans going forward.[85] This was a bizarre, but fitting, end for a law school that had survived ABA probation and a DOE freeze on federal loans but could not dodge the reaper forever. It was a little like the end of the movie *The Departed*, where the villain survives while most other characters die, only to be killed in the last instance by the least likely character. Here, the State of North Carolina played the role of the straw that broke the camel's back.

THE TRUE ENEMY REVEALS ITSELF, BUT TRUMP'S ELECTION RESETS THE CLOCK

Charlotte and many other law schools had apparently been operating under the assumption that as long as they remained ABA accredited, they would be fine. The DOE actions against Corinthian and especially ITT happened too quickly for Infilaw to recognize its more immediate regulatory threat: the DOE. The DOE's treatment of Charlotte was terrifying for any other law school in hot water with the ABA. Following the Charlotte precedent, the DOE could suspend loans to any law school the ABA found "out of compliance."

Yet the defeat of Hillary Clinton and the reboot of DOE priorities meant that these schools were again saved by the bell. Law schools still face an awakened ABA and a tough market profile going forward (albeit aided by the Trump Bump), but for now the threat that the DOE could cut off federal loans following any ABA action has been removed.

Two other closures show us that there are other, obscurer dangers. State regulators felled Charlotte, and if the DOE is disinterested in chasing down law schools, state regulators may pick up the baton, especially in blue states where state attorney general's offices are itching for ways to join the "resistance" against Trump.

Whittier and Valparaiso show another possible route—the power of shame. This route will typically only apply to law schools that are part of broader universities, rather than freestanding schools. As the introduction describes, the board of trustees voted to shutter Whittier Law School despite relatively workable finances. And yet the administration decided to quit rather than float a struggling law school, basically due to optics. Bill Henderson predicted this exact possibility in a 2013 *National Law Journal* op-ed, which argued that university presidents facing problematic law schools might opt to close them rather than run them at a loss or allow them to lower standards too far.[86] Valparaiso presented a more market-based closure, but still, it was the board of trustees that pulled the plug, not the law school itself.

A last route that may also motivate central administrators to consider shuttering a law school is university-wide accreditation. For example, the Southern Association of Colleges and Schools Commission on Colleges accredits the University of Tennessee. While it does not accredit the law school in the first instance, they might well raise a struggling law school as an issue for the central university. If the pressure was bad enough, the board of trustees might more strongly consider closure.

UPSHOT

So where does all of this leave us? Amazingly, it looks as if most law schools will again skate by. Start with the market-based closures. Law schools looked likely to make it even before the Trump Bump in applications. If law schools are indeed going to see larger classes inspired by an anti-Trump wave, they can breathe a happy sigh of relief. Market-based closures may be even less likely going forward. Many law schools have already done the hard work of shrinking costs to meet lower revenues. If revenues rise, the good times could return relatively quickly.

The Trump Bump might also help on the ABA front. Higher enrollment of better students can only help bar passage and attrition. And regardless, the DOE at least seems likely to hibernate until 2021 or later. This is welcome news for struggling law schools because in a thicket of potential threats, the DOE action against Charlotte School of Law was easily the scariest and most pressingly existential. The ABA process has multiple layers of review and appeals. In Charlotte's case, the DOE gave the school less than a month to prepare for a world without federal loans.

The ABA may also note a lessening of DOE pressure to enforce accreditation standards and thus may feel comfortable sliding back into relative sloth. The loosening of distance learning requirements suggests this process may already have begun. The disaccreditation of Arizona Summit and other censures of law schools suggests otherwise. We shall see. The ABA has shown signs of life but without the stick of real DOE oversight that approach could reverse at any time.

One of my favorite trends of this decade is the explicit discussion of the role of luck in success, based partially on Robert Frank's excellent book *Success and Luck*.[87] If it is truly better to be lucky than to be good, then we have seen a remarkable spate of good luck for law schools at risk of closing. While they are hardly out of the woods, things look brighter now than they have since 2012. In fact, the fear that law schools will dust themselves off and learn nothing from the events of 2011–18 is one of the main reasons I named this book *Fixing Law Schools*. We have come too far and endured too much to learn no lessons from the last decade.

THE MIDDLE CLASS SWEATS IT OUT

We began by covering the law schools that are likeliest to close, because they are facing the gravest dangers. But every American law school is under stress and facing tough times, even after the Trump Bump. This chapter discusses the vast middle of law schools. There are about twenty American law schools that think they are a top-fourteen type school. We will cover these schools in chapter 9. On the opposite end of the spectrum, a large number of schools reside in tier 2 of the *U.S. News and World Report*'s rankings, or at the very bottom of the ranked schools, and have no aspirations of being an above-average or top-hundred law school. By and large, these are the law schools we covered in the previous three chapters.

Here we cover everybody else. Generally, these schools are regional. Most of the students come from within a few hundred miles of campus. When they graduate, the bulk of the students find jobs in that same geographic area. Most of these schools are part of a broader university, although the health and prestige of these universities (and thus their willingness to float a law school's finances for a while) varies widely. Most of these law schools have been around for a while, so they have a significant alumni base, likely including important members of the judiciary and the state and local government in their region. Many of the partners in local law firms and the general counsels for local corporations will also be alumni.

IS IT OK TO LUMP MORE THAN ONE HUNDRED LAW SCHOOLS TOGETHER INTO ONE CHAPTER?

The law schools in this category are located all over the country. They range from flagship public law schools to long-standing private law schools and to newish law schools such as the University of Nevada, Las Vegas, School of Law. How is it useful to discuss such a mass of institutions in broad strokes? The similarities vastly outweigh the differences among these schools. By nature and because of American Bar Association (ABA) regulation, American law schools that are not at the very top or very bottom of the market have herded together into virtual indistinguishability.

I can list a multitude of legal scholars making this same point, but the easiest way to prove it is to invite you to compare law school websites.[1] The list of AALS member schools should suffice.[2] Just randomly click on any two law schools on the list that are not one of the twenty or so law schools that think they are among the top fourteen, and you will see a remarkable amount of similarity. Seriously, go to this site and just start clicking and scrolling through. I promise that if you cover up the names of the school and the geographic location and just read the descriptions, you will have a very, very hard time figuring out which law school you are reading about. The faculties basically look the same, with older white males still pretty dominant along with a smattering of younger, female, and racially diverse recent hires. The curricula look basically identical: same first-year classes, same upper-level mix of bread-and-butter classes such as Evidence or Commercial Transactions, same claims of clinical and externship offerings that will produce "practice-ready" graduates, and similar random seminars based on the interests of the tenured faculty.

Some readers will immediately object to the claim that these law schools are in fact very similar. Take clinical offerings, for example. It is unquestionably true that there are wide variations among law schools in the depth and breadth of their "experiential" offerings. But compare these actual differences to how they are presented on law school websites. Most every law school makes some sort of claim to be "experiential" and interested in creating "practice-ready" graduates. The fact of difference is less important than the effort to appear the same.

There can be some differentiation based on law school specialties or centers (some schools have a special track in advocacy, technology, environmental law, or sports law, for example), but again, these small-ish differentiators actually highlight the vast sameness. Most of these programs are cobbled together from classes that almost every law school will have, plus a few extra classes or experiences. Given that the first year and other required classes are very similar across schools, these programs serve as different flavors of icing on identical cakes. Some of these programs are also more show ponies than workhorses. You can usually tell the difference by looking to see if the program has any data (in comparison to anecdotes), suggesting that graduates obtain jobs in the specialty. Programs in sexy areas such as entertainment law or sports law are especially likely to fail this test.

The few law schools that are truly different are the exceptions that prove the rule. The City University of New York (CUNY) School of Law and Northeastern University School of Law, for example, have a legitimate claim to run differently focused, public-interest law schools with unusual curricula. But they are just two of 100 to 150 schools. So why are middle-class law schools so similar? Let's start by discussing some disincentives to differentiation.

CASE STUDY ONE: NO GOOD DEED GOES UNPUNISHED— WASHINGTON AND LEE

Part of the reason law schools herd so much is that the few law schools that have gone out on a limb to change have not seen great returns. CUNY and Northeastern are both fine schools with good reputations in their specialized areas, but their individuality has hardly resulted in a boost in overall law school rankings. Most law schools (sadly) measure success by their *U.S. News* rankings, so CUNY and Northeastern have not engendered many imitators.

Washington and Lee University School of Law (W&L) is a more recent example. W&L is a smallish, private law school located on the campus of Washington and Lee University in bucolic Lexington, Virginia. Lexington is a college town with a population of about seven thousand located in the heart of the scenic Shenandoah Valley. It is also home to the Virginia Military Institute (more popularly known as VMI), so it has a weird mix of W&L undergrads at an elite liberal arts university and the VMI cadets, surrounded by farmland.

The location is lovely, but it presents a challenge for an aspirational top-twenty law school. W&L is three hours from Washington, D.C., two hours from Richmond, and an hour from Roanoke. The town is pretty, but in terms of drawing faculty it is a little too isolated, especially for what academics call "trailing spouses." Lexington thus faces a one-two punch geographically. It is likely a hard place to be single, since the social scene is limited and dominated by undergraduates. It is a pleasant place to raise a family, as long as you are not looking for a dual-career family. Given the educational achievements of the law faculty at W&L, however, and current social mores among the elite, the lack of career options for spouses and partners is a significant drawback.

W&L also finds itself in a crowded Virginia/D.C. marketplace for law schools. Virginia has eight law schools. D.C. has another six. Many of these law schools are direct competition for W&L in terms of applicants and job placement. Among beautiful rural Virginia law schools, W&L finds itself behind the University of Virginia (UVA) and basically tied with William and Mary, the oldest law school in America. Among D.C. area schools, W&L finds itself behind Georgetown, and probably George Washington, with the relatively new Antonin Scalia Law School at George Mason University suddenly pushing its way up the rankings. W&L cannot even claim a stranglehold on job placements in Richmond, Virginia, as UVA and William and Mary send graduates there, as well as the in-town and relatively strong Richmond School of Law.

And yet, W&L has done a good job of holding its own over the years, bouncing around between number twenty-two and number thirty in the *U.S. News* rankings from 2005 to 2010, making W&L's self-image as a solid top twenty-five law school, rather accurate. But faced with the challenges described above, and aware of the eternal critique of the lack of practical training in law schools, W&L decided to take a (relatively) bold risk to raise its profile and try something new. In 2008, W&L announced a plan to replace the traditional third-year curriculum with an entire required year of experiential courses.[3] The year was designed to include a mix of "two-week immersions, clinics, externships, practicum courses (elaborate simulations), [and] law-related service."[4] The *Wall Street Journal* called it "the boldest move" to date in legal curriculum reform.[5] The *Washington Post* called it "a revolutionary change."[6] The *ABA Journal* named W&L dean Rodney Smolla a "Legal Rebel" for 2008.[7]

As with any bold move, there was some grumbling in academia. Some longtime boosters of clinical/practical legal education thought the change was more hat than cattle. Other law schools already required simulation or clinical classes for graduation, just not all together in the third year. On the other side, some professors sniped that wasting the entire third year on practical courses would leave W&L's students at a disadvantage in terms of substantive law, not to mention the bar examination. The location was also a concern, as externships and clinics might be harder to staff in rural Virginia than in a metro .

Regardless of these (in my opinion relatively petty) critiques, here at last was a bold claim to a new model of legal education and a response to the question "what's the use of a third year of law school?" During a period of relatively negative coverage of law schools, W&L seemed to have hit gold.

The program ran as a pilot for the first few years because the school did not want to change the graduation requirements for students who had applied and matriculated before the standards were in place, but they went live with fully required participation in 2011–12.[8] The early returns were promising. One of legal academia's most influential commentators, Bill Henderson, called W&L the "biggest legal education story of 2013."[9] Henderson posted a long write-up on W&L's gains in application volume and student satisfaction (as measured by the Law School Survey of Student Engagement). In 2012, W&L had too many first-year enrollees and had to offer financially attractive deferments to students, hardly a common problem at other schools.

But the news shifted rather quickly following a precipitous fall in the *U.S. News* law school rankings. A change in the way employment numbers were counted, combined with a weak year of placement and bar passage for W&L, resulted in a tumble from twenty-sixth to forty-third in the rankings.[10] W&L blamed the fall on employment and bar passage, and argued that eventually the focus on practice-ready graduates would help, although it would "take five to 10 years for the benefits of the program to become apparent."[11] The next two years brought miniscule relief, as W&L moved from forty-third to forty-second and then fortieth, seemingly mired about fifteen slots behind where they thought the law school should be. Bar passage and job placement remained the main culprits.

The positive press turned much darker, and in 2015 W&L published a "strategic transition plan."[12] The plan included several moves meant to help the rankings and student selectivity, including a permanent shrinkage of the school to one hundred students per class and "financial aid, which will continue to be allocated beyond historical norms," but "will gradually return to sustainable levels."[13] W&L's incoming class in 2016 was 40 percent smaller than its graduating class of 2015 (the largest enrollment drop in the country that year), and the school's finances deteriorated.[14] The plan allowed the school to dip into its endowment to cover deficits, which were projected to continue through 2018, with the budget "projected to be back in balance by the 2018–19 academic year."[15] Budgets were cut by 10 percent, and faculty and staff positions were also eliminated.[16] These moves were extreme enough to draw the attention of the *Washington Post* and the *Chronicle of Higher Education*.[17]

The really strange part was that W&L's employment outcomes actually worsened following the adoption of the new third-year program. Deborah Merritt wrote a long blog post noting the perversity of this outcome.[18] After doubling down on preparing "practice-ready" graduates, W&L actually did worse than its peer schools in job placement.

W&L has seemingly righted the ship since, moving up twelve spots in the 2018 rankings to number twenty-eight and to number twenty-six in 2019.[19] Yet their gain comes at the cost of law school innovation. W&L has basically abandoned its third-year experiment and replaced it with a more generic requirement of eighteen credit hours of experiential classes taken sometime during the second and third years of law school.[20] In fairness to W&L, eighteen credit hours is a lot and is likely on the higher end among law schools in the US. I emailed James Moliterno, the head of the program, to ask about the changes, and he replied that "although somewhat modified, the experiential curriculum reform is alive and well." Given that requiring eighteen credits is still a significant commitment to experiential learning, that is a fair response. But in comparison to a self-declared effort to redesign the third year of law school, the change is a pretty substantial retreat.

It is not just a change in how the credits are allocated, because the school seems to have decided to soft sell the entire topic, at least for now. If you visited the W&L website in the summer of 2017, you would have found nary a mention of a revolutionary and new third-year program, or a particularly robust commitment to experiential education. The front page of the website had a longish video describing the features and advantages of W&L: small classes, engaged faculty, lovely town, and so forth. Near the end of the video it mentions that W&L students will take a clinic or externship before graduation, but the mention is notable for how low key it is. Just four years earlier W&L was presenting its third-year program as *the* differentiating feature of the school. Now W&L seems hard to distinguish on this basis at all.

Longtime observers of the market for law schools will find this retreat astounding and a little sad. Rereading Bill Henderson's 2013 love letter to W&L is particularly discouraging, as all of the links from Henderson's piece to the W&L third-year program are now dead. When the law school voted to reformat their third year in 2008, they trumpeted the change as a bold and fundamental shift in the nature of W&L and of law schools as a whole.[21] But after a brief period of radical change, W&L has retreated back to the pack, happy to look and act like its peer schools, rather than appearing as a bold innovator. Fans of *Flowers for Algernon* or *Awakenings* will be reminded of a bittersweet period of blossoming and individuality followed by a rapid decline back to the status quo.

While it is hard to get too charged up over law school requirements, the W&L story is unhappy in several ways. First and foremost, Deborah Merritt's insight that changing curricula do not change hiring practices (at least for now) is very discouraging. Nor is it just W&L. On a self-serving note, the University of Tennessee College of Law (where I teach) has the oldest continually operating law school clinic in America and has had a very strong emphasis on practical legal education since the end of World War II. As far as I can tell, it has had a very limited effect on our placement results.

Why doesn't hiring follow reform? Law firms have consistently complained that law grads are not prepared to hit the ground running. Why not sort law school grads based on their practice readiness? One possibility is that even when they try really hard, law schools are not good at creating practice-ready graduates. So, although law firms do actually look at this criterion, law schools fail to deliver.

A second possibility is that the hiring partners at law firms both small and large don't put much weight on the curricula of the law schools they hire from. Instead, law firms have relied on a simple hiring metric: the first cut for consideration is the rough ranking of the law school combined with the class ranking of the student. So roughly the top 50 percent of UVA's class competes with the top 20 percent of W&L's class for the same jobs in D.C. The actual differences between the schools in terms of curricula are pretty much ignored. Given that the students who go to UVA are statistically pretty similar to the students that go to W&L and given the general lack of evidence that class rank or school ranking are determinative of success as a lawyer, the reliance on these metrics is puzzling.

Of course, hidebound adherence to precedent is not only a law school problem. It is endemic throughout the American legal field. Law firms hire this way because that's how law firms have done it from time immemorial. What other reason do they need? If this strikes you as a very reductionist and silly way to hire a lawyer, you may be right, but that does not change the preferences and behavior of law firms. Law firm hiring remains and has always been very hierarchical, and a change in the curriculum, even a move toward better-prepared graduates, apparently does nothing to move the needle.

It is also disconcerting that these changes do not seem to affect incoming student choices. Students rely more heavily on rankings than any other factor in choosing which law school to attend.[22] Scholarships or special programs or geography may draw some students at the margins, but the rankings are the single biggest factor.

Law professors have long decried the oversized effect of the *U.S. News* rankings, and every single one of those critiques is fair. The rankings let the tail wag the dog. The rankings focus on the wrong things. The rankings drive schools to compete only on the ranked criteria and discourage innovation. The critiques are unending. Regardless, the rankings matter in a number of ways, including inputs (law students and potential law professors often choose schools based on rankings) and outputs (the rankings affect law firm and other hiring). Because the rankings matter, schools pay close attention to them.

Sadly, W&L thus teaches us that innovation does nothing to improve three of the main indicators of law school success: rankings, the quality of incoming classes, or job placement. In fact, the W&L story can be used as a cautionary tale that changes lead to bad results and downsizing! Correlation does not equal causation, but that will not stop observers of the W&L experiment from noting that their rankings dove following the big changes and bounced back when they abandoned/downplayed them. The truth of the matter is much more complicated, and the job placement and bar passage numbers were the primary drivers. But still, perception is king, and it will be a long time before another law school announces a radical shake-up to their curriculum.

The most important metric underlying the *U.S. News* rankings is peer and lawyer evaluations of quality. Whether curricular changes affect those rankings at all is an open question (they probably do not). But even the impression that looking different might negatively affect rankings is enough to discourage innovation. Why risk it?

HERDING AND THE AALS

W&L explains some of the disincentives to change. But the sameness of these schools is also a result of the many hidden advantages of herding. A good place to start the discussion is to explain the role that the Association of American Law Schools (AALS) plays in the nature of middle-class law schools.

Every middle-class law school is ABA accredited. Because ABA accreditation is required to sit for the bar in most states, those are table stakes. Yet virtually all of these schools are also members of a voluntary association of law schools, the AALS. They are thus subject to another layer of membership requirements, procedures, and rules. Despite being fully voluntary, AALS and its requirements have been enormously influential over the years and have encouraged schools to look and act the same.

You may be wondering why we just started talking about AALS requirements, an older and in some ways more influential body than the ABA, this late in a book on law schools. This book is not alone. If you look at the indexes to *Failing Law Schools* or Robert Stevens's excellent history of American law schools, discussion of ABA accreditation dominates over the AALS membership review process. Former law school dean Larry Dessem wrote a 2005 law review article describing the "ABA/AALS Sabbatical Site Inspection" process that theoretically covers both the ABA and the AALS but basically only discusses the ABA's standards and procedures.[23]

This is partially because, as chapter 6 notes, ABA accreditation is an existential issue for law schools. It is also because for years AALS membership review has basically piggybacked onto ABA accreditation.[24] The AALS membership review now takes place simultaneously to the ABA accreditation process. The AALS representative serves double duty as an ABA site visitor, and the AALS process includes all of the documents produced for the ABA.

The requirements for AALS membership also closely resemble the requirements for ABA accreditation. We will discuss the oddness of the current overlap in a minute, but remember from chapter 1 that this was not always the case. To the contrary, AALS membership standards were originally much more stringent than ABA standards, and they grew more stringent continuously from 1899 into the 1930s.[25]

In the end, AALS membership shrank over this period, while the number and enrollment of night and proprietary law schools exploded. The AALS recognized that its battle over the nature of American law schools was failing. Simply banding together and arguing that AALS schools provided a better education was not enough. From 1915 forward, the AALS made an explicit attempt to get the ABA to push for higher standards for law schools and to require an elite-model law school education as a prerequisite for entering the bar. ABA accreditation was the solution. In 1917, the ABA created its Council on Legal Education.[26] The new section wrote its own accreditation requirements in 1921. At first ABA accreditation was not attached to bar membership, so the immediate effect was muted.

Throughout the 1920s, the AALS membership requirements and the ABA accreditation requirements grew more demanding, and by the end of the decade they had largely converged.[27] In the battle between the elite model and the proprietary model, the ABA had finally and completely chosen a side. When the Great Depression hit and state supreme courts grew more concerned about lawyer quality and lawyer overpopulation, the list of ABA-accredited law schools was just sitting there on the shelf as an easy and defensible new requirement for taking the bar. The transition to requiring graduation from an ABA-accredited law school essentially ensconced the AALS model as the dominant one nationwide. What the AALS had struggled to do via the market became reality through regulation: the elite model became *the* model for law school education.

This brief recap of the history of the ABA and the AALS helps clarify why so many law schools look the same. As of now, the AALS and ABA requirements are almost identical.[28] ABA accreditation and AALS membership have also largely converged. In 2018, there were 179 AALS-member law schools and 201 fully ABA-accredited law schools.[29]

The overlap speaks volumes about the nature of the ABA accreditation process. From its inception in 1900, the AALS has been an aspirational group of law schools, seeking "to uphold and advance excellence in legal education."[30] The goal is *excellence*, not minimum safe quality. The ABA's mission, by contrast, is to "provide a fair, effective, and efficient accrediting system for American law schools that promotes quality legal education."[31] Thus the ABA's stated mission is to provide quality, not excellence. This makes sense for a quasi-governmental accrediting process that is theoretically focused on consumer protection. And yet the requirements for both groups are almost identical, suggesting that excellence (as defined primarily by the AALS and its members) is the true standard. The ABA and the AALS accreditation requirements thus result in a great deal of herding, as the majority of law schools seek to meet the dual standards and to embody the same aspirational goal of excellence.

Note that this overlap of criteria also makes managing a law school much easier than it would be in a free-flowing marketplace. Some readers in legal academia will immediately scoff at that idea—*easier*? Hardly! Meeting these requirements and their various parts and subparts is the bane of many an administrator and faculty's existence. Yes, it is very hard to get ABA accreditation and to join the AALS. Yes, the process requires a good deal of work and often requires faculties to make hard choices to stay in compliance.

But do you know what is much harder? Market pressure to innovate and present a different, more competitive product over time is harder. One of the reasons the post-2010 time period has been so painful for law schools is that it was the first time in a long while that they couldn't just look like every other law school, open their doors and expect to enroll plenty of students at whatever price point they set. For years prior to the crash, the ABA and AALS processes have basically outsourced thinking about what excellence in legal education looks like, allowing law schools to herd around a single model. Remember that one of the main advantages to a closed market/oligopoly is that the market participants are freed from having to try too hard to compete, through either pricing or product differentiation.

This effect is compounded by the rise of the *U.S. News* rankings. These rankings essentially allowed law schools to outsource the definition of "excellence" to a third-party publication. Rankings have proven remarkably influential throughout academia, but nowhere are they more powerful than in law. Law schools have decided to compete come hell or high water on these rankings.

There are obviously advantages to the *U.S. News* rankings. Prospective students receive a (relatively) clear set of criteria to judge the comparative quality of law schools. The rankings have been (mostly) the same over the years, so they also allow for longitudinal comparisons. Yet the rankings competition has resulted in much destructive behavior. Many law schools, regardless of level, have been caught cheating by padding their employment statistics, presenting misleading postgraduate salary numbers, or simply lying about the nature of the school itself.[32]

Weirdly, the cheating is less worrisome than the gamesmanship. Schools have hired their own graduates and shrunk their first-year class size to game the LSAT and undergraduate GPA numbers. Other schools have boosted their incoming transfers (transfers do not count for the *U.S. News* rankings) and used their precious scholarship moneys to draw students with the highest LSAT and undergraduate GPA numbers, regardless of whether those students truly need the tuition breaks. Because poverty often correlates with lower test scores, this has the perverse result that the "bottom" of many schools' entering class pays full freight, essentially supporting the discounts for the (often wealthier) applicants with the shinier statistics.

The strangest behavior is the mass decision to shrink the size of incoming classes and that of the faculty and the staff. All over the country, law schools that could lower their incoming students' undergraduate GPA and LSAT numbers and still fill their school to a 2011 version of capacity have chosen not to. This has been a painful decision for these schools. We offer the University of Cincinnati College of Law as an example of just how painful this decision has been.

CASE STUDY TWO: BALANCING THE BOOKS CAUSES A MINOR REVOLT—CINCINNATI

First, a note of fairness. I know several current and former faculty members at the University of Cincinnati (including their former dean), and I have had, and continue to have, a favorable impression of all of the players in this drama. I am also not suggesting that Cincinnati is an outlier. To the contrary, the whole point of the case study is to draw attention to the struggles of the many law schools that resemble Cincinnati. I chose Cincinnati because their very public dispute with their former dean over cost-cutting highlights the challenges a typical law school faced, even long-standing, well-regarded, state-supported institutions like Cincinnati.

Plus, any time the *New York Times* covers the suspension of your dean at length, you have opened your school to greater scrutiny.[33] Jennifer Bard was hired as the new dean at Cincinnati in 2015.[34] She has since stated that she was hired with an explicit mandate to address "multimillion-dollar" operating deficits.[35] When you read the details of how bad the 2011–14 stretch was for Cincinnati, you are likely to believe Dean Bard. Dean Bard claims that she took reasonable steps to address the shortfall, including folding the law library into the university library system, cutting back on faculty travel, increasing teaching loads, and trimming back the use of school operating funds to pay the supplemental salaries of senior faculty members holding endowed chairs.[36]

Note that lowering entry standards and keeping the school the same size were not on the list. As a matter of deduction, we can thus assume that Cincinnati and its faculty were willing to take the above steps, each of which made life at Cincinnati worse for the faculty and staff, ahead of just enrolling the same number of students they did in 2011 and continuing on as they had been doing. The harder path was likely taken for the salutary purpose of maintaining the school's "quality" (whatever that means), but honestly the decision was probably more a result of fear about the rankings. If the LSAT or GPA numbers went down, the rankings might go down. When the rankings go down, fewer students apply, and those students are of a lower quality. Cincinnati (like most other schools) fears this downward spiral even more than faculty and staff layoffs and salary cuts.

This is not to say that the changes made by Dean Bard were greeted with equanimity. In fact, all hell broke loose. In a series of thorough and well-sourced articles, the *Cincinnati Business Courier* painfully detailed the full scope of the debacle.[37] In 2016, a group of faculty responded to Dean Bard's suggestions by pushing for a vote of no confidence. The university management eventually placed Dean Bard on administrative leave.[38] She hired a lawyer and received a sizeable settlement: two years off at her full salary of $300,000 per year, plus retention of her tenured position as a law professor resuming in 2019–20.[39]

So what happened at Cincinnati? Here's a little historical background: The University of Cincinnati College of Law was founded in 1833 and claims to be the fourth-oldest continuously operating law school in the country.[40] William Howard Taft, the only person to serve as both the president of the United States and the chief justice of the U.S. Supreme Court, is an alumnus and served as the school's dean.[41] Cincinnati was a charter member of the AALS and has, by any measure, a storied history.

During Bard's deanship, the University of Cincinnati as a whole was in the middle of an expensive campaign to improve its national reputation. Consider, for example, its aggressive architectural plan, including buildings designed by world-renowned architects like Frank Gehry, Michael Graves, Peter Eisenman, Bernard Tschumi, and Thom Mayne.[42] Taken together, the history of the law school and the ambitions of the central university should have provided the law school some cover in a downturn.

And yet the post-2011 crash was quite unkind to Cincinnati. Ohio has nine law schools and five different public law schools—Akron, Cincinnati, Cleveland Marshall, Ohio State, and Toledo.[43] This makes for a tough market for both law schools and law graduates. In 2015, Matt Leichter compared the Bureau of Labor Statistics projections for new lawyer jobs with the ABA count of law school graduates, and he concluded that there were more than 2.5 law grads in Ohio competing for every new job, making Ohio the seventeenth-worst state for law graduate overproduction that year.[44]

By 2013, applications and enrollment were significantly down at all of Ohio's public law schools.[45] Cincinnati was hardly in the worst spot, as Cleveland State and Toledo faced much larger declines in enrollment.[46] But times were hard for sure. The ABA has collected the required disclosures for every law school since 2011 and published them online, so comparisons over 2011–16 are easy to make. Cincinnati's disclosures tell a pretty clear story of why Dean Bard was hired in 2015 with a mission to cut costs and balance the budget.

Start with applicants and matriculants. In 2011, 1,572 applied to Cincinnati. In 2015, just 779 did, a 50 percent decline in applications. This was worse than the national trend at the time.

Cincinnati attempted to hold the line on the incoming statistics of its first-year classes over this period, so it shrank the size of its incoming classes.[47] In 2011, 119 students started at Cincinnati as first-year law students (1Ls). In 2014, the year before Dean Bard was hired, only 73 did, almost half of the size of the entering class of 2009. One sign that Dean Bard was hired to balance the books is the return to more typical class sizes for the school. The class of 2016's 126 matriculants was larger than 2011's.

Cincinnati also took a relatively radical recruiting step in 2014: it lowered its out-of-state tuition. In 2013, out-of-state students faced a sticker price of $41,044. In 2014, out-of-state tuition was cut to $29,010.

Cincinnati has essentially frozen its tuition since then: in 2017, in-state tuition was $24,010, and nonresident tuition was $29,010 for the fourth straight year.[48]

Despite lowering tuition costs, Cincinnati actually *increased* the percentage of students receiving a discount on their tuition over the period. In 2012, 65 percent of the entering class received a discount. A jaw-dropping 94 percent of Cincinnati's student body received a tuition discount in 2017, *despite the school cutting tuition in 2014* and maintaining the discounted tuition through 2017! The median grant award at Cincinnati from 2011 to 2014 remained constant at $6,500, before rising to $10,000 in 2016 and again to $12,500 in 2017—a 92 percent rise. In 2016, the net tuition for law students at Cincinnati was just $15,233.[49] If you were wondering why Dean Bard recommended some deep cuts for the school, just imagine the revenue numbers under these circumstances.

Even with the extreme measures taken in 2014, Cincinnati saw a slide in matriculant numbers. Between 2011 and 2014, median undergraduate GPA fell from 3.57 to 3.45 and median LSAT from 160 to 155. The good news was that Cincinnati increased its class sizes in 2015 and 2016 and maintained its LSAT and GPA credentials (the 2016 median LSAT was 155, and the median GPA was 3.47), possibly by offering more and larger discounts to incoming students.

The decline in GPA and LSAT scores did not significantly sink Cincinnati's rankings, although there has been a minor slide from its 2011 position on the list. *U.S. News* ranked Cincinnati fifty-sixth in 2011, sixty-ninth in 2013, bottoming out at eighty-second in 2016, and rebounding to sixty-fifth in 2019.[50] So the trend is improved from the 2016 nadir, despite growing the class and cutting costs. Yet Cincinnati has not regained its pre-2011 rankings in the fifties.

Another sign of cost-cutting was a gradual shrinkage of the full-time faculty and a significant cut in part-time faculty. In the fall of 2012, Cincinnati had thirty-two full-time faculty members, nine "deans, librarians & others who teach" (largely administrators), and thirty-three part-time faculty members, for a total of seventy-four. By fall 2016, there were twenty-seven full-time faculty members, nine administrators, and only twenty-three part-time faculty members, for a reduced total of fifty-nine, a 20 percent decrease.

Note that by cutting the part-time faculty Cincinnati was trying to keep its full-time faculty busy and useful. One way to distinguish the schools that are trying to maintain their rankings (like Cincinnati) from the schools that are just trying to hold on for dear life (the schools discussed in the last three chapters) is the scale of the cuts to the full-time faculty, and whether the number of part-time faculty members has grown to compensate.

Cincinnati is a cautionary tale for budget cutting. A review of the school's finances sounds grim, but changing the budget risks faculty ire, and law schools have a long tradition of faculty governance, for better or worse. Dean Bard's ouster will make other deans think twice before bringing the squeeze.

CINCINNATI IS HARDLY ALONE: CASE STUDIES— CATHOLIC AND MINNESOTA

If you have been paying attention, you will note that each of the law schools covered in this chapter started by taking extreme measures to maintain their rankings, often at great cost to the bottom line. Both Cincinnati and W&L, for example, ran in the red for a few years before normalizing through budget cuts and stabilizing the size of their incoming classes. Even more extreme examples of the size of the losses and the lengths necessary to balance the budget come from Catholic and Minnesota.

The Catholic University of America, Columbus School of Law (CUA Law) was founded in 1897.[51] CUA Law was accredited by the AALS in 1921 and by the ABA in 1925. *U.S. News* ranked Catholic eighty-second in 2013, and it has a fine academic reputation.[52] Nevertheless, in order to maintain its ranking in 2013, the school shrank its incoming class enough that the *entire university* was required to take a 20 percent operational cut.[53] If you have been wondering whether the floodwaters have reached many or most law schools, contemplate this remarkable story. CUA Law's revenue and enrollment drop did not just require a 20 percent cut in the law school's budget. Its woes required a 20 percent reduction of the *entire* university budget. The woes continued into 2018, when the provost announced another 9 percent cut to the tenured faculty and increased teaching loads.[54] Of course, the law school itself was not spared. CUA Law shed more than half of its faculty between 2010 and 2016, confirming the magnitude of their budget problems.[55] The cost to the rankings? A slide to 110 in 2019.[56]

The story at CUA Law also highlights that the challenges have proven especially acute in some geographic regions. In Washington, D.C., for example, CUA Law is not alone in its struggles. Including CUA, three of Washington's best private law schools have all shed faculty at alarming rates since 2010: American shed half its faculty and George Washington roughly a third.[57]

Minneapolis is another regional market that has been particularly hard hit. The 2018 *U.S. News* rankings placed the University of Minnesota Law School twentieth.[58] Minnesota is widely considered a top-twenty-five law school and among the best public law schools in the country. But applications fell by more than half since 2010, and the law school had to cut enrollment by a third between 2010 and 2015.[59] From 2012 through 2018, the university gave the law school $39.9 million to cover budget shortfalls.[60] That figure is not a typo: a top-twenty-five law school ran at an almost *$40 million* deficit during the crash. The law school cut faculty by 21 percent and staff by 14 percent since 2014 and hopes to be out of the woods by 2021. As of 2019 the school was running a smaller deficit and on track to make the 2021 deadline for self-sufficiency.

Minnesota was not the only Minneapolis law school to struggle. In 2015, Hamline University School of Law and William Mitchell College of Law chose to combine into a single school (and cut their combined faculties by half or more) to try to ride out the storm.[61]

Even mighty Northwestern announced plans in 2018 to cut staff and teaching positions in light of "challenging financial circumstances."

Tenured faculty remained untouched, but the addition of Northwestern and Minnesota on the list of financially troubled law schools suggests that even the very top American law schools are struggling.

UPSHOT

W&L, Cincinnati, Minnesota, and CUA Law all show different versions of the same story. The narrative begins with some radical moves to maintain "quality" despite the collapse in applications. Cut the size of the class, and offer more and larger scholarships to try to maintain rankings and class quality. Lose money. Hope that the university will carry you for a while (or permanently, one never knows!). When the university grows weary, cut costs where you can, including by shrinking the faculty and staff and making other unpleasant decisions such as growing the size of the class.

As the examples above establish, a law school's mileage may vary with these strategies. When the bill comes due, the combination of cuts announced at Cincinnati and W&L sound like a pretty obvious snapback: shrink the faculty through attrition, raise teaching loads, cut costs in the library and elsewhere, and hope to balance the books without destroying the school's reputation or bar passage results.

Note that we know a lot about each of these schools because they made very public announcements about their money troubles and their plans for balancing the books. Most middle-class law schools are still somewhere in the "lose money and hope it all eventually works out" phase of the plan. If the Trump Bump is permanent and applications and matriculation rebound, it all may be just an unpleasant blip on the radar. But if the bump proves illusory, expect more stories like those described above. This situation will affect individual law schools, but it may also result in more collateral damage at the lower end of the spectrum. If every middle-class school decides to boost their incoming class sizes to near their 2011 levels, life might get very dicey for the law schools that are already faced with the hardest times.

THE GOOD NEWS AND THE BAD NEWS
FROM THE T14(ISH)

"T14" refers to the fourteen law schools that, with some internal bouncing around, have filled the top fourteen slots in the annual *U.S. News
and World Report* rankings every year since 1987.[1] They are, in alphabeti-
cal order, Columbia University Law School, Cornell Law School, Duke
University School of Law, Georgetown University Law Center, Harvard
Law School, New York University (NYU) School of Law, Northwestern
University Law School, Stanford Law School, the University of California Berkeley School of Law, the University of Chicago Law School, the
University of Michigan Law School, the University of Pennsylvania Law
School, the University of Virginia School of Law, and Yale Law School.[2]
The top slot has been held by Yale every year since 1987. The number
two slot has bounced around between Harvard and Stanford (although
mostly Harvard), and the rest of the T14 has been more fluid, with schools
rising and falling within the fourteen slots. But the overall makeup of the
top fourteen schools has been remarkably consistent. The year 2018 was
the exception that proves the rule, as the University of Texas snuck up
to fourteenth, pushing Georgetown to fifteenth. This caused some panic
at Georgetown as well as a long (and hilarious) *Above the Law* debate
about what it all *meant* for the term "T14."[3] Thank *goodness* Georgetown
returned to fourteen and Texas to fifteen in 2019, restoring order to the
universe.[4]

The "shakeup" in 2018 serves to show just how static the T14 has
been. Given that the rankings have gone through various changes in
methodology since 1987 and that schools have been doing anything and

everything to improve their rankings since at least the 1990s, it is remarkable that these schools have remained ensconced at the top. But the longer you study American law schools, the more examples of long-term sameness you find.

So aside from a *U.S. News* ranking, what are the characteristics of this top tier of law schools? Expense is one. As we'll cover below, the T14 schools have the highest sticker prices of all law schools and have led the charge on tuition growth over the years. These schools are all attached to larger, name-brand universities. The obvious examples are the five Ivy League schools in the T14, but each and every law school in the T14 is associated with a university that considers itself among the very best in the United States and in the world. Harvard, Yale, and Stanford are without peer in the country, and in some ways peerless in the world (although Princeton might disagree). Even the public institutions listed count themselves among the best and wealthiest institutions in the world.

These schools tend to have large, well-compensated faculties that emphasize scholarly productivity and quality above all else. These faculties have lower teaching loads. Brian Tamanaha suggests that the baseline teaching load for these schools is three classes per year (two classes one semester and one class the next), with many faculties moving to a 50 percent load (just two classes per year).[5] This is not to say teaching does not matter at these schools, or that they do not have excellent teachers. But by policy and mindset, scholarly promise or production is the coin of the realm, the sine qua non of hiring and tenuring.

This is because these law schools are the most likely to imitate the broader academic institutions around them. T14 schools tend to have more faculty members with PhDs.[6] They tend to have more professors that lack any practice experience at all.[7] These faculties tend to be on the leading edge of various "law and" scholarly trends, from law and economics starting fifty years ago to the current growth of the empirical study of the law.

More than fourteen schools share these attributes, and more than fourteen schools consider themselves as peer institutions to the T14.

This is why I call this group the T14(ish). There is no strict delineation of course, but one easy test is to ask if a non-T14 school considers itself indistinguishable from a similar school in the T14. So Vanderbilt (and maybe Emory) count because Vanderbilt and Emory certainly consider themselves peers with Duke, the other "Harvard of the South." The same is true for the University of Texas, which sees no daylight between itself and Cal or Michigan among top-tier public law schools. The University of Southern California (USC), the University of California, Los Angeles (UCLA), and Washington University in St. Louis are all in this camp as well, in my opinion.

By contrast, Minnesota, Iowa, or Arizona State (other top-twenty-five-type law schools) might greatly desire to become T14 type schools, but they recognize a clear difference between themselves and the absolute top state institutions. Their students are more local. Their employment is more local. They have smaller endowments and lower tuition (albeit still much higher than it used to be). Their buildings are less grand, and their faculties (while packed with climbers) are less turbocharged. I do not attempt to defend this grouping statistically, because it is more of a state of mind than an empirically definable group. The main point is that a certain group of American law schools consider themselves the very tippety-top institutions, and they behave, spend, and charge accordingly.

This chapter presents a brief overview of the behavior of these schools in the post-collapse law school world. I begin by criticizing the schools for being excessively selfish and for plowing the road for some of the worst law school behavior described in this book. These schools hold themselves out as shining exemplars of legal education, yet they have exhibited a particularly despicable brand of self-interested behavior.

I start with the bad news, but I'll give credit where it is due: these schools have also launched some of the most interesting and promising programs at law schools in the United States or around the world. You can decide for yourself whether the good news makes up for the bad.

WHY IT'S FAIR TO BE SO CRITICAL

Lawyers have always played an outsized role in American life. Evidence for this claim abounds. Lawyers have dominated all three branches of the government. Most American presidents have been lawyers. The American judiciary is virtually all lawyers. Lawyers have always been overrepresented in state and federal legislatures. We look to law to settle our most divisive and challenging social issues. As early as 1831, Alexis de Tocqueville noted that "there is hardly a political question in the United States which does not sooner or later turn into a judicial one."[8] Consider gay marriage or second amendment rights if you think that Tocqueville's quote is outmoded today. The point is that lawyers matter a great deal to the country as a whole. And since law schools are essentially the single gateway into the profession, they matter as well—maybe not as much as some law professors think, but still, the point stands.

These T14(ish) schools have been the dominant force in the nature and structure of law schools since at least World War II. Nor was this responsibility thrust upon them. These same law schools were all founding or guiding members of the Association of American Law Schools (AALS) and the American Bar Association (ABA) Council on Legal Education. The AALS was not just a trade group for elite schools, as is the Ivy League itself. They did not ignore other law schools, while celebrating their own excellence. The AALS and the elite schools argued that other schools were deficient diploma mills and should not be allowed to survive. They insisted that the elite model was the *only* appropriate model for law school education.

Some of you will think the T14 behaved appropriately in setting a high bar of excellence for all law schools. Others will see elitism and self-protection. Either way, I hope we can all agree that if you present your type of law school as the model and flagship for all law schools, you have at least some responsibility to the broader ecosystem you helped create. For example, Harvard carries a special duty because of its outsized influence on legal education. The "History" section of the Harvard

Law's website (appropriately) makes much of Dean Langdell's creation of the case method and the first-year curriculum.[9] It is certainly fair to say that no single institution has had more influence on American legal education than Harvard.

But with great power comes great responsibility. These schools owe their peers, and the entire country, the duty of good management. It is not enough for these schools to manage their affairs to maximize their own benefit. ABA-accredited law schools have been granted a monopoly over the training of American lawyers, and the T14 sets the tone for law schools countrywide. With this public trust comes a public responsibility. Yet in recent years the T14 have behaved as if they owe little to anyone outside themselves. There are three examples of this self-centered behavior. The first concerns tuition and the second the Graduate Record Examinations (GRE). Third is the drift away from teaching and studying the practicalities of the actual work of lawyers, but this example is a closer call between costs and benefits.

RUNAWAY TUITION

The average tuition for a T14 school has risen from $32,588 a year in 2004 to $57,400 in 2017, a 76 percent increase over that period.[10] Out-of-state tuition at Virginia almost doubled over that period, going from $31,100 in 2004 to $61,300 in 2017. Needless to say, these increases were well above inflation. If the average T14 tuition had just risen along with inflation every year since 2004, the 2017 tuition would be under $43,000.

The tuition increases at T14 schools have had a significant effect on the larger law school market. Note in figure 9.1 the rise in T14 tuition as compared to all other law schools over the period. T14 defenders might point out that there is no proof that they led this trend, although it is undeniable that they at least followed the trend. T14 defenders might also ask why they should bear any additional responsibility for the cost of law school? If these law schools are the best, why shouldn't they charge the most?

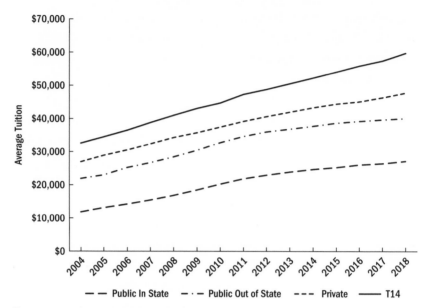

FIGURE 9.1. Average tuition, 2004–2018.

If you agree that these tuition increases are problematic, there is no way to defend the T14 as just part of an overall trend. If the T14 had chosen not to raise their tuition, or to just increase by inflation for a few years, it might have had a significant effect on other law schools downriver. This effect might in fact have come via *shaming*, as no school from outside the T14 would want to be significantly more expensive than the schools within the T14. More importantly though, remember that the federal government will loan students 100 percent of the cost of a law school education, as determined by the law school itself. These maximum loan amounts are subject to Department of Education (DOE) oversight, however, and in approving tuition, fees, and living expenses, the DOE is naturally affected by the market as a whole. If the T14 had held the line on tuition, the DOE might have noticed when markedly lesser law schools grew more expensive than T14 schools.

The same is true for the total debt load carried by graduates of T14 schools. Because the T14 schools are considered a potential road to riches for the students, the debt load for graduates look more reasonable. In turn, the T14 debt loads make comparatively lower debt loads at other schools seem more palatable, even if they are twice or three times what law graduates carried just a decade or so ago.

The T14 has plowed the road for some of the most despicable behavior by more rapacious law schools. In some ways, the behavior of the T14 has been worse, however, because they were not forced to do it; they *chose* to. The Charlotte School of Law or Thomas Jefferson had to radically cut costs and boost revenues to stay in business. By contrast, T14 law schools are among the richest academic institutions in the world. Yale Law School's endowment was $984 million in 2012.[11] In 2008, Harvard Law School's endowment was more than $1.7 billion.[12] Stanford Law School's endowment is estimated to be somewhere between $600 and $700 million.[13] Other T14 schools may be less wealthy, but even so, there is no reason for these schools to be shaking the money tree so hard.

MAYBE IT'S OK BECAUSE THE STUDENTS WORK AT FIRMS AND MAKE A FORTUNE?

When I asked a dear friend who teaches at a T14 school if the tuition problem was on her radar, she answered quite frankly, "No." When asked why not, she said, "The students that are going to firms can afford it. Those who go into public interest can do loan forgiveness. Who is hurt?" To my ears this was a less virulent version of the "this is a market economy, we should charge what the market can bear" justification for rising tuition and debt loads. Is it true that a T14 education may be comparatively even more valuable in a post-2011 employment outcomes world? Sure. Does that justify charging as much as possible? No.

The market explanation is especially galling. These are all nonprofit educational institutions, not for-profit Infilaw schools. If these schools want to charge whatever the market will bear, they should forfeit their status as nonprofits and stop seeking donations. Moreover, this is hardly a functioning market, because of the virtually unfettered growth of government-guaranteed loans. The government pays for the tuition up front, backed by each student's pledge to pay the money back over time. The only party that bears no risk in these transactions is the law school. It should thus not be surprising that prices have risen faster than inflation.

Moreover, even though the T14 employment results have been the best among all law schools they hardly establish a T14 degree as an ironclad investment. Keep in mind that one of the main drivers of tuition hikes in the T14 is the applicant's belief that attending one of these schools will be worth it because of the increased access to big firm starting salaries, often in the neighborhood of $180,000. This is the unstated assumption of T14 administrations and faculties as well. This assumption alone is faulty, since the median starting salary for working in a corporate law firm was only $135,000 in 2016.[14]

But the bigger problem is that most T14 graduates do not end up in these high-paying jobs. Nor is it true that every graduate of a T14 school can find employment. In law school, we grade on a curve, so yes, the T14 presents a better employment picture than other types of law schools. That said, an un- or underemployed T14 graduate who paid anything close to full freight has good reason to be disappointed.

The chart below shows the 2018 employment results (which are substantially better than the results from 2011–15), including the percentage of graduates who found full-time, long-term (FTLT) work that required a JD, and also the percentage that ended up in a non-JD-required position, employed by their law school, or unemployed:

T14 school	% FTLT, JD required	% non-JD position/ law school position/ unemployed
California Berkeley	89%	7%
Chicago	91%	7%
Columbia	94%	4%
Cornell	91%	6%
Duke	91%	5%

T14 school	% FTLT, JD required	% non-JD position/ law school position/ unemployed
Georgetown	82%	11%
Harvard	86%	6%
Michigan	89%	7%
NYU	90%	9%
Northwestern	90%	4%
Penn	89%	6%
Stanford	85%	6%
Virginia	93%	6%
Yale University	77%	16%
T14 average	88%	7%

Based on these numbers, a significant portion of T14 graduates graduate un- or underemployed, somewhere between 4 and 16 percent. As an aside, Yale is clearly an outlier because their graduates are so much less likely to seek full-time work as lawyers. Likewise, while Georgetown's results look relatively poor on this chart, its 2018 numbers were a significant improvement over 2016, when all the D.C. law schools had disappointing results.[15] Eyeballing these two columns, it is fair to say that somewhere between 7 and 12 percent of T14 graduates in 2018 faced disappointing employment results.

Some may object that the T14 graduates that work in JD-preferred or non-JD-preferred jobs are equally happy to be employed. I refer those readers back to chapter 4—unsurprisingly, law grads who do not use their license are the least pleased with their decision to go to law school and their careers and are the most likely to be seeking other work.

Others may argue that it is not fair to treat graduates working in law-school-funded positions as if they are unemployed. There is no available data on the satisfaction levels of these students, but I feel confident that insofar as some or all of them borrowed enough to pay full freight, they are not terribly excited to be working for their law school in what many consider to be short-term fig-leaf jobs aimed at making the employment figures look better.

The number of un- and underemployed T14 grads alone casts doubt on the "we are still a good deal at any price point" message. But even among the full-time, long-term, JD-required folks, not everyone will work in a job earning six figures. Here is the percentage of T14 graduates that got jobs at the largest firms (501+ lawyers) according to the 2018 employment data (and remember that this represents the best hiring year since 2009):

T14 school	Percentage in 501+ law firms
California Berkeley	44%
Chicago	47%
Columbia	65%
Cornell	57%
Duke	52%
Georgetown	48%
Harvard	51%
Michigan	44%
NYU	63%
Northwestern	62%
Penn	63%
Stanford	47%
Virginia	60%
Yale University	24%
T14 average	52%

These numbers again range from 24 to 65 percent, and just barely more than half of graduates land these jobs. The rest of the students find work at smaller law firms, in government, clerkships, or public interest. Not all of these students are unhappy about those placements, and believe me when I say I am *not* measuring law school success solely by big firm placement. To the contrary, I was pleased to see that one of the very best law schools on this list, Yale, sends a relatively lower percentages of their graduates into BigLaw. That said, if the justification for the sky-high tuition is that the students can afford it because of BigLaw, it seems relevant that roughly half of these graduates do not work in BigLaw. The T14 cannot have it both ways: pleased and proud that their graduates are pursuing public interest or government careers that benefit all of us and assuming that all their grads earn enough to repay their massive debt loads.

BUT WE GIVE SO MUCH FINANCIAL AID THAT NO ONE PAYS STICKER PRICE

At this point, some T14 folks may point out that not all students pay full freight and that the T14 schools are especially generous with financial aid. Thus the sticker price is a red herring, because the true cost to the students is much lower.

First, it is not clear that T14 schools are especially generous in this regard. The ABA publishes a spreadsheet covering grants and scholarships for every ABA-accredited school.[16] If you sort the schools by the percentage of students receiving grants/scholarships in 2016, the highest-ranking T14 school is Chicago, at number sixty-four out of more than two hundred schools. If you sort by the fiftieth-percentile grant amount, the highest-ranked school is Northwestern, at twenty-one.

One way to measure how much students are actually paying is to look at the cumulative debt numbers. According to the *U.S. News* rankings on indebtedness at law schools, the T14 schools do not appear to be especially generous or worried about their graduates' debt loads. Here are the T14 schools, including their average debt, the percentage of graduates with debt, and their numerical ranking within all of the law schools ranked by *US News* on debt in 2017:

US News debt ranking	Average total debt	Percentage of graduates with debt
4. NYU	$167,646	64%
5. Georgetown	$166,027	74%
8. Columbia	$159,769	63%

US News debt ranking	Average total debt	Percentage of graduates with debt
11. Cornell	$158,128	65%
13. Penn	$156,725	71%
14. Virginia	$155,177	67%
15. Northwestern	$154,923	65%
18. Harvard	$153,172	77%
30. Michigan	$146,309	73%
31. Berkeley	$145,260	72%
42. Duke	$137,829	72%
43. Stanford	$137,625	75%
50. Chicago	$134,148	62%
70. Yale	$121,815	68%

None of the T14 is even in the bottom half of law schools for average student indebtedness. Somewhere around two-thirds of T14 graduates carried law school debt. The average amount of that debt ranges from $121K to $167K. Suffice it to say that however you count it, the T14 is not being more generous than other law schools. Their students are paying and borrowing a lot.

Even if the T14 was correct to say that the effective price is much lower than the sticker price, that is worse, not better! High T14 tuition offers cover to some of the most rapacious law schools in America. If the T14 does not actually need to have such a high sticker price, they're enabling bad actors for a very limited benefit. They are presenting the cost of law school to the world as somewhere between $60K and $70K in tuition, keeping the run-up in tuition alive year after year, and then actually collecting much less from their students. These discounts are often strategic, of course, and are used to convince students to come to one school rather than another, often for purposes of boosting GPA and Law School Admission Test (LSAT) numbers for the eternal rankings battle.[17] It is certainly true that the T14 is not alone in this behavior, but if you believe that the self-proclaimed elite among us should hold themselves to higher standards, you will surely be disappointed by their post-2010 role in tuition and debt increases.

HARVARD, THE T14, AND THE GRE

Recall chapter 5's discussion of law schools moving to accept the GRE as well as the LSAT. The movement started when three middle-class law schools announced a study of the GRE as an admissions test: Wake Forest, Arizona, and Hawaii.[18] Of the three, only one, Arizona, immediately started accepting the GRE.[19]

In a total stealth attack, Harvard Law School announced in March 2017 that it would accept the GRE as well as the LSAT.[20] Harvard argued that the change would "diversify" its applicant pool, and Harvard being Harvard, schools scrambled to copy them. For admissions year 2018–19, the following T14(ish) schools have joined Harvard: Chicago, Columbia, Cornell, Georgetown, NYU, Northwestern, Penn, Texas, UCLA, USC, and Virginia.[21]

Before we turn to the impact on other law schools, a moment on Harvard's decision. First, and most obviously, Harvard did not need to accept the GRE to survive a downturn. Harvard was fine, I promise. That said, it was curious that the 2018 *U.S. News* rankings were leaked two days before Harvard's announcement and that Harvard had slid from second to third.[22] If rankings played any part in the decision, *U.S. News* mania has truly reached a new (and unfortunate) nadir.

How does accepting the GRE possibly help with rankings? Arizona and Harvard may have hoped to hide lower-scoring GRE students, but in 2017 the *U.S. News* rankings announced that GRE scores would now be included.[23] There are still two, albeit lesser, rankings advantages. The rankings include a student selectivity portion, so if an extra five hundred random GRE takers apply and all are rejected, that alone would help in the rankings. There is also the first-mover advantage. Harvard, Arizona, and the other first movers are the only schools to accept the GRE, so for now they are the sole choice of GRE-only applicants. Over time, and especially with Harvard plowing the road, that advantage will dissipate, but for the first few years of publicity and applications, the earliest birds will be receiving more than their share of worms.

Harvard's decision makes the rapid acceptance of the GRE much more likely. Like the decision to keep jacking up tuition, this decision will offer cover to law schools with less pure intentions and will also not prove particularly helpful to the T14 schools that are leading this parade.

First, as chapter 5 argued, accepting the GRE will offer a vast new group of students the opportunity to apply to the more predatory American law schools. When these students are accepted, they will have the opportunity to borrow $180,000+ with limited hope for passing the bar or gaining employment. Harvard and other T14 schools will not be directly responsible for these trends, but they will have played their part in normalizing the GRE. ABA acceptance of the GRE is also much more likely with Harvard, as well as with two-thirds of the T14 as early adopters.

But let's assume you believe Harvard owes no duty to other law schools. Is this move still a good idea for Harvard, on the merits? Color me skeptical. One reason Harvard in particular should require the LSAT is because a special, exclusive test discourages college graduates from applying to law school on a lark or applying to ten history graduate programs and ten law schools just to see what happens. The LSAT acts as a natural damper on law school applications—and in our current job placement situation, that may not be a bad thing. Because Harvard can take most any applicant they would like, they are hardly in need of broadening the pool to include students who are otherwise lukewarm about going to law school. I have no empirical basis for this prediction, but I'll bet dollars to donuts that the students who take the GRE and are planning on going to some other type of graduate program, apply to law school "just to see what happens," and then shift course to attend law school will do worse in school and in the profession than the students who want to attend law school enough to take the LSAT. For years, law school has suffered as the graduate school of last resort for confused history/English/political-science majors who could not think of anything else to do after graduation. The law school downturn slowed that process, and accepting the GRE is an explicit attempt to reopen the spigot.

Moreover, the explanation that this move will create an influx of racial or gender diversity is specious, given the nature of the GRE. Studies show that GRE scores, like other standardized test scores, tend to run higher for white males. The *Atlantic* summed it up: "The Problem With the GRE: The exam 'is a proxy for asking 'Are you rich?' 'Are you white?' 'Are you male?'"[24]

The GRE has also been shown to be a poor predictor of success in PhD programs, with GRE scores having limited correlation with completing a PhD.[25] Since the test is not succeeding at its primary job, what are the odds it will be better than the LSAT at predicting success in law school or, even less likely, success as a lawyer? Harvard may hope to diversify the educational backgrounds of its students for salutary reasons, and maybe they are right about the effect this change will have on Harvard. I predict the overall effect for law schools and the profession will be less positive.

THE ORIGINAL SIN: ELITE SCHOLARSHIP, PHDs, AND THEORY *UBER ALLES*

I put this critique last because it is the most obvious, the least original, and the most overwritten. From the very beginning of the case method, the weaknesses of the Harvard model have been clear to all. Building law schools around a scientific study of law and filling the building with full-time law teachers who focus mainly on scholarly pursuits naturally meant a shift away from a pure apprenticeship model, where the education was, by nature, practical. If it is true that personnel is policy, the original choice to rely on full-time faculty that writes scholarship set the course a century and a half ago.

It is unsurprising that the victory of the elite model in the 1920s to the 1940s also meant that the equilibrium between practical experience and teaching and scholarship would continue to slide toward the academic side over the years. The elite model has always wanted to be an academic discipline first and foremost, and rationally so. The elite model's claim to legitimacy is based almost solely on the idea that the academic study of the law is superior to the practical study of law. If the practical study was better, why abandon apprenticeships?

Once you have a faculty of experts, it makes sense to let the experts design the program. Both the ABA and the AALS make clear that accredited/member law schools *must* be faculty governed. In the world's least surprising development, faculty governance has meant the ongoing academicization of law schools.

Again, personnel is policy. Where would we find academic law professors who will produce scholarship? We find them as the most promising students at the most elite schools. When these faculty members join middle-class schools, which model of law school will they seek to imitate? They'll imitate the law school they attended of course. How will they remake their school in the model of Yale or Harvard? They'll put more emphasis on scholarship. And so the cycle goes.

The effect itself is empirically obvious. Law school faculties have put more emphasis on scholarship over the years by reducing teaching loads, adding summer research grants as part of the compensation package, and hiring more law professors with PhDs and little or no practice experience.

The complaints have been constant and increasing in volume over the years. In 2002, D.C. Circuit judge Harry Edwards published a *Michigan Law Review* article excoriating law schools and legal scholarship for abandoning the practice of law.[26] A more ironic and recent overview of this trend comes from former law professor and federal judge Richard Posner.[27] Posner's complaint is ironic because there is probably no individual law professor who is more responsible for the rise of the "law and ——" movement than Posner, who almost single-handedly founded the study of law and economics. The year 2007 saw two more excellent additions to the canon: the Carnegie Foundation–supported *Educating*

Lawyers and Roy Stuckey's *Best Practices for Legal Education.*[28] At heart, 2012's *Failing Law Schools* is also about this trend. I find *Failing Law Schools* to be particularly trenchant, as you would be hard pressed to find a more serious or prolific legal scholar than Brian Tamanaha to launch a broadside on the concept of scholarship *uber alles.*[29]

The empirical support for whether the trend is actually detrimental is harder to find. There is no accepted metric to decide whether law school graduates in 2018 are worse prepared than law school graduates in 1958 or 1978, despite the obvious change in the nature of law faculties and thus law schools themselves. There is likewise limited evidence for the commonsense idea that if professors spend most or all of their energy on scholarship, their teaching will suffer. I conducted a large-scale empirical study on whether there is a correlation (negative or positive) between scholarly productivity and teaching evaluations. The study found no correlation between teaching and scholarship. This meant that the "scholarship is key to effective teaching" trope was unproven. The same was true for the "scholarly emphasis is killing teaching" argument. Basically, scholarship and teaching are two different activities, and they do not seem to have a consistent effect on each other.

Regardless of the absence of empirical evidence establishing any particular harms to students or the profession from the law school obsession with scholarship, you may agree as a matter of logic that there is no reason every law school in America should look like a T14 law school. Because most law professors come from a relatively narrow background, they tend to measure "excellence" in a law school based on that background. If you agree that has warped law school priorities over the years, you can lay much of the blame at the feet of the T14 itself.

SOME GOOD NEWS: THE ELITE HAVE LED IN SOME POSITIVE DIRECTIONS AS WELL

Leading is hard, and so it is understandable that the T14 has stumbled in spots. But they have led in positive ways as well of course. If there is a trend in modern legal education that you like, it is very likely that it started, or received a significant boost, from a T14 school. I'll highlight two examples here, but there are more.

CLINICAL LEGAL EDUCATION

If you know anything about the history of clinical legal education, you know that T14 schools have repeatedly been its pioneers. Duke Law School was the first law school to offer an in-house, for-credit clinical program, starting in 1931.[30] Prior to Duke's program, clinics had been volunteer, noncredit programs that often did not even involve any faculty at all. Legal realist and Yale Law professor Jerome Frank thought enough of the idea to publish a 1933 law review article entitled "Why Not a Clinical-Lawyer School?"[31] Yale Law School's main clinical program is now named for Frank.[32]

When clinical education really started to take off in the 1960s and 1970s, the T14 played a primary role. Gary Bellow came to Harvard Law School in 1971 to head up their nascent program and, along with Bea Moulton and Jeanne Charn, laid the academic and intellectual groundwork for the new clinical education movement. Clinics were more than just an in-house externship or a new style of apprenticeship: they were a totally new and innovative teaching method based in legal realism, adult learning research, and a comprehensive theory of law teaching. Law school clinics are the single biggest innovation of the last fifty years in law school education (with legal writing programs a close second), and the efforts at T14 schools to create and support these programs (albeit frequently at differential or lower levels of tenure, job security, and salary) have been invaluable.

LAW AND TECHNOLOGY PROGRAMS

Clinical legal education is what passes for a modern innovation in law schools, and these programs are, in fact, steeped in modern thinking on character and skills development. Nevertheless, they are at heart a very old-school and human-driven enterprise, from the focus on real-life clients and issues to the intense one-on-one supervision. The T14 has also taken the lead in a newer-school area: the combination of law and technology.

Stanford has three different centers focusing on reimaging the profession and the provision of legal services. The Codex Center for Legal Infomatics leads the world in the study of the automation and mechanization of legal analysis by computers. Here's their mission statement:

> Legal technology based on Computational Law has the potential to dramatically change the legal profession, improving the quality and efficiency of legal services and possibly disrupting the way law firms do business. More broadly, the technology has the potential to bring legal understanding and legal tools to everyone in society, not just legal professionals, thus enhancing access to justice and improving the legal system as a whole.[33]

Codex is also working with the US Department of Justice on data mining and prosecution to build "evidence-based, data-driven" prosecutorial decision-making.

Stanford also hosts the Center on the Legal Profession, built by and around Deborah Rhode and her decades of leadership in legal ethics, feminism, and access to justice. It is not an exaggeration to say that no single person in the US has thought more, or worked harder, on these issues than Rhode, and the center is a reflection of her outstanding body of work.

The Legal Design Lab is housed within the center. The lab is headed up by the inimitable Margaret Hagan and focuses on what she calls "human facing" technology, creating apps and programs that help ordinary folks navigate complicated court processes and legal problems. A list of their projects is fun and heartening. If Stanford is going to charge a king's ransom and snowdrift funds, it is hopeful to see that they are opening the Scrooge McDuck vault for these sorts of projects.

Harvard Law School has likewise founded the A2J lab, spearheaded by Jim Greiner; the lab focuses on using data and blind trials to assess the effectiveness of various efforts to provide access to justice to the indigent.[34] As goofy as it seems, the idea of doing best-in-class research on where, when, and how legal work makes a difference (or fails to make a difference) in people's lives is a radically new idea in law schools, and Harvard is lapping the field in this area. Harvard also offers a law, science, and technology program that includes a suite of classes both inside the school and across the campus aimed at raising tech literacy and entrepreneurship among its graduates.

Georgetown Law School offers a program in legal technologies that gives students the chance to create online legal applications for the indigent in the technology innovation and law practice practicum. Students then present their apps in the Iron Tech Lawyer competition with prizes for excellence in design and all-around best app.

In some ways, praising these programs is hypocritical, because part of the reason they exist is the sheer volume of money sloshing around in T14 schools these days. But schools with lower tuition and much smaller budgets, especially the industry leader Chicago-Kent and others like University of Southern California and Miami, make clear that there is not a one-to-one ratio between tuition hikes and innovation.

With great power comes great responsibility, and in many ways the T14 has failed us. They are entrusted with educating the best and brightest in the legal field and are wealthy from donations and tuition. Yet these institutions have behaved in a manner likely to enrich the schools and their faculties at the expense of their students, and the country as a whole.

◆ 10 ◆

SHOULD I, MY CHILD, MY BUDDY, OR ANYONE GO TO LAW SCHOOL?

I've studied and written about law schools for years, and as such, I've spent a fair amount of time answering the question "Should I go to law school?" I am also a law professor and a lawyer. If you know many of those folks, you will not be surprised that the answer to this question is, "It depends!" If you do the due diligence and research that I suggest in this chapter and you still want to go to law school, this is an excellent time to go. Professor Gillian Hadfield has aptly noted that we live in a "law-thick world"—law permeates and controls more of our activities than ever before.[1] This means that finding smart, creative, and hardworking people who have a realistic view of what lawyers actually do and sending them to law school is critical for American businesses, American government, and the country as a whole.

On the flip side, if you are considering law school because (a) you like the TV shows *Suits* or *The Good Wife* and you want to make a boat-load of money; (b) you really want to do "something" to help the world, without any idea of what you would be doing to help whom; (c) you're a history major with no other career ideas; or (d) you are looking for a degree or career that can guarantee job security and an upper-middle-class salary without requiring you to be entrepreneurial, now is a particularly bad time to go to law school. Honestly, these have always been bad reasons to attend law school, but the degree costs a lot more now and the job prospects are weaker than they were a generation ago, so the costs of entering law school for the wrong reasons are higher than ever—too high really. So, please do the work, make a wise decision, and then arrive at your studies with your eyes open and ready to work. This chapter unpacks this advice into some pre-law-school steps for due diligence.

BEWARE OF CATEGORICAL "YES OR NO" RESPONSES TO THIS QUESTION

My first piece of advice is to look out for binary "always yes or always no" answers to whether law school is a good idea. There is no one-size-fits-all answer. Unfortunately, one-size-fits-all advice abounds. On the one hand, Paul Campos's *Don't Go to Law School (Unless)* is not quite a blanket "no" for law school, but it is very close.[2] In some sections of his book, Campos intimates that you should not go to law school unless you get a free ride to a T14 school or you have a guaranteed job at a family business waiting for you. In 2016, David Barnhizer wrote a pretty scathing paper arguing that students in the Great Lakes region should think carefully before attending a midwestern law school. Three of the reasons he gives are as follows:

> The region's lawyer job markets are saturated to the point that there are not a significant number of new jobs being created and the replacement market that depends on the deaths or retirement of lawyers currently in practice is slow moving.
>
> Public budgets for local and state governments in the Great Lakes/ Midwest region are under significant stress with the result that those institutions represent a largely static or declining employment market for lawyers.
>
> A significant number of the region's "top" law jobs will be "cherry-picked" by graduates of law schools such as Harvard, Yale, Michigan, Ohio State and a few others.[3]

Jerry Organ compared the law school debt numbers for the class of 2011 with their reported starting salaries and concluded that more than half of the law grads that year would struggle to pay off their debts or own a home, hardly an advertisement for attending law school.[4]

On the other hand, strong "yes" advice has also bubbled up. One classic example is Jordan Weissmann's two-part 2014 series in *Slate*, arguing that now is a "great time to go to law school."[5] Weissmann theorized that because law school attendance had shrunk precipitously, the eventual graduates of these smaller classes (the classes of 2017 and 2018) were bound to end up with better employment results. To be specific, if the number of jobs held roughly constant and the number of law grads fell, more law grads would find jobs:

> Here is the key number to keep in mind: 36,000. That is roughly the number of new J.D.s we should expect to graduate in 2016. [Among 2013 graduates,] 32,775 found full-time, long-term work, meaning the job lasted at least a year. Of those jobs, 26,337 required passing the bar, meaning they were typical legal jobs. An additional 4,714 were in fields that technically did not require law degrees, but where employers preferred to hire J.D.s anyway—think congressional staffers, labor organizers, or NGO workers. Finally, 1,724 were in jobs completely unrelated to law, which sounds bad, but the reality is that a certain number of graduates always do something unconnected to their degree.
>
> Let's say those numbers hold. In that case, we can expect that about 91 percent of the class of 2016 will find long-term, full-time work, compared with about 72 percent last year. About 73 percent would be in full-time, long-term legal jobs, compared with 58 percent last year.[6]

Unfortunately for Weissmann (and, more importantly, for the class of 2016), there is not a set number of new jobs available in law in any given year, and while the class of 2016 did fare slightly better by percentages than the class of 2013, a large number of 2016 law grads still struggled to find full-time work as a lawyer. In 2013, 64.4 percent of the class had jobs requiring a JD nine months after graduation. In 2016, 67.7 percent of the class had jobs requiring a JD ten months after graduation.[7] Weissmann was dead wrong in his hope that the 2013 number of jobs would hold.

Despite the improvement in employment percentages in 2016 and again in 2017, the total number of jobs declined.

Frank McIntyre and Michael Simkovic (the authors of the controversial "million-dollar law degree paper") wrote a follow-up paper entitled "Timing Law School."[8] The paper was supported by funding from the Law School Admissions Council and the Access Group, an industry group for law schools formed to encourage law school attendance.[9] The basic argument of the paper was that there is never a bad time to go to law school, even now, because of the historical trends in the earnings of JD holders. I addressed this argument more fully in chapter 4, but for now I'll note that while historical trends are often the most accurate way to predict future earnings, this is merely a general rule of thumb, not an ironclad rule of physics. This is especially so when some law schools have slid into what looks like open enrollment, suggesting that a different cohort of students are entering law school today than in the past.

Regardless, the main point is to be leery of blanket answers devoid of context. Success in law school requires a great deal of nuanced thinking and a comfort level with operating in gray areas where there are few black-and-white answers. The decision to apply to law school is the same.

HOW TO DECIDE IF LAW SCHOOL IS RIGHT FOR YOU: DUE DILIGENCE

If you're considering law school, the very first thing you should do is research the work that lawyers actually do and the lives that lawyers actually live. Before borrowing $100,000 or more for law school, spend a little time thinking about what kind of work you might like to do as a lawyer. Because America has a unitary legal degree and profession, law school graduates end up doing a wide variety of things. So, it is a good idea to find more than one possible job that you might enjoy. Then see if you can find people near you who have one of these jobs, and ask them out to lunch or coffee to ask them, "How do you like the job? How did you get where you are now? Can I follow you for part of a day?" You may be shy about doing this, but you would be surprised by how generous lawyers, even very busy lawyers, are with their time (assuming you are likewise considerate in the demands you make).

The point of these meetings is to get a flavor for the work and the life. Most lawyers do not earn a million dollars a year and drive Ferraris, and most lawyers don't actually spend much time trying cases before a jury. Before you go to law school, make sure that you actually want to be a lawyer. This is no-brainer advice, but if you attend law school, you will be shocked by the number of students who have given no thought to whether they actually want to be a lawyer and what type of lawyer they might like to be.

Hey, Ben Barton, you ask, *what if I want to be a sports agent and Rob Pelinka (my law school classmate who was the agent for Kobe Bryant and is now the general manager of the Los Angeles Lakers) won't return my calls? Or what if I really want to do equine law (horse law) or plaintiff's side environmental justice work, and I can't find anyone near me who will talk to me about it?*

Far be it from me to crush anyone's dreams, and I do know actual people who have desperately wanted these jobs and now are happily doing them. That said, if there aren't very many people who want to do your proposed job near you, or there are so few of them and they are so busy that you can't reach them, that is probably not a good sign. It's not a showstopper necessarily, but (a) you should expect to struggle to find one of these jobs, and you should assume you are going to have to fight to keep one; and (b) you should have a backup plan, just in case you get to law school and change your mind about your life's passion.

Same with the laudatory goal of trying to use law to change the world or fix a particular social problem. There is no end of need for quality legal services, especially in an effort to make the world a better place. For example, if the Trump Bump is real and results in a wave of new lawyers dedicated to improving the lives of impoverished immigrants, or protecting transsexual soldiers, I will personally be thrilled. My concern for these students would be the need to make a living, and while there *are* lawyers who do this work, the funding for it is limited, and the competition for the existing jobs is challenging. This is not to say it's impossible, just that one should enter the quest with eyes wide open and few illusions.

Or your problem may not be an abiding but unrealistic passion; your problem may be confusion about what kind of lawyer you might want to be. At this point you may think to yourself, "I have no idea what I want to do. That's why I need to go to law school, to find out!" If this describes you, reread that sentence and rethink going to law school. There are cheaper and more rewarding ways to find yourself, I promise.

On the other hand, if you are sincerely interested in being a lawyer but just have no feel for what kind of law to pursue, that's fine too! The main point is to research and talk to a sampling of different kinds of lawyers to see if any of them could fit the bill. The more the better, as there is a likelihood you'll change your mind in law school or as you grow older. So talk to a public defender, a prosecutor, and a corporate lawyer, and see if any or all of them appeal. If none of them appeal, try a few more. Still nothing? Business school may be better for you, my friend.

THAT SOUNDED SORT OF DISCOURAGING; CAN'T YOU SAY MORE?

Sure. Let me start by saying that I practiced law for two years at a big law firm before I started teaching law, and then I worked another thirteen years as a clinical law professor (which means I supervised and taught students who were handling actual cases for actual indigent clients), so I have years of field experience as a lawyer. It is a terrific job for the right kind of person. There are very, very few jobs that offer a better combination of intellectual challenge, the opportunity to write for a living, and sheer variety of human experience than the practice of law. I often tell potential students, Law is a people job, a helping job, and an intellectual puzzle job. If you like those things, you will like or even love being a lawyer.

If you or your family know more than a few lawyers, it is likely that you know one who is not crazy about their job. That happens. But you probably also know a lawyer that can wax rhapsodic about "the life of the law." These happy lawyers are not unicorns; they actually exist. If you look at the lawyer satisfaction surveys, you will find that lawyer happiness is *not* determined by salary. In fact, some of the most discontented lawyers are the wealthiest. The happiest lawyers love the work itself. Some of these folks earn a lot, but others earn less. For example, lawyers who work in-house for corporations are on average happier than their cohorts who work at large firms serving corporate clients, despite earning less than BigLaw lawyers. That's puzzling! Similarly, solo practitioners report higher rates of satisfaction than law graduates who are working in more highly paid jobs that do not require a JD.

In-house lawyers are happier because they have more control over their schedules and are engaged in the cooperative work of helping an organization succeed. That is exactly the sort of job that creative humans love! Solo practitioners have a harder lot in life. They often have to work in multiple different areas of the law and hustle to get clients and to collect their bills. But they get to practice law and use their work and degree to help people directly. And they get to run their own small business, giving them more control than most professionals over the timing and nature of their work. This is naturally more satisfying than many non-lawyer jobs, where the special skills and desires that led someone to go to law school are not necessarily used.

OK, I WANT TO BE A LAWYER; AM I DONE NOW? DUE DILIGENCE 2: SCHOOLS

If you have done the work and decided that you actually want to be a lawyer, you are off to a good start! Unfortunately, your due diligence is only beginning. The next step is to decide if there is a law school that fits your goals. If all of this sounds like a lot of hassle, remember the price tag. Before you spend the time and money on a particular law school, make sure it is right for you. And by the way, if you do not like doing this sort of research, you may not care much for being a lawyer.

This book is packed with data, and most of that data is publically available in print and online. First and foremost, spend some time looking at the job placement data for the schools you are interested in. The website http://employmentsummary.abaquestionnaire.org has a list of the employment results of every law school in the country from 2010 forward. Look at the data for each school that interests you, and examine also the aggregate data for the corresponding year for comparison. This data is not granular enough to tell you about the likelihood of landing any particular job, such as state prosecutor, but it can give you a ballpark estimate of what graduates do. In particular, it can tell you what percentage of graduates obtain full-time work as a lawyer.

Because law schools are required to gather this data, you should be able to call the admissions office of any law school and (politely) ask for some data on your chosen field. For example, you could say, "I'm interested in becoming a public defender. Can you send me the names and contact information of several recent grads who are public defenders so I can speak to them?" The more specific your desire, the more important it is to drill down on the school's performance. For example, if the school advertises a specialty in entertainment law or the music business, don't accept glossy pictures of second-year law students working as interns; ask for names of recent graduates actually working as entertainment lawyers, and in what capacity. Then contact some of them. If the school can't or won't present this information, I wouldn't consider it a good sign.

Say your heart's desire is to work at a large corporate law firm in New York City. Start by finding out how many graduates each of your potential law schools sent to large law firms in New York City over the 2010–16 period. If the answer is "not many," that may mean you should try a different school, adjust your career goals, or not attend law school.

Then return to the employment data, and take a minute to consider the unpleasant possibility that law school may not turn out as you would hope. So, let's say that about 15 to 20 percent of the graduating class ends up in one of the highest-paying law firm jobs. That would actually be a pretty strong result outside of the T14. And yet, without taking other factors into account, this data suggests you only have a 20 percent chance of meeting your goal. If you could be content with a different job, say working in a small firm for a lower salary or in state government, then consider the odds of doing that job as a graduate from your law school. Basically, you should not attend law school if the data from the school you are considering indicates that half or more of the graduates end up in employment settings you would not like. Why? Because this is the likeliest result from the law school you're attending!

Also look at the financial aid information, which is publicly available from the American Bar Association (ABA) at http://www.abarequired-disclosures.org. The school reports will tell you what percentage of students receive aid each year and what the average amount is. Carefully balance the amount you're likely to pay against the employment results and other factors. Whatever you do, do not simply go to the "best" law school you get into (per the *U.S. News* or any other rankings) with no regard for cost. Lawyers spend a lot of time weighing probabilities, possible outcomes, and costs in order to choose the path likeliest to result in the most success at the least cost. This is exactly what you should be doing when choosing a law school. In fact, consider having a "total cost" ceiling in mind, and just eliminate schools that come in above it. If the only school you can afford has poor placement statistics, strongly consider walking away and applying again another year, or pursuing a different career.

TECHNOLOGICAL ERADICATION?

But what about technology? Won't technological change swallow up the practice altogether? The more relevant question is, Will technology change the practice of law, and if so, how? The answer to the first part of this question is unreservedly *yes*. The practice of law is as small *c* conservative as it gets—resistant to change and scared of the new. This has kept it relatively unaffected by the technological revolution occurring all around us. But hiding one's head in the sand does not actually make change disappear. Change is coming.

For younger people thinking about entering the profession, the move toward incorporating technology is not necessarily a bad thing. On the contrary, who would you expect to better adapt to a brave new world of virtual offices and legal chatbots handling client interviews, someone my age or someone the average age of a typical law student? The great bulk of folks entering law school today are digital natives; they have spent their whole lives working with computers, cell phones, and other technologies. This does *not* mean they are naturally good at programming or other advanced computer skills. Most technologically adept folks are pursuing computer science or engineering degrees rather than law. But it does make it more likely that these new law students will understand the concept of a digital office, for example, better than someone who has been practicing law for years. The lawyers who do the best job of holding down fixed costs and spending the most time actually practicing law are the lawyers who will triumph going forward. These lawyers are much likelier to be the digital natives graduating right now, not the lawyers who graduated last century.

ARE YOU AN ENTREPRENEUR/HUSTLER AT HEART?

Technological innovation will also change the game in terms of who succeeds in the market. For decades, and possibly for as long as there has been a T14-type law school, there were certain types of corporate and big-firm jobs that were *only* accessible via a certain type of pedigree. Over time, though, we will increasingly see that the lawyers who are best able to adjust to the brave new world of technology will be the ones to break through in new business models.

Consider Jane Allen, who is the founder of Counsel on Call, a new model legal services company that connects law firms, corporate clients, and specialist lawyers.[10] Bill Henderson describes Counsel on Call as a national leader in "managed services—a new category of legal firms that build systems to handle high-volume, repetitive work—and how they're making millions of dollars from the effort."[11] In short, Jane Allen is a massive success in the new legal economy. She is a proud University of Kentucky College of Law graduate, and while she did work at a well-known regional Nashville law firm, she is hardly an example of credentialism. To the contrary, she is an example of hustle, moxie, and a great idea triumphing over credentials.

Business author Daniel Pink's book *To Sell Is Human* famously made the point that all Americans are now in sales, whether we're selling our own "brand" or boosting our employer's profile, or actually selling goods or services.[12] Whether this is true nationally or not, it is absolutely true for law. The days when a law school graduate could expect a comfortable middle-class existence solely based on passing the bar and hanging up a shingle are firmly over, if they ever existed. Even lawyers in relatively "safe" jobs like academia or government will need to continuously think about the value they add to their organization, or they may eventually find themselves exiting that organization due to budget cuts or other causes.

Gillian Hadfield has noticed that there is a great dearth of the types of lawyers that high-level corporate clients really need—lawyers who can think across business models and country borders to address tomorrow's global legal challenges.[13] Hadfield points out that today's law schools and law firms produce way too few of these sorts of professionals. Today's lawyers are in many ways ill suited for our technological and global challenges. Frankly, tomorrow's lawyers have a much better chance to fill this growing need. Neither the world nor the law is getting simpler any time soon, I promise.

Again, this is great news for the right kind of person. Law is growing less hidebound, and this means that hustle, grit, and ability will be more likely to win out now than ever before. If you are "in" for that competition, being a lawyer and attending law school may be perfect for you. If you are not, think hard about it.

UPSHOT

Weirdly, this is both the best of times and the worst of times to go to law school. There has never been a worse time for people who are unsuited to law school or the practice of law to attend. Baby boomers experienced a relatively forgiving employment market and low law school tuition. Law school now costs a fortune—usually paid via student loans—and offers a less certain return. This is especially so if students enter without a relatively clear-eyed focus on why they are there and what they want to do with the degree.

On the other hand, if students have done the work to decide that they want to be a lawyer, and they choose a school that is a cost-effective vehicle for their goals, it is a great time to go. Schools are more aggressively negotiating tuition prices and are anxious to have students come. This puts today's students in the position to drive a hard bargain with the right school.

Likewise, some economists wax eloquent about what they call "creative destruction," the process in a market economy where some legacy businesses fail and are then replaced by new, more innovative businesses. This is definitely what is currently happening in law. Creative destruction offers many opportunities to the nimble of foot and those not wedded to old ways of doing things. Today's law graduates are uniquely situated to take advantage of these changes, assuming they choose their law schools and later careers wisely.

So, in a nutshell—do the work to make sure law school (or business school or accounting school, for that matter) is right for you. If you have done the work, then please come! The world very much needs more intelligent, hardworking, young lawyers; of that, I am sure.

CONCLUSION

This conclusion covers two topics: what should happen in law schools and what is likely to actually happen in law schools. I cover both because too many discussions of law schools and their woes devolve into free-for-alls of unlikely or flatly impossible reforms. Here we stick to three reform proposals that might actually happen and leaven even those with a discussion of the likelier result: that for the near term little will change.

WHAT SHOULD HAPPEN

Hopefully by now you are convinced that law schools find themselves in a precarious and challenging position. Applications and enrollment are down (although maybe the Trump Bump will save us all). Job placement has been and remains soft. Schools have lost faculty, colleagues, and a handful of peer institutions. Even former law professor Barack Obama suggested the third year is a waste of time.[1]

You could forgive law faculties for feeling as if they have been through struggles and that now is the wrong time to press forward on anything new. Law schools have, in fact, changed a lot in the last decade. Unfortunately, almost all of those changes have been to address financial and enrollment challenges, not the fundamental problems that led to the crisis.

But at least there is a shared recognition that law schools need reform. In 2011 and 2012, many rejected the idea that any changes were needed at all. That argument has been buried for now, so maybe there has never been a better time for reform. Here are four improvements that might actually happen, and that may in fact be necessary for long-term survival.

LOWER THE PRICE AND DEBT LEVELS

The easiest place to start is with the price. Many law schools have had to tighten their belts since 2010, including losing faculty colleagues and staff, facing salary cuts, and losing perks like travel and summer research grants. Even with a bump in applications and attendance, now is an inopportune time to tell these folks that they need to cut back further on income.

But they have to cut back further on income. If something cannot go on forever, it will not go on forever, and the run-up in tuition and debt must end, sooner rather than later. A 2018 Gallup poll showed only 23 percent of law school graduates thought their education was worth the cost and only 20 percent thought law school prepared them well for life after graduation.[2] This was the lowest among all types of graduate school.

There are political, logistical, and moral reasons for urgency here. Politically, law schools of all stripes, but especially the schools that expect students to graduate with six figures in law school debt (on top of their undergraduate debts), are asking too much of their students and of the US government. Consciously or unconsciously, these schools have taken advantage of the hopefulness of their students and the generosity of a federal government that intends higher education to be a ladder into the middle class.

As it becomes more apparent that law school (and other graduate school) debt is sometimes not a ladder but an anchor, and as the venality of some law schools becomes ever clearer, the government will very likely renegotiate the deal. Calls to cap or scale back federal loans and loan forgiveness programs are loud and getting louder. Law schools seem to be assuming that a renegotiation of the deal is a problem to put off until tomorrow, and that at worst it will cap future tuition growth where it stands now. This explains why schools seem to be rushing to lock in tuition gains and concomitant higher loan amounts. They want to start any renegotiation over federal loans at a high baseline.

Unfortunately, there is no guarantee that today's tuition amounts will lock in tomorrow's debt limits. The worse that higher education looks, the more likely it becomes that Congress might adopt more stringent reforms. Possibilities include a cap on federal loans, abandoning the federal government's role in higher education loans altogether, and requiring institutions to take some "skin in the game" as insurance against loan defaults.

The moral issue is also hard to ignore. Deborah Jones Merritt has argued that we are seeing a massive intergenerational wealth transfer, as Millennials take out loans to pay out the salaries of their boomer and gen X professors.[3] Yes, law schools have had to tighten their belts. As a result of this process, being a law professor has gotten to be a slightly less sweet deal than it was a decade ago, and speaking against my own personal interest, that trend is wise and should continue. There is surely fat to be trimmed here, as salaries rose and teaching loads shrank pretty continuously for decades before 2011. Likewise, the ABA's move to outcome-based regulatory measures should allow schools to cut costs in terms of libraries and staff positions that do not directly benefit today's law students.

Asking today's students (and probably eventually US taxpayers) to take on a lifetime's debt to float these schools while employment outcomes remain uncertain for a third of graduates is a tough sell. Tuition cuts and lower debt loads are necessary. The years 2017–18 finally brought some good news in this regard, as debt loads fell slightly. Let this be the beginning of a much-needed trend.

FIND SMART WAYS TO TEACH TECH

In HBO's *Game of Thrones* seasons 5 through 7 (and in the even better J. R. R. Martin books), the residents and rulers of fictional Westeros find themselves utterly exhausted and spent after years of civil war and rotating kings and queens running various portions of the continent. The irony is that while all of these internecine wars are occurring, Westeros faces a truly existential threat, an army of undead approaching from the North. For multiple reasons, the warring rulers of Westeros choose to ignore this threat. Some do not believe it exists. Some think that strategically they are better off fighting with each other than addressing a common enemy. Some assume that if the enemy is as described, they are all doomed anyway, so why fight it at all? And others are too exhausted to even contemplate a new and more daunting war against supernatural foes.

Law schools find themselves in a similar spot with the new wave of legal tech. After a relatively brutal decade, they are suddenly confronted with stories of artificial intelligence (AI) lawyers and other technologies destroying their livelihoods. Recall chapter 3's discussion of British futurist Richard Susskind's prediction that the work of most small firm and solo practitioners will disappear as soon as the next decade. This is a daunting prospect for law schools (let alone lawyers), and given that some of these technologies—such as true AI or using blockchain to create a new kind of interactive contract—are mind-bending, you can forgive law schools for going to extremes by either (a) ignoring the problem altogether or (b) chasing after the most forward-looking and advanced technologies on the horizon while ignoring the more near-term technologies.

Both of these approaches are erroneous. To paraphrase Kanye West, it's best to crawl before you ball, y'all. On the one hand it is silly to try to teach students the most advanced and futuristic versions of these technologies. If legal AI gets so good that there are few or no jobs for human lawyers, law schools and lawyers will be finished regardless of what we try to teach today. There is no upside to trying to train law students to create or operate the technology that underlies this possible version of the future. No one is going to hire a Stanford law graduate to code ahead of a Stanford engineer.

But this does not excuse law schools from addressing advances in legal technology. This responsibility arises on three fronts: (1) tomorrow's lawyers will need to understand how to use technology to streamline their practices; (2) tomorrow's lawyers will also need to be prepared in some spots to compete against computers; and (3) we can all play a part in combining computers and human efforts to expand access to justice for poor and middle-class Americans. A new type of law school course has emerged that spans all of these seemingly disparate goals, allowing law schools to do well while doing good.

Before describing this new approach, let me offer a reminder regarding several interlocking trends buffeting law schools and lawyers. Lawyers are not currently losing work to AI-driven programs that imitate human thinking and interaction. Instead, they are facing competition from computer programs that replace repetitive human tasks like document review, or programs like the interactive forms on LegalZoom and Rocket Lawyer that break the drafting of legal documents down into question-and-answer decision trees, using relatively simple questions to create forms like wills or simple divorce papers. Law students need to understand how these programs work, and how humans can work *together* with these technologies, mechanizing whatever work they can while preserving the areas in which human judgment adds unique value to the process.

Even as these new programs are coming online, America remains mired in a miserable access-to-justice crisis, one that affects not just the poor but the middle class as well. Deborah Rhode and Gillian Hadfield have gathered the most damning data. For our purposes, here is a brief summary: as law grows more complex and important in the lives of Americans, most Americans cannot afford to hire a lawyer for even basic and truly necessary services such as handling a contested divorce or child custody matter, disputing a debt-collection matter, or defending an eviction or foreclosure.[4]

But hey, you ask, didn't you spend almost a whole chapter complaining that almost a third of law graduates cannot find full-time work as lawyers? How is it possible that needy middle-class consumers can't find a lawyer? The answer is that lawyers and law students have been trained to handle each legal case, even a relatively simple or run-of-the-mill matter like a divorce, individually. Imagine how much your clothes would cost, and how many pairs of pants you would own, if all clothes were custom-made and created individually just for you by an individual licensed tailor. The middle class cannot afford legal work, because even if a solo practitioner charges $100 an hour (and the average rate for a small firm lawyer in America was $232 per hour in 2016), the costs add up quickly for even a mildly complicated matter like a DUI charge or a contested child custody matter.[5]

This is an issue for law schools because of how we teach our students. Law schools spend almost all of their time on gray areas in the law. In some ways this makes sense. The most lucrative work for American lawyers is in interpreting and exploiting gray areas. In other ways it is a disaster, especially if it means that middle-class people cannot afford to hire a lawyer and lawyers can't earn a middle-class living.

These trends seem quite distinct, but law schools can address all of them at once by teaching technology more intelligently. The lowest-hanging fruit would be to just add a class in eDiscovery or advanced legal research, working with the latest technologies. My colleague at the University of Tennessee, Paula Schaeffer, taught one of the first eDiscovery classes in the country, instructing students in the nuts and bolts of the current state of the art. More importantly, the course familiarizes the students with the idea that an algorithm (with proper human guidance) can save time and money and increase efficiency. The students at the University of Tennessee are unlikely to go work at a massive law firm in New York City or Los Angeles where eDiscovery is most prevalent, but this actually makes the class more valuable. These students will learn to seek out technological solutions in practice and will press eDiscovery vendors to lower prices to serve middle-class and small-business audiences.

A slightly more complex option is to engage the students in actually creating web-based legal services for the poor. In this area, Chicago Kent Law School has no peer. For a school of its relative rank and size, the Chicago-Kent College of Law has an amazing array of tech offerings, from an Institute for Science, Law, and Technology to a Law Lab that offers a specialized curriculum and a certificate program in "Legal Innovation and Technology."

Chicago-Kent's crown jewel is the oldest and most influential law tech/access to justice program in America (and probably the world), the Center for Access to Justice and Technology. Founded in the late 1990s, the center has been at the forefront of web-based self-help software geared for the indigent.[6] In 2004, the center began developing its very first "A2J Author" software, a user-friendly platform that allows developers to create question-and-answer websites that guide users in creating legal documents.[7] A2J Author is now in version 6.0. It is cloud based and accessible on a smartphone.[8] A2J has generated more than two million documents since 2005, and some version of A2J Author is operating in almost every state in the union. It's an amazing technology that has changed the availability of legal services for millions of indigent Americans. More importantly for our purposes, it has helped teach a generation of law students how to break complicated legal problems down into smaller steps and how to create a document assembly program that is simple enough to be useful but complex enough to be accurate.

Chicago-Kent pioneered this technological approach, but law schools around the country have used A2J Author in a similar manner. Tanina Rostain at Georgetown runs one of the standout programs. Every spring she teaches a class entitled "Technology, Innovation, and Law Practicum." The students work in teams for nonprofit or government partners that need an access-to-justice website or mobile app. The teams work all semester to create an app or website from scratch, starting with interviewing the client entity, then researching the relevant law, and then placing the law into a flow chart of branching logic suitable for a website or app. The students then pause and rewrite what they have into plainer language, at the reading level of the target audience. Following this preliminary work, students create the app/website itself, with the help of Neota Logic on coding and Professor Rostain on other design and drafting elements. The students then show the beta version to the client and test it for functionality, addressing additional concerns and fixing the inevitable bugs. At the end of the semester, the student teams present their projects to the rest of the class, showing how each program works but also discussing the design process, the challenges they faced, client relations, and so on.

The portion of the class in which the students break down their legal problem into a flowchart of questions and branching logic based on the answers is called "storyboarding." It is, in my opinion, the truly critical part of the students' education. Instead of finding gray areas, the students must discover ways to simplify the law and render it as a flow chart, reducing a legal problem to cognizable bite-sized pieces and arranging these pieces in a logical order. Storyboarding is, of course, a necessary skill for creating an A2J website. Much more importantly, it is the precise twenty-first-century lawyer skill that our graduates should master, alongside the traditional gray-areas approach.

As automation becomes a more common part of legal work, jobs for lawyers will divide into two hemispheres. In one hemisphere, there will be lawyers that handle only very complicated or *sui generis* legal work that cannot (for the near term at least) be automated. We will call these lawyers "rich." Note that this split has already begun as BigLaw, and other highly priced lawyers separate themselves from the rest of the profession.

In the other hemisphere, there will be lawyers that handle more regularized work. These lawyers are presently struggling, partially because even run-of-the-mill work takes so many individualized hours. But automation and the storyboarding process that underlies creating an interactive website can provide a solution for these lawyers: do more work, at lower rates, but more efficiently. If the various access-to-justice surveys are even partially right, there is a mass of unmet need out there, and there is no reason only LegalZoom or Rocket Lawyer should harvest it. Lawyers using the skills they gain in an A2J Author–type class will be well suited to find ways to automate their work around the edges. These classes should be expanded and offered all over the country.

On a related note, small-firm and solo practitioners also struggle because they spend so little of their time on billable work. In 2016, the legal billing program Clio produced a study of amalgamated data from all fifty states that showed that the average American lawyer who uses Clio (almost all of whom are small firms or solos) spends only 2.2 hours a day on billable work.[9] Of that time, they only actually bill clients for 1.8 hours a day (we call this number the "realization rate"). Of the billed time, only 1.5 hours is actually collected (the "collection rate"). No matter what you charge per hour, it is hard to make a decent living getting paid for only 1.5 hours of your time per day! These lawyers spend the rest of their times hustling to find work and handling the administrative tasks associated with owning a small business.

Law schools have always done an embarrassingly bad job of teaching the nuts and bolts of the practice of law (how to get clients, how to set a billing rate, how to collect on bills, etc.). This is partially because some law professors have no experience working in private practice, and even the ones who do often left because they hated the hassle of the billable hour. It is also partially because law schools have considered themselves academic units, and what could be less academic or interesting than the *business* of the practice of law.

This gap is especially harmful today because technology allows for lawyers to automate more and more of their nonlegal work. For example, technology makes an office or a staff a luxury for new solo practitioners. Along with how to use technology to assist in the practice of law, we should also teach students to use technology to streamline and automate the business of law. In the future, the main street lawyers that make it will be the ones who spend more time billing clients and less time doing everything else. Law school can and should help prepare students for this future.

LET A THOUSAND FLOWERS BLOOM: MOVING TO OUTPUT REGULATION

This book has been pretty critical of the regulation of American law schools. I have also been critical of law schools herding and looking the same, even when differentiation might be in their interest in a competitive marketplace. Many have argued that the regulation itself has stifled innovation, but after years of study I have concluded that the regulation operates more as a cover story for the lack of innovation than an actual bar.

One way to prove this point is to ask any individual dean or faculty member who is complaining about the constraints of the regulations, "What exact innovation did you have in mind, and what exact regulation barred it?" When pressed, this person will likely say that it's the general requirement of expenditures on a full-time faculty or library that ties their hands, not a specific prohibition. OK, maybe so. Or maybe the regulations just make it easier for law schools to go along and get along without having to make it in a competitive marketplace. Competitive marketplaces tend to produce innovation and differentiation, and concomitant advantages for customers and pressures on providers.

So maybe we should deregulate altogether or mostly? The problem here is that when given the chance to "innovate," many law schools just use the opportunity to cut costs and quality and increase profit margins. The rise of the for-profit law school is the perfect example. For-profit law schools could have tried to create a better product that costs less. Instead, their primary innovation has been to take the least likable aspects of predatory nonprofit schools and turn them up to maximum volume. Open enrollment, the smallest faculty possible, a traditional curriculum taught poorly, and poor bar exam and placement results are hardly innovations, except in profitability.

Even if I am right that current regulation is not a direct barrier to innovation, the question of how to increase innovation is more difficult to answer. Right now, the ABA is in the middle of a shift to more outcome-based regulation (on things like bar passage and job placement), rather than input regulations covering things like the nature of the curriculum or the faculty. This seems like a wise move. As noted in chapter 6, input regulations are hard to enforce and lead to bean counting and technical compliance, rather than a focus on whether the law school at issue is serving the interests of its students and the public. Competing over outcomes is a good first step toward innovation, as law schools will have clear goals in mind in terms of results for their graduates but limited requirements in terms of how they reach those goals.

Maybe this will result in radical cost-cutting and some of the other behaviors I have criticized earlier. Sure, but if the results are good, who cares? A two-year online law school program that resulted in above-average bar passage rates and 80 percent employment in JD-required jobs would be more than A-OK with me. I would lead the parade in support. As of yet, for-profit and other lower-ranked schools have not been able to produce good results in terms of employment or bar passage, but if they did, we should all applaud (and take notes). The bright light of attention on results for graduates would also help focus the attention of applicants on the numbers that really matter.

With the new output measures in hand, the ABA should double down on its suddenly robust enforcement of those standards. Arizona Summit is by some measures the worst law school in America, so pushing forward on disaccreditation there was a good start. Nevertheless, if you double back and read the various lists of struggling law schools (highest debt loads, worst bar passage, and job placement), you will see that Arizona Summit is not so different from some of its peers. The ABA should not hesitate to take action against these law schools as well.

LET A THOUSAND FLOWERS BLOOM: EMBRACE NEW PROGRAMS, BUT DON'T BE EVIL!

The single biggest recent change in American law schools is the growth in the non-JD student body. Law schools of all stripes, sizes, and locations are rapidly creating a bevy of non-JD programs, from more traditional in-person master of laws (LLM) programs to more innovative online-only masters in law programs.

On the one hand this is great news. The ABA currently does little to regulate these programs, so law schools at last have a laboratory where they can try out all sorts of new models of teaching, including online or other computer-based methods. Law schools can use this experimental space to decide what works and does not work and then let it bleed over into the traditional program if it proves successful. This book spends a lot of time criticizing JD programs for looking the same and failing to innovate. Given that the opposite is the case in the non-JD space, perhaps law schools will solve their problems in the less regulated spaces first and then use those lessons to save the JD programs.

On the other hand, I can't help but be skeptical of many of these programs. Many non-JD programs may be sincere attempts to offer value to their students in terms of transferable skills and job placement. I worry that many of them are just efforts to fill empty seats by hook or by crook. The flip side to the lack of regulation in this space is the possibility of predatory schools seeing a whole new and untapped group of students who can borrow full freight for degrees of dubious value. Many of these programs are new, especially the masters and undergraduate programs, so there has not been enough time to establish a track record of success in placing students or a rubric to uniformly test what they have learned. Nevertheless, the bar passage rate for foreign LLM students and the speculative nature of the usefulness of a "master's in law" make me worry that some (many?) of these programs will prove to be a worse value than the worst JD programs.

I have a simple two-step test when assessing any of these programs. The first question is, could this program operate as a scam? By "scam" I mean, could the value proposition between tuition/federal loans be so far out of whack with what the students learn during school and earn after graduation that the program resembles the JD programs of America's most predatory law schools? The second, related question is, does this program seek to cash out the perceived value of a legal education without actually delivering the utility that a JD offers? One of the worst aspects of law school behavior since the 1990s is the way that schools sold out their reputational capital for near-term profit. Schools of all stripes relentlessly raised tuition and grew in size through 2011 regardless of whether the market could support so many law graduates. Many current non-JD programs seem even more likely to suffer from these defects, thus my skepticism.

Again, it is too soon to either wholly condemn or roundly praise these programs. In some ways any change at all is good for legal education. Nevertheless, law schools have already tarnished their reputations in the last decade. The last thing we need is a new arena to further sully our names.

WHAT I THINK *WILL* HAPPEN

The problems this book covers are on the ABA's radar. In 2017, the ABA created a new Commission on the Future of Legal Education, and the membership on the committee is promising. The commission is chaired by Dean Trish White of Miami Law School, who has been one of the most innovative deans in the country. Members include British futurist Richard Susskind, as well as top critics of the current model such as Gillian Hadfield, Deborah Jones Merritt, and David Wilkins. If personnel is policy, the committee is starting off strongly.

Nevertheless, I try not to get too excited about these things anymore. The ABA's last Task Force on the Future of Legal Education just released its final report in 2014![10] That task force was likewise staffed by excellent and well-meaning people. The ABA also published a different report on the financing of legal education in 2014, based on another task force staffed by yet other very able people.[11] In 2016, a different ABA commission, again staffed by some truly outstanding folks, published a report on the future of legal services in the United States.[12]

When I asked someone familiar with the ABA's thinking why a commission was being appointed almost immediately after the publication of a lengthy report by a task force of the same name, they started to explain to me the difference between a "task force" and a "commission" in ABA nomenclature. Bureaucracies are tough to navigate, let alone bureaucracies created by America's finest lawyers.

The problem here is not a lack of insight, or another report no matter how well meaning. The problem is finding the will to take chances and make changes in light of a changing market. In defense of the ABA and law schools, the way forward is hardly obvious, especially if regulators and law schools look too far out on the horizon toward an imagined lawyerless future.

But regardless of whether radical change would be a good idea, for the near future I predict two different flavors of "not much change." Which flavor we get depends on whether the Trump Bump and the adoption of the Graduate Record Examinations (GRE) as an entry exam presage a return to high application volumes. If you look at the Law School Admission Test (LSAT), application, and enrollment totals over the years, they do tend to move together (meaning that more LSAT takers usually mean more applicants and more enrollees). These three numbers also tend to bounce up and down in relatively slow waves, meaning that a five- to ten-year period of upward growth is followed by a peak, then a fall for a few years, then a trough, and then a repeat of the cycle. Just eyeballing the last thirty years, we are due for a rally.

If 2018–19 is indeed the beginnings of a rally, you can expect almost no change from law schools, except to slow down on cost-cutting and to try to increase selectivity with an eye on bar passage, job placement, and (sadly) the *U.S. News* rankings. Schools will likely maintain their current skinny profile in terms of smaller class sizes and faculties for a few years to see if the bounce-back sticks, but otherwise expect a lot of happy exhaling and some crowing from the folks who have taken a beating for predicting a rosier future since 2011.

If the recent uptick is a dead-cat bounce or flattens out, we will see a slightly different status quo, as schools continue the process of shrinking budgets and class sizes and growing non-JD programs to address the new normal. Just as schools such as Minnesota, Washington and Lee, Cincinnati, and Mitchell Hamline have taken steps to move back to balanced budgets, others will join them, unless the uptick turns into a flood of new matriculants.

But to the great disappointment of some, despite the market and tech changes of the last seven years, the status quo is likely to hold. Consider faculty governance. Brian Tamanaha's *Failing Law Schools* is absolutely correct when it says that American law schools have largely been run by and for law professors.[13] Not surprisingly, law deans are finding their faculties disinterested in any sweeping changes that will make their jobs harder. An aptly titled *Chronicle of Higher Education* article says it all: "As They Ponder Reforms, Law Deans Find Schools 'Remarkably Resistant to Change.'"[14] Schools facing closure will obviously have a mandate for a change. Schools that face struggles, but not extinction, will likely stay the course as long as they can.

Law schools, state supreme courts, and the ABA are all small-*c* conservative institutions by nature. In the common-law system, every successful lawyer is at heart a traditionalist because of the centrality of precedent to legal reasoning. Change happens incrementally, and the answer to many questions is, "Let's look backward to see what we've done in the past." This mode of thought has powerful effects on lawyers and law schools, and especially in a time of crisis, the instinct will be to batten down the hatches and ride out the storm, even if it means a few captains go down with their ships.

CODA

If there is a single lesson from the current state of American politics, it is that cynicism is corrosive. Over time we have been so critical of the motives and actions of our cultural, educational, religious, and educational institutions that we have come to think that most all of them are some kind of hustle or scam. One possible explanation for the rise in cynicism is that so many of our institutions have failed us in recent years. From churches to political parties, to rating agencies and banks, the cynics have had a good run of explaining human behavior. This may, in fact, not be a new problem. Perhaps all human institutions devolve over time into selfish and self-destructive behavior.

Regardless, I am aware that at times in this book I have tipped over into cynicism about the behavior of American law schools. I hope I have been fair overall, but readers may disagree. I want to be cognizant of my responsibility and role. I am writing a book about an institution, legal education, that I have dedicated my life to and still very much believe in. The last thing I want to do is corrode an institution I love further through cynicism, regardless of how well earned.

So, as a brief coda for the book, please forgive me the indulgence of stating what I hope is obvious. I critique legal education and the legal profession because I love it so. There are few people in America or in the world who are as fortunate as I have been professionally. But with great love comes great responsibility, a responsibility I take very seriously. I hope this book has lived up to that goal.

ACKNOWLEDGMENTS

I owe a great debt of gratitude to the other scholars and researchers working in this space. In this book I am truly standing on the shoulders of giants. There are two books in particular that I read and reread for knowledge and inspiration: Brian Tamanaha's exceptional *Failing Law Schools* and Robert Stevens's *Law School: Legal Education in America from the 1850s to the 1980s.*

This book attempts to amalgamate a lot of data and trends into a single overview. The book probably cites Paul Caron and his website *TaxProf Blog* more than any other source. Caron's blog is a must-read if you are interested in this topic. I also relied a lot on a number of different scholars who have been doing analysis of law school trends over this period. Professors William Henderson, Jerry Organ, Derek Muller, and Daniel Katz stand out for special recognition. Again, if you are interested in this topic, you should definitely read their websites Legal Evolution (Henderson), the Legal Whiteboard and *TaxProf Blog* (Organ), *Excess of Democracy* blog (Muller), and *Computational Legal Studies* blog (Katz).

I am also greatly indebted to two data-rich websites run by nonacademics: *The Last Gen X American* blog (aka *The Law School Tuition Bubble*) and *Law School Transparency*. These sites have amassed and analyzed a *ton* of data on law schools and the legal profession and have greatly affected and enriched my thinking.

I have also had a great deal of help from colleagues who have read and commented on this manuscript. Deborah Rhode, Glenn Reynolds, Russell Pearce, Renee Knake, and Brannon Denning were particularly generous (foolish?). They each read and commented on multiple drafts and improved this book immeasurably. They also serve as shining examples of an academic life lived well.

I presented an early version of the book during the Legal Ethics Schmooze at UCLA Law School in 2017 and received a number of excellent comments. Special thanks to Swethaa Ballakrishnen, Scott Cummings, Bruce Green, Brad Wendel, Nora Engstrom, Kate Kruse, Susan Fortney, Eli Wald, and Becky Roiphe. I am also extremely grateful for comments from my colleagues Wendy Bach, Doug Blaze, Paula Schaefer, Maurice Stucke, Penny White, and David Wolitz. The University of Tennessee College of Law is a great place to work.

My wife Indya read the book and offered super-helpful feedback. She also cut me a lot of slack as I wrote. My daughters Dahlia and Georgia were likewise very understanding.

One of my dearest friends from Haverford College, Paige Britton, just so happens to be an amazing editor and future law student, so she read and line edited the manuscript. It is hard to express how helpful she was in this process.

Last, but certainly not least, I was lucky enough to work with a dedicated group of student research assistants on "TEAM BARTON!" Thanks to Danny Bihrle, Julia Hale, Elizabeth Holland, Julia Johnson, Kevin Morris, Alexa Sengupta, Evan Sharber, and Paige Worthington.

NOTES

Introduction

1 *Whittier College History*, Whittier College, https://perma.cc/U3V5-BFZB (last visited Apr. 24, 2018).

2 *Whittier College*, WIKIPEDIA, https://perma.cc/YW7W-6Z82 (last visited Apr. 24, 2018).

3 *About Whittier College*, Whittier College, https://perma.cc/7XNB-MLTH (last visited Apr. 24, 2018).

4 *Patricia Leary's Address at the 50th Anniversary Celebration*, Whittier Law School, https://perma.cc/9QUM-MJNB (last visited Apr. 24, 2018).

5 Elizabeth Olson, *Whittier Law School Says It Will Shut Down*, N.Y. TIMES, Apr. 19, 2017, https://www.nytimes.com.

6 Lawdragon News, *Southwestern Receives Over $6M in Endowments*, LAWDRAGON, Nov. 1, 2013, https://perma.cc/RAK2-ENYZ.

7 Jill Switzer, *Requiem for My Law School*, ABOVE THE LAW (Apr. 26, 2017), https://perma.cc/758Y-E44Y.

8 *Id.*

9 *Consumer Information*, WHITTIER LAW SCHOOL, https://perma.cc/XT96-9AWR (last visited Apr. 25, 2018).

10 *History*, WHITTIER LAW SCHOOL, https://perma.cc/8N34-VB5J (last visited Apr. 25, 2018).

11 *About*, ASSOCIATION OF AMERICAN LAW SCHOOLS, https://perma.cc /TFK5-AQG4 (last visited Apr. 25, 2018).

12 All the facts in this paragraph come from Motion for Preliminary Injunction at 2–3, Whittier Coll. v. Am. Bar Ass'n, No. 07-1817 PA (FMOx) (C.D. Cal. May 7, 2007), *available at* https://perma.cc/57QQ-6V3Z.

13 Admin, *Whittier's Diversity Numbers Make Historic Rebound*, NAT'L JURIST PRELAW, Oct. 10, 2013, https://perma.cc/SS8K-54CF.

14 Am. Bar Ass'n, ABA STANDARDS AND RULES OF PROCEDURE FOR APPROVAL OF LAW SCHOOLS 24–25 (Am. Bar Ass'n ed., 2014), *available at* https://perma.cc/6GXM-5U97.

15 Whittier Coll. v. Am. Bar Ass'n, No. 07–1817 PA (FMOx) at 5–6.

16 Admin, *supra* introduction, note 13.

17 *Id.*

18 *Whittier Law School Changes Bearing Fruit*, WHITTIER LAW SCHOOL, Feb. 20, 2014, https://perma.cc/RNF3-9A27.

19 Staci Zaretsky, *California Bar Exam Rates by Law School (2016)*, ABOVE THE LAW (Dec. 13, 2016), https://perma.cc/7PTS-265F.

20 Sonali Kohli, *Whittier Law School Is Closing, Due in Part to Low Student Achievement*, L.A. TIMES, Apr. 20, 2017, https://perma.cc/EB8C-T8RK.

21 Brian Tamanaha, *Information About Law Schools, Circa 1960: The Cost of Attending*, BALKINIZATION, May 22, 2011, https://perma.cc/43UB-JD86.

22 Derek Thompson, *Your Brain on Poverty: Why Poor People Seem to Make Bad Decisions*, ATLANTIC, Nov. 22, 2013, https://perma.cc/3JPQ-YY5A.

23 Rick Seltzer, *What Comes after Whittier Shutdown?* INSIDE HIGHER ED, Apr. 25, 2017, https://perma.cc/4B8M-6DH9.

24 *Id.*

25 Plaintiff's Ex Parte Application for a Temporary Restraining Order and Order to Show Cause Why a Preliminary Injunction Should Not Be Issued, Cohen v. Whittier Coll., No. BC675825 (Cal. App. Dep't Super. Ct. Apr. 18, 2017), *available at* https://perma.cc/JT9U-9NWR.

26 Stephanie Francis Ward, *Arizona Summit Loses Accreditation Approval, Which May Be a First for an Operating Law School*, ABA J. (June 11, 2018), https://perma.cc/WEX9-AUT8.

27 Anne Ryman, *Arizona Summit Law School Details Plans to Eventually Close Its Doors*, ARIZONA REPUBLIC, Oct. 25, 2018, https://perma.cc/BH2W-3DCN.

28 Fatima Hussein, *Indiana Tech Will Shut Down Law School*, INDY STAR, Oct. 31, 2016, https://perma.cc/6GBE-2VWN.

29 Staci Zaretsky, *Valparaiso Law School Will Stop Accepting New Students, May Wind Down (Updated)*, ABOVE THE LAW (Nov. 16, 2017), https://perma.cc/KR8V-E83R.

30 Tyler Roberts, *Savannah Law School Is Closing after Seven Years*, NAT'L JUR., Mar. 23, 2018, https://perma.cc/M7LE-Y9KC.

31 Nathan Bomey, *Cooley Law School Closing Ann Arbor Campus*, DETROIT FREE PRESS, Oct. 9, 2014, https://perma.cc/Y2TA-D8MN.

32 On the Trump Bump, *see* Sara Randazzo, *Law School Is Hot Again as Politics Piques Interest*, WALL ST. J., Dec. 15, 2017, https://www.wsj.com.

33 All of the facts in this paragraph come from David B. Grusky et al., THE GREAT RECESSION 3–4 (2011).

34 Eli Wald, *Foreword: The Great Recession and the Legal Profession*, 78 FORDHAM L. REV. 2051, 2051–52 (2010).

35 Celia Ampel, *Sticky Fingers: Attorney Thefts from Clients Spiked in Great Recession*, DAILY BUS. REVIEW, Mar. 9, 2018, https://perma.cc/PZU7-GBBE.

36 Rebecca R. Ruiz, *Recession Spurs Interest in Graduate, Law Schools*, N.Y. TIMES, Jan. 9, 2010, https://www.nytimes.com.

37 *See, e.g.,* Noam Scheiber, *An Expensive Law Degree, and No Place to Use It*, N.Y. TIMES, June 17, 2016, https://www.nytimes.com; Dorothy A. Brown, *Law Schools*

Are in a Death Spiral; Maybe Now They'll Finally Change, WASH. POST, Mar. 9, 2015, https://perma.cc/C68U-SESA; and Joe Palazzolo, *Law Grads Face Brutal Job Market*, WALL ST. J., June 25, 2012, https://www.wsj.com.

38 Daniel Coogan, *Drop in LSAT Scores for Law Students Could Affect Applicants*, U.S. NEWS, May 3, 2016, https://www.usnews.com; Staci Zaretsky, *Law Schools in Trouble: Several Schools May Soon "Wither Away" into Closure*, ABOVE THE LAW (Mar. 13, 2016), https://perma.cc/N897-B8CL.

Chapter 1. The Original Sin

1 Jerome Frank, *A Plea for Lawyer-Schools*, 56 YALE L.J. 1303 (1947).

2 Karl N. Llewellyn et al., *Report of the Committee on Curriculum*, 1944 AALS PROC. 159, 168.

3 Roy Stuckey et al., BEST PRACTICES FOR LEGAL EDUCATION (2007); William M. Sullivan et al., EDUCATING LAWYERS: PREPARATION FOR THE PRACTICE OF LAW (2007).

4 David Segal, *What They Don't Teach Law Students: Lawyering*, N.Y. TIMES, Nov. 19, 2011, https://www.nytimes.com.

5 David Margolick, *The Trouble with America's Law Schools*, N.Y. TIMES, May 22, 1983, https://www.nytimes.com; Sean Patrick Farrell, *The Lawyer's Apprentice: How to Learn the Law without Law School*, N.Y. TIMES, July 30, 2014, https://www.nytimes.com.

6 *ABA Approves New Accreditation Standards to Require More "Experiential" Learning Opportunities*, LEGAL SKILLS PROF BLOG (Aug. 12, 2014), https://perma.cc/68QE-UUXV.

7 Roscoe Pound, THE LAWYER FROM ANTIQUITY TO MODERN TIMES 221–50 (1953).

8 *Id.* at 251–81.

9 *Id.* at 271.

10 Robert Stevens, LAW SCHOOL: LEGAL EDUCATION IN AMERICA FROM THE 1850S TO THE 1980S 3–10 (1983); Nate Oman, *The Oldest Law School*, CONCURRING OPINIONS, Aug. 15, 2006, https://perma.cc/J32L-86UK.

11 Stevens, *supra* chapter 1, note 10, at 3.

12 Robert W. Gordon, *The American Codification Movement*, 36 VAND. L. REV. 431 (1983).

13 Steven P. Croley, *The Majoritarian Difficulty: Elective Judiciaries and the Rule of Law*, 62 U. CHI. L. REV. 689, 689–794 (1995).

14 Benjamin H. Barton, THE LAWYER-JUDGE BIAS IN THE AMERICAN LEGAL SYSTEM 105–26 (2011).

15 *See* Stevens, *supra* chapter 1, note 10, at 7–9.

16 Unless otherwise noted, the facts in this paragraph come from Ben Barton, *A Comparison Between the American Markets for Medical and Legal Services*, 67 HASTINGS L.J. 1331, 1355–58 (2016).

17 *Id.*

18 N. S. Davis, HISTORY OF THE AMERICAN MEDICAL ASSOCIATION FROM ITS ORGANIZATION UP TO JANUARY, 1855 56 (1855).

19 29 ABA REP. 601–02 (1906).

20 Stevens, *supra* chapter 1, note 10, at 91–94.

21 Bruce A. Kimball, *The Proliferation of Case Method Teaching in American Law Schools: Mr. Langdell's Emblematic "Abomination," 1890–1915*, 46 HIST. ED. Q. 192, 192–93 (2006).

22 *Id.* at 192–202.

23 Stevens, *supra* chapter 1, note 10, at 35–72.

24 *Id.*

25 4 ABA REP. 265 (1881).

26 *See* Barton, LAWYER-JUDGE BIAS, *supra* chapter 1, note 14, at 113–22.

27 Benjamin H. Barton, GLASS HALF FULL: THE DECLINE AND REBIRTH OF THE LEGAL PROFESSION 136 (2015).

28 Jerold Auerbach, UNEQUAL JUSTICE (1977).

29 Stevens, *supra* chapter 1, note 10, at 25.

30 *About Nashville School of Law*, THE NASHVILLE SCHOOL OF LAW, https://perma.cc/R3ZD-MQDA (last visited Apr. 26, 2017).

31 Stevens, *supra* chapter 1, note 10, at 96–97.

32 Carl C. Monk and Harry G. Prince, *How Can an Association of Law Schools Promote Quality Legal Education?* 43 S. TEX. L. REV. 507, 508 (2002).

33 Stevens, *supra* chapter 1, note 10, at 97.

34 *Id.* at 97–98.

35 *Id.* at 173–74.

36 Richard Abel, AMERICAN LAWYERS 277–78 (1989).

37 *Id.*

38 Herb D. Vest, *Felling the Giant: Breaking the ABA's Stranglehold on Legal Education in America*, 50 J. LEGAL ED. 494, 497 (2000).

39 Stevens, *supra* chapter 1, note 10, at 173–74.

40 Vest, *supra* chapter 1, note 38, at 497.

41 *Id.*

42 Abel, *supra* chapter 1, note 36, at 55.

43 Alfred Z. Reed, TRAINING FOR THE PUBLIC PROFESSION OF THE LAW (1921).

44 *Id.* at 11–19.

45 *Id.*

46 Ruth C. Engs, THE PROGRESSIVE ERA'S HEALTH MOVEMENT 14–15 (2003).

47 Reed, *supra* chapter 1, note 43, at 28.

48 *Id.* at 418.

49 Stevens, *supra* chapter 1, note 10, at 116.

50 William M. Sullivan et al., EDUCATING LAWYERS: PREPARATION FOR THE
    PRACTICE OF LAW (2007).

Chapter 2. The New Problem

1 Amir Efrati, *Hard Case: Job Market Wanes for U.S. Lawyers*, WALL ST. J., Sept. 24,
   2007, https://www.wsj.com.

2 Ashby Jones, *As Students Fret over Jobs, Law Schools Get Creative*, WALL ST. J.,
   Apr. 16, 2009, https://perma.cc/F5EL-Y7DJ.

3 David Segal, *Is Law School a Losing Game?* N.Y. TIMES, Jan. 8, 2011, https://www
   .nytimes.com.

4 Joe Palazzo, *Law Grads Face a Brutal Job Market*, WALL ST. J., June 25, 2012,
   https://www.wsj.com.

5 J. Maureen Henderson, *Why Attending Law School Is the Worst Career Decision
   You'll Ever Make*, FORBES, June 26, 2012, https://perma.cc/T2A8-NBPJ.

6 Eric Posner, *The Real Problem with Law Schools: Too Many Lawyers*, SLATE,
   Apr. 2, 2013, https://perma.cc/KFJ6-PQY4.

7 Adam Cohen, *Just How Bad Off Are Law School Graduates?* TIME, Mar. 11, 2013,
   https://perma.cc/E33S-KF9T.

8 Dimitra Kessenides, *The Employment Rate Falls Again for Recent Law School
   Graduates*, BLOOMBERG (June 20, 2014), https://perma.cc/G45H-NZRK.

9 Noam Scheiber, *An Expensive Law Degree, and No Place to Use It*, N.Y. TIMES,
   June 17, 2016, https://perma.cc/FY87-6KUN.

10 Jacob Gershman, *Law School Graduate Employment Data Shows Decline in Legal
   Jobs*, WALL ST. J., May 2, 2016, https://blogs.wsj.com.

11 Steven J. Harper, *Too Many Law Students, Too Few Jobs*, N.Y. TIMES, Aug. 25,
   2016, https://www.nytimes.com/2015/08/25/opinion/too-many-law-students-too-
   few-legal-jobs.html.

12 Greg Toppo, *Why You Might Want to Think Twice before Going to Law School*, USA
   TODAY (June 28, 2017), https://perma.cc/8G94-WW87.

13 Here is an illustrative series of articles. First, BigLaw layoffs: Jamie Heller and
   Nathan Koppel, *Why Big Law Is Bracing for a Leaner 2008*, WALL ST. J., Feb. 25,
   2008, https://www.wsj.com. Next, BigLaw is done hiring: Nathan Koppel, *Need
   Proof That BigLaw Summer Hiring Is Down? Here You Go*, WALL ST. J., July 21,
   2010, https://perma.cc/6PUK-FG8D. Finally, BigLaw is doomed: Noam Scheiber,
   Yes, Big Law Really Is Dying, NEW REPUBLIC (July 28, 2013), https://perma
   .cc/52VD-X4TA.

14 Staci Zaretsky, Salary Wars Scorecard, Above the Law (June 5, 2018), https://
   abovethelaw.com.

15 *See* Am. Bar Ass'n, *ABA National Lawyer Population Survey, Historical Trend
   in Total National Lawyer Population, 1878–2017* (2017), https://perma.cc
   /HTY3-YFXN.

16 *Id.* The census population data is from US Census Bureau, *Section 31 20th Century Statistics* (1999), https://perma.cc/YP38-3MAG; https://perma.cc/8HPS-CF8E; and https://perma.cc/UT7F-KGNZ.

17 A 2013 estimate stated that India had 1.3 million lawyers that year, more than the US count of 1,268,011. *RTI Reveals: 1.3m Advocates; 1 in 300 Delhi-ites a Lawyer; Maharashtra Lawyers "Richest,"* LEGALLY INDIA (Feb. 18, 2013), https://perma.cc /U9MV-AWNZ.

   A later report suggested that as many as 30 percent of Indian lawyers are unlicensed. A Subramani, *30% of Lawyers in India Are Fake, Bar Council Chief Says*, TIMES OF INDIA (July 26, 2015), https://perma.cc/8HPB-D63L. That suggests that the India lawyer count is somewhat fuzzier than America's. For the Israel per capita figure, *see* Tomer Zarchin, *Israel First in World for Lawyers per Capita, Study Finds*, HAARETZ (Aug. 3, 2011), https://perma.cc/S5NT-9XGM.

18 Bureau of Economic Analysis, *Chapter 5: Personal Consumption Expenditures*, https://perma.cc/T4KL-BNZF (last visited May 9, 2017). *Real Personal Consumption Expenditures: Legal Services (Chain-Type Quantity Index)*, FED. RESERVE BANK OF ST. LOUIS, https://perma.cc/P4BF-JVGP (last visited May 9, 2017).

19 *See* Barton, GLASS HALF FULL, *supra* chapter 1, note 27, at 33–49.

20 NALP Bulletin, *Employment Rate of New Law Grads Unchanged as Both the Number of Graduates and the Number of Jobs Found Decline*, NATIONAL ASSOCIATION FOR LAW PLACEMENT (Oct. 2016), https://perma.cc/6VEB-PXVC. From 1985 to 2000, the category I measure was called "percentage employed legal full time," and from 2000 to 2015, it was called "percentage employed in positions requiring bar passage." For the 2016 data, I used NALP, *Class of 2016 National Summary Report*, https://perma.cc/79ZX-UFVN (last visited May 11, 2018).

21 You can figure this out by multiplying the "percentage employed in positions requiring bar passage" numbers from this chart, https://perma.cc/DA93-CZ89, with the "total number of jobs reported" number from this chart: https://perma .cc/ZEN3-9EPW.

22 Marc Gans, *Not a New problem: How the State of the Legal Profession Has Been Secretly in Decline for Quite Some Time*, SOCIAL SCIENCE RESEARCH NETWORK (June 24, 2012), https://perma.cc/23M9-4ZSF.

23 NALP, *Class of 2016 National Summary Report*, https://perma.cc/USV4-699V (last visited May 11, 2018).

24 Robert Morse, *U.S. News Changes Methodology for Best Law Schools Rankings*, U.S. NEWS (Mar. 10, 2015), http://www.usnews.com.

25 Paul Caron, *50% Of Law Schools Selected for Random ABA Audit Flunked Placement Data Documentation*, TAXPROF BLOG (Nov. 1, 2017), https://perma .cc/2YL4-YAGS.

26 James G. Leipold, *The Stories behind the Numbers: Jobs for New Grads over More Than Two Decades*, NALP BULLETIN, Dec. 2016, https://perma.cc/MSB9-8EP5.

27 Hildebrandt Consulting, 2017 CLIENT ADVISORY, *available at* https://perma
.cc/FP6X-9BCD (last visited May 11, 2018); Thomas S. Clay and Eric A. Seeger,
LAW FIRMS IN TRANSITION (2017), *available at* https://perma.cc/4W7B-TB7A.

28 Clay and Seeger, *supra* chapter 2, note 27, at ii.

29 ABA, *Council Approves Changes in Collection and Publication of Law Graduate
Placement Data*, Dec. 3, 2011, https://perma.cc/6FD2-7CV4.

30 Jordan Weissmann, *Now Is a Great Time to Apply to Law School*, SLATE, June 30,
2014, https://perma.cc/B9YN-3YGE.

31 Steven Freedman, *#1—Intro—Enroll Today!* FACULTY LOUNGE, Apr. 10, 2014,
https://perma.cc/WD8F-YKS4.

32 Eli Wald, *A Primer on Diversity, Discrimination, and Equality in the Legal Profession
or Who Is Responsible for Pursuing Diversity and Why*, 24 GEO. J. LEGAL ETHICS
1079, 1097 (2011).

33 Michael Simkovic and Frank McIntyre, *The Economic Value of a Law Degree* 6, 43
J. LEGAL STUD. 249 (Apr. 13, 2013), https://perma.cc/A5UA-FHKD. If you want to read
about the controversy and disagreements on this figure, just Google search "Simkovic
million dollars" and read the *Above the Law* and thelawyerbubble.com entries.

34 Jane Yakowitz, *Marooned: An Empirical Investigation of Law School Graduates
Who Fail the Bar Exam*, 60 J. LEGAL ED. 3 (2010), https://perma.cc/T7C4-258W.

35 American Bar Foundation, AFTER THE JD: FIRST RESULTS OF A NATIONAL
STUDY OF LEGAL CAREERS (2004); AFTER THE JD II: SECOND RESULTS OF
A NATIONAL STUDY OF LEGAL CAREERS (2009); AFTER THE JD III: THIRD
RESULTS OF A NATIONAL STUDY OF LEGAL CAREERS (2014).

36 American Bar Foundation, AFTER THE JD II, *supra* chapter 2, note 35, at 48;
AFTER THE JD III, *supra* chapter 2, note 35, at 53.

37 American Bar Foundation, AFTER THE JD III, *supra* chapter 2, note 35, at 52.

38 *Id.* at 30.

39 Michael Simkovic and Frank McIntyre, *see supra* chapter 2, note 33. *See also*
Nicole Sanseverino, *Graduates Utilize Law School Degrees in Unexpected Ways*,
DAILY TEXAN, Oct. 19, 2011, https://perma.cc/3CGS-3R54.

40 The full account of Gans's analysis can be found at *supra* chapter 2, note 22. He
generously shared his data with me, and it ended in 2011. I have updated his data
through 2017.

41 There were 916, 264 licensed physicians in the US in 2014. Aaron Young et al.,
A Census of Actively Licenses Physicians in the United States, 2014, 101 J. OF MED.
REG. 2, http://www.fsmb.org (last visited May 11, 2018).

42 Samuel Weigley et al., *Doctor Shortage Could Take Turn for the Worse*, USA
TODAY, Oct. 20, 2012, https://perma.cc/AJ6Y-GHNT.

43 I cover this at length in GLASS HALF FULL, *supra* chapter 1, note 27, at 33–49.

44 For the full scope of the boom years, consider the statistics in the twenty-fifth
anniversary issue of the AmLaw 100. *See* Michael D. Goldhaber, *The Long Run*,
AMERICAN LAWYER, May 2012, at 92.

45 Am. Bar Ass'n, *Lawyer Demographics*, https://perma.cc/9V86-DCD4 (last visited May 11, 2018).

46 If you want to read a long back and forth on this issue, see Stephen Diamond, *Flying Solo: Data Show Lawyers Can Earn a Decent Living on Their Own*, STEPHEN F. DIAMOND (July 25, 2016), https://perma.cc/7XRW-YGWS; Michael Simkovic, *How Much Do Lawyers Working in Solo Practice Actually Earn?* BRIAN LEITER L. SCH. REPORTS (July 26, 2016), https://perma.cc/ZTV2-YH82; Michael Simkovic, *Some Questions for Professor Benjamin H. Barton About His Use of IRS Data to Estimate Solo Practitioner Incomes*, BRIAN LEITER L. SCH. REPORTS (July 28, 2016), https://perma.cc/KA3Y-R73G; Benjamin H. Barton, *Barton Responds to Simkovic and Diamond: IRS and Census Data Not That Far Apart upon Closer Inspection*, TAXPROF BLOG (Aug. 11, 2016), https://perma.cc /CVA2-KW53; Michael Simkovic, *"Glass Half Full" Author Concedes Problems with IRS Estimates of Solo Practitioner Incomes and Headcounts*, BRIAN LEITER L. SCH. REPORTS (Aug. 16, 2016), https://perma.cc/6549-PGUB.

47 *See* Sheldon Danzinger, UNDERSTANDING POVERTY 104 (2009).

48 *See, e.g.*, Allen Rubin, STATISTICS FOR EVIDENCE-BASED PRACTICE AND EVALUATION 77 (2009).

49 *See* Anne VanderMey, *MBA Pay: Riches for Some, Not All*, BUSINESS WEEK (Oct. 1, 2009), https://www.yahoo.com/news.

50 *Class of 2014 Bimodal Salary Curve*, NAT'L ASS'N FOR LAW PLACEMENT (Aug. 2015), https://perma.cc/L9BS-WF2E.

51 *See* Michael Simkovic and Frank McIntyre, *The Economic Value of a Law Degree*, Apr. 14, 2013, https://perma.cc/NYK9-RDQP.

52 *See* Frank McIntyre and Michael Simkovic, *Value of a Law Degree by College Major*, Mar. 7, 2016, https://perma.cc/2AKP-FKFE.

53 Michael Simkovic, *6 Factual Errors and Several Misleading Statements in Recent New York Times Story by Noam Scheiber*, BRIAN LEITER'S LAW SCHOOL REPORTS, June 18, 2016, https://perma.cc/M3K5-EUE9.

54 Michael Simkovic, *Above the Law Needs to Read More*, BRIAN LEITER'S LAW SCHOOL REPORTS, July 22, 2013, https://perma.cc/2CJB-47NC.

55 *See supra* chapter 2, note 46 and accompanying text.

56 Michael Simkovic, *Law Schools' Four Billion Dollar Collective Action Problem*, BRIAN LEITER'S LAW SCHOOL REPORTS, Aug. 25, 2014, https://perma.cc /RE66-TDGZ.

57 Paul Campos, *If I Had a Million Dollars—III*, LAWYERS, GUNS AND MONEY, July 19, 2013, https://perma.cc/533J-VXZA; Elie Mystal, *Another Garbage Study Offering Misleading Statistics on the Value of a Law Degree*, ABOVE THE LAW (July 17, 2013), https://perma.cc/T5D6–4EKS; Brian Tamanaha, *Why the "Million Dollar Law Degree" Study Fails (Final Post)*, BALKINIZATION, July 25, 2013, https://perma.cc/99ND-VLD7; Matt Leichter, *"Economic Value" Paper a Mistrial at Best*, LAST GEN X AMERICAN, September 9, 2013, https://perma.cc

/D4TG-VXKD; Steven J. Harper, *The Dangerous Million-Dollar Distraction*, THE
BELLY OF THE BEAST, July 24, 2013, https://perma.cc/KVS9-7KSS.

58 Jane Yakowitz, *Marooned: An Empirical Investigation of Law School Graduates
Who Fail the Bar Exam*, 60 J. LEGAL ED. 3 (2010), https://perma.cc/7PJZ-67GV.

Chapter 3. Future Shock

1 Maia Szalavitz, *10 Ways We Get the Odds Wrong*, PSYCHOLOGY TODAY, Jan. 1,
2008, https://perma.cc/D7MB-GEBW.

2 Julie Sobowale, *Beyond Imagination: How Artificial Intelligence Is Already
Transforming the Legal Profession*, ABA J. (Apr. 2016); William D. Henderson,
How Managed Services Are Building Systems for Corporate Legal Work, ABA J.
(June 2017), https://perma.cc/GQS9-CYWB; Sharon D. Nelson and John W.
Simek, *How Will Watson's Children Impact the Future of Law Practice*, DICTA,
Apr., 2016.

3 Jason Koebler, *Rise of the Robolawyers*, ATLANTIC, Apr., 2017, https://perma
.cc/2U98-VQWJ; Dan Mangan, *Lawyers Could Be Replaced by Artificial
Intelligence*, CNBC, Feb. 17, 2017, https://perma.cc/4T27-DA48; Jane Croft,
Artificial Intelligence Closes In on the Work of Junior Lawyers, FINANCIAL TIMES,
May 4, 2017, https://perma.cc/L3Q5-CQDY; James Watkins, *Why Artificial
Intelligence Might Replace Your Lawyer*, Ozy.com, Feb. 10, 2017, https://perma
.cc/2Q5L-AUVN.

4 Watkins, *supra* chapter 3, note 3, at 3.

5 Hugh Son, *JP Morgan Software Does in Seconds What Took Lawyers 360,000
Hours*, BLOOMBERG, Feb. 27, 2017, https://perma.cc/J548-GSUB.

6 Lisa Calhoun, *Marc Andreessen Predicts 2 Types of Jobs in the Future: Which One
Will You Have?* INC., July 18, 2016, https://perma.cc/HW6F-EUKH.

7 *See, e.g.,* Gary Lea, *The Struggle to Define What Artificial Intelligence Actually
Means*, POPULAR SCIENCE, Sept. 3, 2015, https://perma.cc/8G5SWEH5.

8 David Schatsky et al., *Demystifying Artificial Intelligence*, Deloitte University Press,
Nov. 4, 2014, https://perma.cc/CFA2-9MUY.

9 *See* Daniel Martin Katz, Chicago-Kent College of Law, https://perma.cc/Y765–
2CGM (last visited May 11, 2018).

10 Daniel Katz, *Artificial Intelligence and Law: A Primer*, COMPUTATIONAL LEGAL
STUDIES, Mar. 18, 2017, https://perma.cc/HN9Z-EGQN.

11 One great example of this is the *Consumer Reports* review of LegalZoom and
Rocket Lawyer; *see Legal DIY Websites Are No Match for a Pro*, CONSUMER
REPORTS, Sept. 2012, https://perma.cc/9C5N-9MLB.

12 *See* Benjamin H. Barton, *Some Preliminary Thoughts on Liability Standards for
Online Providers of Legal Services*, 44 HOFSTRA L. REV. 541, 552–56 (2015),
available at https://perma.cc/WPF2-JN97.

13 *See* Charles Duhigg, *How Companies Learn Your Secrets*, N.Y. TIMES, Feb. 16,
2012, https://www.nytimes.com.

14 Jordan Weisman, *iLawyer: What Happens When Computers Replace Attorneys?* ATLANTIC, June 19, 2012, https://perma.cc/EAV2-HXQK; Joe Palazzolo, *Why Hire a Lawyer? Computers Are Cheaper,* WALL ST. J., June 18, 2012, https://www.wsj.com.

15 Joe Palazzolo, *How a Computer Did the Work of Many Lawyers,* WALL ST. J., Jan. 17, 2013, https://blogs.wsj.com.

16 Dana Remus and Frank S. Levy, *Can Robots Be Lawyers? Computers, Lawyers, and the Practice of Law,* SSRN, Dec. 11, 2015, https://perma.cc/47MB-M8RJ.

17 Alan Turing, *Computing Machinery and Intelligence,* MIND, Oct. 1950, *available at* https://perma.cc/SR3W-6VH7.

18 Steve Lohr, *A.I. Is Doing Legal Work. But It Won't Replace Lawyers, Yet,* N.Y. TIMES, Mar. 19, 2017, https://www.nytimes.com.

19 For chess, *see* Chris Baraniuk, *The Cyborg Chess Players That Can't Be Beaten,* BBC, Dec. 4, 2015, https://perma.cc/9PS2–5GYP. For baseball, *see* Michael Lewis, MONEYBALL (2004). For law, *see* Barton, GLASS HALF FULL, *supra* chapter 1, note 27, at 78–83.

20 *See* Martin Ford, RISE OF THE ROBOTS: TECHNOLOGY AND THE THREAT OF A JOBLESS FUTURE (2016).

21 *See* Richard Susskind, EXPERT SYSTEMS IN LAW: A JURISPRUDENTIAL INQUIRY (1988); Richard Susskind, THE END OF LAWYERS (2010).

22 Richard Susskind, TOMORROW'S LAWYERS (2013); Richard Susskind and Daniel Susskind, THE FUTURE OF THE PROFESSIONS (2017).

23 Susskind, TOMORROW'S LAWYERS, *supra* chapter 3, note 22, at 57.

24 John O. McGinnis and Russell Pearce, *The Great Disruption: How Machine Intelligence Will Transform the Role of Lawyers in the Delivery of Legal Services,* SSRN, May 13, 2014, https://perma.cc/E868-JZE4.

25 Daniel Martin Katz, *Artificial Intelligence and Law: A Six Part Primer; Professor Daniel Martin Katz,* COMPUTATIONAL LEGAL STUDIES, Mar. 18, 2017, https://perma.cc/8CBW-8WVR.

26 Dana Remus and Frank S. Levy, *Can Robots Be Lawyers? Computers, Lawyers, and the Practice of Law,* SSRN, Nov. 27, 2015, https://perma.cc/HW7S-C7HV.

27 Benjamin H. Barton, *The Emperor of Ocean Park: The Quintessence of Legal Academia,* 92 CAL. L. REV. 585, 593–95 (2004).

28 Benjamin H. Barton and Stephanos Bibas, REBOOTING JUSTICE 201–4 (2017).

29 *Automation and Anxiety,* ECONOMIST, June 25, 2016, https://perma.cc/3KWW-YL2F.

30 Barton, GLASS HALF FULL, *supra* chapter 1, note 27, at 191–224.

31 Gideon Lewis-Kraus, *The Great A.I. Awakening,* N.Y. TIMES MAGAZINE, Dec. 14, 2017, https://www.nytimes.com.

Chapter 4. Boom to Bust for Law Schools

1 *See ABA Approved Law Schools,* ABA, https://perma.cc/VDR5-46GU. For more on UMass Dartmouth, *see* Karen Sloan, *UMass-Dartmouth Gets ABA Accreditation,* NAT'L L. J. (Dec. 8, 2016), https://perma.cc/K6QC-GZPZ.

2 Lynda McDaniel, *Law and Community Service: The Appalachian School of Law*, Appalachian Regional Commission, https://perma.cc/Y7EU-2E3M (last visited May 11, 2018).

3 Ry Rivard, *Saving the Law School, Hurting the Town*, INSIDE HIGHER ED, Apr. 3, 2015, https://perma.cc/TM38-VHZB.

4 Danya Perez-Hernandez, *Valley Legislators File Bills Asking for a Law School in the Area*, MONITOR, Nov. 24, 2016, https://perma.cc/V8XH-DG2Y.

5 Michael Gordon, *Charlotte School of Law Crisis Resurrects Talks of a Law School at UNCC*, CHARLOTTE OBSERVER, Jan. 12, 2017, https://perma.cc/2C95-LJE9.

6 Derrick Nunnaly, *UW Tacoma Law School Vision Remains Years Away*, NEWS TRIB., Feb. 17, 2017, https://perma.cc/4KGG-FZNL.

7 *Tuition Tracker*, Law School Transparency, https://perma.cc/377X-PE3D (last visited May 11, 2018).

8 *CPI Inflation Calculator*, Bureau of Lab. Stat., https://perma.cc/52D8-RV2P (last visited May 11, 2018).

9 Mark Cohen, *Law School Building Boom—Really?* BLOOMBERG BIG L. BUS. (Sept. 23, 2015), https://perma.cc/368M-NZ43.

10 *See* Paul Campos, *Has the Increased Cost of Law School Improved Legal Education?* 50 WAKE FOREST L. REV. 101, 102–3 (2015).

11 Brian Z. Tamanaha, FAILING LAW SCHOOLS 39–53 (2012).

12 Ruiz, *supra* introduction, note 36.

13 For a full description of the law school scamblog movement, *see* Lucille A. Jewel, *You're Doing It Wrong: How the Anti-Law School Scam Blogging Movement Can Shape the Legal Profession*, 12 MINN. J.L. SCI. & TECH. 239, 263–74 (2011).

14 Mary Beth Marklein, *Grads Taking Law Schools to Task for Poor Job Market*, USA TODAY (Aug. 24, 2010), *available at* https://perma.cc/TLC6-2246; John Eligon, *Jobs Data More Vital to Her than Food*, N.Y. TIMES CITY ROOM BLOG (Aug. 27, 2010, 12:51 PM), *available at* https://cityroom.blogs.nytimes.com; Annie Lowrey, *A Case of Supply and Demand*, SLATE, Oct. 27, 2010, https://perma.cc/FB5X-F6TN.

15 This quote is often misattributed to Mahatma Gandhi but is of uncertain derivation. Dan Evon, *First They Ignore You, Then They Vote for You?* Snopes.com, Mar. 1, 2016, https://perma.cc/VHY3-96QK.

16 For a list of all of *Third Tier Reality*'s law school profiles, *see Nando's Law School Profiles*, LAW SCH. SEWAGE PIT PROFILES, https://perma.cc/JJB2-DTGC. *Third Tier Reality* ceased publication in early 2018.

17 Law School Transparency, https://perma.cc/MSX9-9JZ7 (last visited May 11, 2018); LAW SCH. TUITION BUBBLE, https://perma.cc/EPQ9-LTU8 (last visited May 11, 2018).

18 Campos actually stopped posting on the site in 2013, but it is still all online here: INSIDE THE L. SCH. SCAM, https://perma.cc/VF28-GHVJ (last visited May 11, 2018).

19 Deborah Cassens Weiss, *Law Prof Blogging on "Law School Scam" Is No Longer Anonymous*, ABA J. (Aug. 22, 2011), https://perma.cc/3E44-WERD.

20 Paul Campos, DON'T GO TO LAW SCHOOL (UNLESS) (2012).

21 Tamanaha, FAILING LAW SCHOOLS, *supra* chapter 4, note 11.

22 *Educators Debate: Are Law Schools in Crisis?* NAT'L L. J., Nov. 7, 2011, https://perma.cc/3RH3-CFV2.

23 Elizabeth Olson, *Law Graduate Gets Her Day in Court, Suing Law School*, N.Y. TIMES, Mar. 6, 2016, https://www.nytimes.com.

24 *See* Alexandra Gomez-Jimenez v. New York Law School, 956 N.Y.S.2d 54 (N.Y. 2012).

25 Maura Dolan, *Law School Graduates Aren't Finding Much on the Employment Docket*, L.A. TIMES, Apr. 1, 2013, https://perma.cc/WFE3-MZRL.

26 Joe Palazzolo and Jennifer Smith, *Law Grads Claim Schools Misled*, WALL ST. J., Feb. 2, 2012, https://www.wsj.com.

27 Matthew Shaer, *The Case(s) against Law School*, N.Y. MAGAZINE, Mar. 4, 2012, https://perma.cc/2V5T-U39Z.

28 *See, e.g.,* Palazzolo, *Law Grads, supra* introduction, note 37.

29 Here are two of the most-viewed YouTube videos: *Don't Go to Law School—Find Out Why*, YOUTUBE (Mar. 26, 2010), https://www.youtube.com; *Dear Me, Don't Go to Law School*, YOUTUBE (Feb. 29, 2012), https://www.youtube.com.

30 On YouTube's popularity with younger Americans, *see* Todd Spangler, *Millennials Find YouTube Content More Entertaining, Relatable than TV: Study*, VARIETY, Mar. 3, 2015, https://perma.cc/2YEN-FPSB.

31 This data comes from the Law School Admission Council (LSAC), *Total LSATs Administered: Counts and Percent Increases by Admin and Year*, https://perma.cc/Q7ZX-WZQB (last visited May 11, 2018).

32 *What Is CAS?* Powerscore, https://perma.cc/LV83-22Y6 (last visited May 11, 2018).

33 The list of ABA-accredited schools requiring the CAS can be found here: *US ABA-Approved Law Schools*, LAW SCH. ADMISSION COUNCIL, https://perma.cc/2LEK-5F36 (last visited May 11, 2018). Note, the LSAC has a separate count of what it calls "applicants," but the LSAC changed the way they count that category in 2015–16, so the LSAC count works better for longitudinal comparisons. *End-of-Year Summary: ABA (Applicants, Applications and Admissions), LSATs, Credential Assembly Service*, Law Sch. Admission Council, https://perma.cc/4MXV-SYG9 (last visited May 11, 2018).

34 LSAC, *supra* chapter 4, note 31.

35 Paul Caron, *Proportion of Law School Applicants with LSATs > 160 Is Down 35% since 2010; < 150 Is Up 146%*, TAXPROF BLOG, June 12, 2017, https://perma.cc/Y94R-ZUVQ.

36 John A. Byrne, Why the MBA Is Now the Most Popular Master's, Poets and Quants, May 26, 2014, https://perma.cc/KTW3-PQME.

37 Jeffrey J. Selingo, MBA Enrollment Is Down Again: What's the Future of the Degree? Wash. Post, Oct. 7, 2018, https://perma.cc/BB58-C8KD.

38 Benjamin Wermund, *Shrinking Applicant Pool Has Law Schools Competing to Cut Costs*, HOUSTON CHRON., May 31, 2014, https://perma.cc/7SFP-UNPL.

39 Matt Leichter, *2015: Full-Time Law Students Paying Full Tuition Fell ~5 Percentage Points (Again)*, LAW SCH. TUITION BUBBLE, https://perma.cc/P93J-LT7S (last visited May 11, 2018).

40 Bernard A. Burk, Jerome M. Organ, and Emma Rasiel, *Competitive Coping Strategies in the American Legal Academy: An Empirical Study*, SSRN, Oct. 17, 2018, https://perma.cc/T3VQ-AUM6.

Chapter 5. Why Haven't More Law Schools Closed? Part I

1 Paul Caron, *Decline in LSAT Test-Takers Portends "Death Spiral" for Low-Ranked Schools*, TAXPROF BLOG (Mar. 20, 2012), https://perma.cc/E3PH-FNSE.

2 Glenn Reynolds, *Higher Education Bubble Update, Legal Education Edition*, INSTAPUNDIT (Mar. 20, 2012), https://perma.cc/B9PS-K3YQ.

3 Phillip J. Closius, *American Law Schools in Crisis*, BALTIMORE SUN, June 4, 2012, https://perma.cc/4SAL-DGKL.

4 News editor, *Law School Faculties 40% Larger than 10 Years Ago*, NAT'L JURIST, Mar. 9, 2010, https://perma.cc/A2LJ-HZSX.

5 *See* Tamanaha, FAILING LAW SCHOOLS, *supra* chapter 4, note 11, at 63.

6 Matt Leichter, *Which Law Schools Are Shedding Full-Time Faculty? (2016 Edition)*, LAST GEN-X AMERICAN, https://perma.cc/BEZ9-MQPH (last visited May 11, 2018).

7 Derek Muller, *As Full-Time Law Faculty Numbers Shrink, Law School Administrator Numbers Grow*, EXCESS OF DEMOCRACY (Jan. 21, 2016), https://perma.cc/MU7M-6Q9N.

8 For stories on staff shrinkage, *see* Jake Jarvis, *WVU Invites Employees to Leave through "Voluntary Separation Program,"* CHARLESTON GAZETTE-MAIL (July 2, 2016), https://perma.cc/2PWU-RK5C; Paul Campos, *Washington and Lee Law School Cuts Salaries, Downsizes Faculty and Staff, Invades Corpus of Endowment*, LAWYERS, GUNS, AND MONEY (Feb. 19, 2015), https://perma.cc/RR95-SVCL.

9 Leichter, *supra* chapter 5, note 6.

10 *Id.*

11 Matt Hongoltz-Hetling, *VLS Cuts Salaries for Faculty in Bid to Close Budget Deficit*, VALLEY NEWS, July 17, 2018, https://perma.cc/T8YC-YQ5N.

12 *See, e.g.,* Vernellia R. Randall, *LSAT Discrimination and Minorities*, RACE, RACISM, AND THE LAW, https://perma.cc/4E59-CZ2G (last visited May 11, 2018); David M. White, *Requirement of Race-Conscious Evaluation of LSAT Scores for Equitable Law School Admissions*, 12 LA RAZA L.J. 399 (2001), *available at* https://perma.cc/TXG8-JK9M.

13 LSAC, *LSAT Scores as Predictors of Law School Performance*, https://perma.cc /FRA9-YL6K (last visited May 11, 2018). The law school GPA data comes with some caveats: (1) While the LSAT is more predictive than UGPA, the combination

of both is the best predictor of success. (2) The correlation between LSATs and law school grades is weaker than one might think and grows weaker when grades from all three years of law school are considered. Alexia Brunet Marks and Scott A. Moss, *What Makes a Law Student Succeed or Fail? A Longitudinal Study Correlating Law Student Applicant Data and Law School Outcomes*, 13 J. EMPIRICAL LEGAL STUD. 205 (2016).

14 *See, e.g.*, Jane E. Cross, *The Bar Examination in Black and White: The Black-White Bar Passage Gap and the Implications for Minority Admissions to the Legal Profession*, 18 NAT'L BLACK L.J. 63 (2004); Milo Colton, *What Is Wrong with the Texas Bar Exam? A Minority Report*, 28 T. MARSHALL L. REV. 53 (2002).

15 Paul Caron, *Updated LSAC Data on the Quantity and Quality of Law School Applicants*, TAXPROF BLOG, Feb. 26, 2018, https://perma.cc/AR5E-GCU4.

16 Keith Lee, *Top University Students Avoiding Law School, 2017 Edition*, ASSOCIATES MIND, https://perma.cc/CTE5-EYFA (last visited May 11, 2018).

17 Karen Sloan, *Law School Applications Are Up, Especially among High LSAT Scorers*, NAT'L L.J., Apr. 6, 2018, https://perma.cc/PE22-Y258.

18 Keith Lee, *New Lawyers 2010 to 2017: Lower LSATs, Lower Bar Passage . . . More DUIs??* ASSOCIATES MIND, https://perma.cc/NK5Z-82MK (last visited May 11, 2018).

19 Jerry Organ, *The Composition of Graduating Classes of Law Students, 2013–2016, Part One*, Legal Whiteboard, Dec. 29, 2014, https://perma.cc/CC2G-HEBQ.

20 For another take on this data, ending in 2015, *see* Jerry Organ, *Changes in Composition of the LSAT Profiles of Matriculants and Law Schools between 2010 and 2015*, Legal Whiteboard, Jan. 18, 2016, https://perma.cc/V7Q5-X98W.

21 Jordan Weissmann, *Desperate Law Schools Are Admitting Way Too Many Poorly Qualified Students*, SLATE, Oct. 29, 2015, https://perma.cc/2GKL-Q3D6.

22 *Id.*

23 LSAC, *LSAT Technical Report Series* 2, https://perma.cc/ACL2-U2BG (last visited Apr. 2, 2018).

24 Josh Mitchell, *The Rise and Fall of a Law-School Empire Fueled by Federal Loans*, WALL ST. J., Nov. 24, 2017, https://www.wsj.com.

25 Florida Coastal School of Law, *Florida Coastal School of Law Files Suit against American Bar Association*, May 10, 2018, https://perma.cc/RC2K-L2MQ.

26 Deborah J. Merritt, *Race, Debt, and Opportunity*, LAW SCHOOL CAFÉ, Mar. 10, 2016, https://perma.cc/PGU6-E37N. The remaining facts in this paragraph come from this source.

27 *Id.*

28 Frank Wu, *Law School Scholarship Policies: Engines of Inequity*, LSSSE, https://perma.cc/M9U7-8N9F (last visited May 11, 2018).

29 Stephanie Francis Ward, *Affluent Students Get Law School Merit Scholarships while Others Foot the Bill, Study Finds*, A.B.A. J., Feb. 8, 2017, https://perma.cc/J4UA-LRHJ.

30 Am. Bar Ass'n, ABA STANDARDS, *supra* introduction, note 14, at 33.

31 Elie Mystal, *ABA Considers Dropping LSAT Requirement for Admission to Law School*, ABOVE THE LAW (Jan. 13, 2011), https://perma.cc/SQ7Z-BREN.

32 Memorandum from Managing Dir. of Am. Bar Ass'n on Standard 503 and Interpretation 503–3 (Jan. 2015), https://perma.cc/3L35-9NCW.

33 Stephanie Francis Ward, *ABA Legal Ed Council Approves Proposed Rule Change to End Admission Test Requirement*, ABA J. (May 11, 2018), https://perma.cc /P2TJ-CU2F.

34 Stephanie Francis Ward, *Plan to Drop Law School Entry Exam Requirement Withdrawn before ABA House Vote*, ABA J. (Aug. 6, 2018), https://perma.cc /PRN2-TB8Z.

35 ABA Standard 503, Interpretation 503-1 (2018), https://perma.cc/QQ7G-8E6E (last visited Nov. 23, 2018).

36 *Wake Forest Law Joins Two Other Schools in Blazing Trail for Possible New Standardized Testing Option*, Wake Forest Sch. of L. (Jan. 27, 2016), https://perma .cc/TZP7-S86Q; Staci Zaretsky, *This Law School Will Pay You to Take the GRE to Save Its U.S. News Rank from the Dreaded LSAT*, ABOVE THE LAW (Jan. 28, 2016), https://perma.cc/VWD6-KJP7.

37 Paul Caron, *Arizona Is the First Law School to Admit Students Based on GRE instead of LSAT*, TAXPROF BLOG (Feb. 11, 2016), https://perma.cc/7LHC-VJ3J.

38 Zaretsky, *supra* chapter 5, note 36.

39 Paul Caron, *Law Schools Replace LSAT with GRE to Goose Enrollment*, TAXPROF BLOG (Feb. 23, 2016), https://perma.cc/7SVA-C84Y.

40 Carrie Jung, *Forget the LSAT; This Law School Will Accept Your GRE Scores*, NAT'L PUB. RADIO ED (May 16, 2016), https://perma.cc/28FP-9VFC.

41 Karen Sloan, *Harvard Becomes Second Law School to Accept GRE for Admission*, LAW (Mar. 8, 2017), https://perma.cc/5RKN-YBV2.

42 *Id.*

43 A list of the 2017–18 GRE law schools can be found here: *Taking the GRE General Test for Law School*, ETS, https://perma.cc/PXG2-3YY6 (last visited May 4, 2018).

44 A current list of law schools that accept the GRE can be found at *Taking the GRE General Test for Law School*, ETS, https://www.ets.org (last visited May 1, 2019).

45 Joshua Craven and Evan Jones, *GRE v. LSAT*, LawSchooli, https://perma .cc/6CM7-TH5J (last visited May 11, 2018).

46 Loretta B. DeLoggio, *Which Is Harder, the GRE or the LSAT?* Quora, Feb. 18, 2016, https://perma.cc/3SUS-3NXC.

47 Ally Marotti, *John Marshall Law School Will Start Accepting GRE as Test Alternative to LSAT*, CHICAGO TRIB., Jan. 30, 2018, https://www.chicagotribune.com.

48 *See supra* chapter 5, note 13, and accompanying text.

49 Am. Bar Ass'n, ABA STANDARDS, *supra* introduction, note 14, at 23.

50 *Id.*
51 Doug Lederman, *Syracuse University Plans Online JD Degree,* INSIDE HIGHER ED, Apr. 19, 2016, https://perma.cc/MF3F-KR4B.
52 Concord Law School, *The First Online Law School,* https://perma.cc/V2UX-9USV (last visited May 11, 2018); California Southern University School of Law, *Introduction to the Juris Doctor (JD),* https://perma.cc/BAF8-JMJT (last visited May 11, 2018).
53 Kaplan University, *Doctrinal Degree in Juris Doctor,* https://perma.cc/KMC5-XM9W (last visited May 11, 2018).
54 California Southern University School of Law, *Business and Professions Code Section 6061.7(a) Information Report for All Locations Reporting Year 2017,* https://perma.cc/4ZNA-93Q8 (last visited May 11, 2018).
55 *Online Master of Laws Degree (LL.M.),* U.S. NEWS, https://www.usnews.com (last visited May 11, 2018).
56 Check out the list of thirty-five schools at College Choice, which includes everything from online schools you have never heard of to Villanova and USC Law. *35 Best Online Law Schools for 2017,* College Choice, https://perma.cc/PS63-8DPZ (last visited May 11, 2018).
57 *Post-JD and Non-JD Programs,* A.B.A., https://perma.cc/N8QR-BBQF (last visited May 11, 2018).
58 Muller, *supra* chapter 5, note 7.
59 Hanover Research, *Alternative Non-JD Programming for Law Schools* (2013), https://perma.cc/KB2A-NL86.
60 Blake Edwards, *The Juris Masters Program: Natural Evolution or Stop-Gap for Struggling Law Schools?* BLOOMBERG LAW (Aug. 17, 2016), https://perma.cc/H8C6-ZTTC.
61 See Derek Muller, *2017 Law School Enrollment: JD Enrollment Flat, Nearly 1 in 7 Are Not in the JD Program,* EXCESS OF DEMOCRACY, Dec. 15, 2017, https://perma.cc/FAW5-W7XJ.
62 Letter from Robert Rhee, professor, Univ. of Fla., to Oscar A. Sanchez et al. (Sept. 9, 2016), https://perma.cc/7L87-YGK2.
63 *Id.*
64 Carole Silver, *What We Don't Know Can Hurt Us: The Need for Empirical Research Regulating Lawyers and Legal Services in the Global Economy,* 43 AKRON L. REV. 1009, 1022 & n. 35 (2010).
65 *Id.*
66 Caroline Kitchener, *Trump Is Driving Some of the World's Brightest Foreign Students Out of America,* VOX (Jan. 31, 2017), https://perma.cc/6BL6-MH6K.
67 Muller, *supra* chapter 5, note 61.
68 Michael Simkovic, *U.S. LLM Programs Probably Benefit International Students (Part 1): Students Who Stay in the U.S.,* BRIAN LEITER'S L. SCH. REPORTS (Nov. 29, 2016), https://perma.cc/4XVQ-QGXW; Michael Simkovic, *U.S. LLM*

Programs Probably Benefit International Students (Part 2): Students Who Return Home, BRIAN LEITER'S L. SCH. REPORTS (Dec. 1, 2016), https://perma.cc /YKZ5-UFBE.

69 *See* C. Aaron LeMay and Robert C. Cloud, *Student Debt and the Future of Higher Education*, J. COLLEGE & U.L. 79, 80–81 (2007).

70 *Id.*

71 Philip Schrag, *Federal Student Loan Repayment Assistance for Public Interest Lawyers and Other Employees of Governments and Nonprofit Organizations*, 36 HOFSTRA L. REV. 27, 31–32 (2007).

72 *Id.*

73 *See University of Michigan Law School Tuition 1950–2009*, Univ. of Mich. (Feb. 2009), https://perma.cc/8KZ6-SPBL.

74 Higher Education Reconciliation Act of 2005, Pub. L. No. 109-71, 120 Stat. 4, 158–60 (2005) (codified as amended in scattered sections of 20 U.S.C.).

75 Schrag, *supra* chapter 5, note 71, at 33–34.

76 *PLUS Loans*, Fed. Student Aid, https://perma.cc/8QR5-FE69 (last visited May 11, 2018).

77 *Student Budget*, T. Jefferson Sch. of L., https://perma.cc/4TCE-R2LN.

78 *Student Expense Budget*, N.Y. Univ., https://perma.cc/LE9F-V7ZH; *Cost of Attendance*, Harv. L. Sch., https://perma.cc/KZ2E-FL59.

79 Barton, GLASS HALF FULL, *supra* chapter 1, note 27, at 158–59.

80 Rick Seltzer, *Law Schools Flagged for Job data*, INSIDE HIGHER ED (Nov. 1, 2016), https://perma.cc/3ZA4-KTPB.

81 Paul Caron, *50% of Law Schools Selected for Random ABA Audit Flunked Placement Data Documentation*, TAXPROF BLOG (Nov. 1, 2016), https://perma .cc/E2N8-D44N.

82 My favorite spot for frothy coverage of salaries and bonuses is *Above the Law; see, e.g.*, Staci Zaretsky, *Salary Wars Scorecard: Which Firms Have Announced Raises?* ABOVE THE LAW (June 13, 2016), https://perma.cc/XV69-DHUJ.

83 Philip G. Schrag, *Failing Law Schools: Brian Tamanaha's Misguided Missile*, 9–11, 26 GEO. J. OF LEGAL ETHICS (Nov. 22, 2012), https://perma.cc/5QFR -NUH9.

84 *Id.*

85 *See, e.g., Loan Forgiveness*, Seattle Univ. Sch. of L., https://perma.cc/56JS-456R (last visited May 11, 2018); *Student Debt Relief*, Cooley L. Sch., https://perma.cc /ZM6K-E4C9 (last visited May 11, 2018); *Student Repayment and Forgiveness*, A.B.A., https://perma.cc/U4H2-CVGX (last visited May 11, 2018).

86 U.S. Gov't Accountability Off., GAO-17-22, FEDERAL STUDENT LOANS: EDUCATION NEEDS TO IMPROVE ITS INCOME-DRIVEN REPAYMENT PLAN BUDGET ESTIMATES (2016), https://perma.cc/BBR4-7RUT.

87 Andrew Kreighbaum, *U.S. Underestimates Cost of Loan Programs*, INSIDE HIGHER ED (Dec. 1, 2016), https://perma.cc/KFD7-R8SM.

88 GAO, *supra* chapter 5, note 86, at 51.

89 *See, e.g.,* Rajeev Darolia, *Should Student Loans Be Dischargeable in Bankruptcy,* BROWN CENTER CHALKBOARD, Brookings (Sept. 29, 2015), https://perma.cc /KL38-M7BB.

90 GAO, *supra* chapter 5, note 86, at 51.

91 Katie Lobosco, *What Is (and Isn't) in the Budget for Student Borrowers,* CNN MONEY, May 26, 2017, https://perma.cc/Q2Y3-44ST.

92 Danielle Douglas-Gabriel, *GOP Higher Ed Plan Would Limit Student Loan Forgiveness in Repayment Program, Overhaul Federal Financial Aid,* WASH. POST, Dec. 1, 2017, https://perma.cc/4EZC-4BWF.

93 Farran Powell, *Proposed Student Loan Changes May Deter Law Applicants,* U.S. NEWS, Feb. 14, 2018, https://www.usnews.com.

94 Jack Crittenden, *Will You Keep Your Conditional Scholarship?* NATIONAL JURIST, July 22, 2015, https://perma.cc/UZD5-8G9Q.

95 *See* Jason Dyer, *Is "One, Two, Many" a Myth,* NUMBER WARRIOR (July 30, 2010), https://perma.cc/A5PW-BYP3.

96 Jacob Alderice, *The Informed Student-Consumer: Regulating For-Profit Colleges by Disclosure,* 50 HARV. C.R.-C.L. L. REV. 215, 249 (2015).

97 *See, e.g.,* Cara Feinberg, *The Science of Scarcity,* HARVARD MAGAZINE, June 2015, https://perma.cc/K6TW-UE9K; Roger D. Johnson, REDISCOVERING SOCIAL ECONOMICS: BEYOND THE NEOCLASSICAL PARADIGM 80–81 (2017).

98 For higher lifetime earnings, *see* Jennifer Cheeseman Day and Eric C. Newburger, *The Big Payoff: Educational Attainment and Synthetic Estimates of Work-Life Earnings,* CENSUS (July 2002), https://perma.cc/7BNH-4WV7. For the rise in graduate school enrollment since 2006, *see* Hironao Okahana et al., *Graduate School Enrollment and Degrees: 2005–2015,* 18 COUNCIL OF GRADUATE SCHOOLS (Sept. 2016), https://perma.cc/4SWG-VMKU.

99 Tamanaha, FAILING LAW SCHOOLS, *supra* chapter 4, note 11, at 78–84.

100 Wendy Nelson Espeland and Michal Sauder, ENGINES OF ANXIETY (2016).

101 Barton, GLASS HALF FULL, *supra* chapter 1, note 27.

102 For similar data ending in 2015, *see* Natalie Kitroeff, *The Best Law Schools Are Attracting Fewer Students,* BLOOMBERG, Jan. 26, 2016, https://perma.cc /XG2Y-GYGA.

103 All of the rankings facts come from Bradley A. Areheart, *The Top 100 Law Reviews: A Reference Guide Based on Historical USNWR Data,* SSRN, Aug. 29, 2017, https://perma.cc/3QF9-6JE5.

104 Staci Zaretsky, *The 2019 U.S. News Law School Rankings Leak: The Top 100,* ABOVE THE LAW (Mar. 13, 2018), https://perma.cc/X2VE-T5TE.

105 *See, e.g.,* Jonah Engel Bromwich, *Lawyers Mobilize at Nation's Airports after Trump's Order,* N.Y. TIMES, Jan. 29, 2017, https://www.nytimes.com.

106 Matt Moody, *Lawyers Are Heroes of the Trump Resistance,* VAULT, Jan. 31, 2017, https://perma.cc/UG57-P6XU.

107 LSAC data, *Total LSATs Administered: Counts and Percent Increases by Admin and Year*, https://perma.cc/2BS5-J7BJ.

108 Karen Sloan, *Number of Law School Applicants Surges, Especially among High Scorers*, Law.com, July 30, 2018, https://www.law.com.

Chapter 6. Why Haven't More Law Schools Closed? Part 2

1 Am. Bar Ass'n, *ABA Standards and Rules of Procedure for Approval of Law Schools, 2016–17* (2016), https://perma.cc/W22W-SX22.

2 *Id.* at 9.

3 *Id.* at 11–13.

4 *Id.* at 27–30.

5 *Id.* at 39–43.

6 *Id.* at 51–78. All of the rest of the procedures listed in this paragraph can be found in these pages.

7 Paul L. Gaston, HIGHER EDUCATION ACCREDITATION: IT'S CHANGING, WHY IT MUST 36 (2014).

8 Maureen E. Lally-Green, *An Idea Whose Time Has Come: Certified Legal Interns as Oral Advocates in the Pennsylvania Appellate Courts*, 49 DUQ. L. REV. 477, 492 n. 35–36 (2011).

9 Corey Adwar, *There's a Way to Become an Attorney without Setting Foot in Law School*, BUS. INSIDER (July 30, 2014), https://perma.cc/PX9V-3UHR.

10 *See* Benjamin H. Barton, THE LAWYER-JUDGE BIAS IN THE AMERICAN LEGAL SYSTEM 105–59 (2011). This source supports all of the claims in this paragraph.

11 If you're interested in this topic and haven't read this work, you absolutely should. The most comprehensive of the articles is George B. Shepherd and William G. Shepherd, *Scholarly Restraints? ABA Accreditation and Legal Education*, 19 CARDOZO L. REV. 2091 (1998). George B. Shepherd, *No African-American Lawyers Allowed: The Inefficient Racism of the ABA's Accreditation of Law Schools*, 53 J. LEGAL EDUC. 103 (2003), is also excellent.

12 Barton, GLASS HALF FULL, *supra* chapter 1, note 27, at 166–67.

13 Peter J. Kolovos, Note, *Antitrust Law and Nonprofit Organizations: The Law School Accreditation Case*, 71 N.Y.U. L. REV. 689, 689–92 (1996).

14 Mass. Sch. of L. at Andover, Inc. v. Am. Bar Ass'n, 937 F. Supp. 435 (E.D. Pa. 1996), affirmed, 107 F.3d 1026 (3d Cir. 1997).

15 *Id.*

16 *See* Terry Carter, *Another Antitrust Win for the ABA*, A.B.A. J., May 1997, at 38.

17 There is a great DOJ page that provides links to all of the major documents in the case: United States v. American Bar Association, United States Department of Justice, https://perma.cc/P32V-QB33 (last visited May 11, 2018).

18 Press Release, Department of Justice, Justice Department and American Bar Association Resolve Charges the ABA's Process for Accrediting Law Schools Was Misused (June 27, 1995), https://perma.cc/Q78E-WRMC.

19 Press Release, Department of Justice, Justice Department Asks Court to Hold American Bar Association in Civil Contempt (June 23, 2006), https://perma.cc /E9ZK-VCD6.

20 Catherine Fredenburgh, *ABA to Shell Out $185K over Accreditations*, LAW360 (July 6, 2006), https://perma.cc/VJM7-UE5T.

21 *ABA-Approved Law Schools by Year*, A.B.A., https://perma.cc/P3NR-UAV2 (last visited May 11, 2018).

22 *Id.*

23 Ameet Sachdev, *Law Deans Linked to Accrediting Task*, CHICAGO TRIBUNE, Feb. 15, 2004, https://perma.cc/4DW3-MPUZ.

24 *Barry Currier Named Managing Director of Accreditation and Legal Education*, A.B.A. (2013), https://perma.cc/FM89-C8Z2.

25 *Section Welcomes Bill Adams as New Deputy Managing Director*, A.B.A. (2014), https://perma.cc/3CJE-6QTM.

26 Elie Mystal, *The American Bar Association Will Have an Online Law School Guy as Its Top Adviser on Legal Education*, ABOVE THE LAW (Apr. 25, 2012), https:// perma.cc/NG6C-Y7DP.

27 North Carolina Board of Dental Examiners v. Federal Trade Commission, 135 S. Ct. 1101, 1108 (2015).

28 Deborah L. Rhode and Benjamin H. Barton, *Rethinking Self-Regulation: Antitrust Perspectives on Bar Governance Activity*, 20 CHAPMAN L. REV. 267 (2017).

29 Matthew B. Fuller, *A History of Financial Aid to Students*, 44 J. STUDENT FIN. AID 42, 48–52 (2014), has a great overview of this background.

30 Lamar Alexander, *Alexander: Accreditation Must Improve, Because neither Congress nor Department of Education Are Up to the Task of Monitoring Quality*, U.S. SENATE COMMITTEE ON HEALTH, EDUC., LAB. AND PENSIONS (June 17, 2015), https://perma.cc/9QSN-KK3J.

31 *Id.*

32 *See, e.g.,* Michael Lewis, THE BIG SHORT (2010).

33 All the facts in this paragraph come from Judith S. Eaton, *Accreditation and the Federal Future of Higher Education*, ASS'N OF AM. U. PROFESSORS (2010), https://perma.cc/JE6R-2RDV.

34 Michael Stratford, *Challenges of an Accreditor Crackdown*, INSIDE HIGHER ED (Nov. 17, 2015), https://perma.cc/7QQZ-7598.

35 *Id.*

36 Am. Bar Ass'n, *ABA Standards and Rules*, *supra* chapter 6, note 1, at v.

37 U.S. Gov't Accountability Off., GAO-07–314, HIGHER EDUCATION: ISSUES RELATED TO LAW SCHOOL ACCREDITATION (2007), https://perma .cc/3RZ2-WC73.

38 Elie Mystal, *American Bar Association Gets Smacked Around by Accreditation Committee, but Keeps Its Power*, ABOVE THE LAW (June 10, 2011), https://perma .cc/L96S-G2JU.

39 Letter from Senator Charles E. Grassley, ranking member, Comm. on the Judiciary, to Stephen N. Zack, president, AM. BAR ASS'N (July 11, 2011), https://perma.cc/6JXN-AMUQ.

40 *U.S. Department of Education Staff Report to the Senior Department Official on Recognition Compliance Issues*, https://perma.cc/XZ6S-8Z7B; Paul Fain, *Accreditor on Life Support*, INSIDE HIGHER ED (June 24, 2016), https://perma.cc/X747-SGVZ.

41 Kyle McEntee, *Transcript Reveals Debate over ABA's Accrediting Power*, BLOOMBERG LAW (Aug. 3, 2016), https://perma.cc/3XNV-PRLS.

42 Stephanie Francis Ward, *ABA Won't Be Suspended from Accrediting New Law Schools*, A.B.A. J., Sept. 23, 2016, https://perma.cc/3VW8-GCWY.

43 Barry Currier, *Report on the Status of the Accreditation Project*, A.B.A. (Summer 2016), https://perma.cc/N8UK-UG7N.

44 *Withdrawal of Approval: Arizona Summit Law School*, ABA, https://perma.cc/FVB5-ERQ8.

45 Kristen Rasmussen, *10 Law Schools Sanctioned by the ABA for Lax Admissions*, Law.com, Nov. 29, 2017, https://perma.cc/6WXL-BZJZ. For the University of Puerto Rico, see Stephanie Francis Ward, *Law School at University of Puerto Rico out of Compliance with Academic Support Standard*, ABA J. (Oct. 12, 2018), https://perma.cc/P599-75D5.

46 Andrew Kreighbaum, *ABA Tightens Up*, INSIDE HIGHER ED (Aug. 31, 2016), https://perma.cc/X5R5-B6H9.

47 Stephanie Francis Ward, *Duncan School of Law Does Not Meet Admissions Standard, ABA Accreditation Committee Says*, ABA J. (Apr. 9, 2018), https://perma.cc/8QYE-8WUS.

48 James Podgers, *Sweeping Accreditation Review May Prompt "Sea Change" in Law School Evals*, ABA J. (June 3, 2009), https://perma.cc/Z8XD-UZEW.

49 Managing Director's Guidance Memo, ABA, June 2015, https://perma.cc/SNZ7-8PGH.

50 On the "psychometric properties" of the MBE, *see* Susan M. Case, *Common Goals with Increasingly Similar Outcomes: Jurisdiction Approaches to Bar Exam Grading, Scoring, and Standards*, TESTING COLUMN, https://perma.cc/A28M-PFMG (last visited May 11, 2018).

51 Staci Zaretsky, *Multistate Bar Exam Average Score Plummets to Three-Decade Low*, ABOVE THE LAW (Apr. 1, 2016), https://perma.cc/R4UX-FBRW.

52 *Repeat Test Taker Scores Drive February 2018 Average MBE Score Decline*, NCBE, Apr. 18, 2018, https://perma.cc/PE85-NWL5.

53 Derek Muller, *February 2018 MBE Bar Scores Collapse to All-Time Record Low in Test History*, EXCESS OF DEMOCRACY, Apr. 19, 2018, https://perma.cc/2KTA-5999.

54 General Statistics Report, *see infra* chapter 6, note 70.

55 Paul Caron, *July 2016 California Bar Exam Results: Nine Law Schools (including UC-Hastings) Are at Risk of Failing ABA's Proposed New Bar Passage Accreditation Standard*, TAXPROF BLOG (Dec. 13, 2016), https://perma.cc/2YLQ-WDZJ.

56 *California Bar Exam Profile*, Bar Exam Stats, http://www.barexamstats.com.

57 Mark Hansen, *What Do Falling Bar-Passage Rates Mean for Legal Education—and the Future of the Profession?* A.B.A. J., Sept. 1, 2016, https://perma.cc/EU6G-2JLW.

58 See Gary S. Rosin, *Unpacking the Bar: Of Cut Scores and Competence*, 32 J. LEGAL PROF. 67, 93 (2008). ("For any given cut score [the score needed to pass the bar], bar passage rates not only fall as law school LSAT scores fall, they fall at increasing rates.")

59 Joe Patrice, *Who's to Blame for School's "Horrific" Bar Results? Maybe the California Bar Examiners*, ABOVE THE LAW (Dec. 6, 2016), https://perma.cc/T5DQ-WH5N.

60 *Id.*; Am. Bar Ass'n, *ABA Standards and Rules*, supra chapter 6, note 1, at 24–25.

61 *Action Items*, Law School Transparency, https://perma.cc/94AP-PNM4 (last visited May 11, 2018).

62 Jay Sterling Silver, *Pedagogically Sound Cuts, Tighter (Not Looser) Accreditation Standards, and a Well-Oiled Doomsday Machine: The Responsible Way Out of the Crisis in Legal Education*, 66 RUTGERS L. REV. 353, 416 (2014).

63 Hansen, *supra* chapter 6, note 57.

64 Stephanie Francis Ward, *Conflicting Views on Proposal to Link Accreditation to Bar Passage Results*, A.B.A. J., Jan. 1, 2017, https://perma.cc/JJ6U-2C3G.

65 *See* Paul Caron, *Deans Endorse ABA's Proposed 75% Bar Passage Accreditation Requirement*, TAXPROF BLOG (Sept. 21, 2016), https://perma.cc/Z52N-8B6C.

66 Stephanie Francis Ward, *Committee Oks Proposal to Tighten ABA Bar Pass Standards; Some Members Hope More Will Be Done*, A.B.A. J., Sept. 12, 2016.

67 *Id.*

68 Kathryn Rubino, *ABA Finally Adopts Tougher Bar Passage Standards for Accreditation—Well, Almost*, ABOVE THE LAW (Oct. 24, 2016), https://perma.cc /MRM6-A4EK.

69 Letter from Deans Steering Comm., Ass'n of Am. Law Sch., to Council of the ABA Section on Legal Educ. abd Admissions to the Bar (Jan. 13, 2017), https://perma.cc/JE5K-DWLP; Letter from Lawrence P. Nolan, president, Mich. State Bar, to Am. Bar Ass'n Delegates (Jan. 18, 2017), https://perma.cc /X6YN-CD8E.

70 *General Statistics Report July 2016 California Bar Examination*, State Bar of Cali., https://perma.cc/ADH2-VCSB (last visited May 11, 2018).

71 Stephanie Francis Ward, *ABA Rejects Proposal to Tighten Bar-Pass Standards for Law Schools*, A.B.A. J., Feb. 6, 2017, https://perma.cc/4P2Z-M4X6.

72 Kristen Rasmussen, *10 Law Schools Sanctioned by ABA for Lax Admissions*, Law. com, Nov. 21, 2017, https://perma.cc/US65-3446.

73 Larry Cunningham, *Collecting Ultimate Bar Passage Data: Weighing the Costs and Benefits*, LAW SCHOOL ASSESSMENT, Nov. 19, 2017, https://perma .cc/7VBW-7GNS.

74 Karen Sloan, *Avoid the Search: Law Schools' Bar Pass Rates Now Found in One Spot*, Law.com, Mar. 22, 2018, https://perma.cc/CTA6-YT54.

75 Am. Bar Ass'n, *ABA Standards, supra* chapter 6, note 1, at 24.

76 Staci Zaretsky, *Which Law Schools Allegedly Paid Students Not to Take the Bar Exam?* ABOVE THE LAW (June 5, 2015), https://perma.cc/8YLN-UATB.

77 Lisa Worf and Greg Collard, *Law School Official: Bar Passage Would Have Been in 20s if Not for Paying Students Not to Take Exam*, WFAE (Jan. 24, 2017), https://perma.cc/ZHA8-DWVX. All of the facts in this paragraph come from this source.

78 Jerry Hartzell, *Infilaw and Student Debt*, N.C. ST. B.J. (Spring 2015), https://perma.cc/LLF2-756C.

79 Michael Gordon, *No Loans, No School, Now No Charlotte School of Law Students Pass Bar Exam on First Try*, CHARLOTTE OBSERVER, Apr. 17, 2018, https://perma.cc/7JED-AY33.

80 *2016 509 Reports*, A.B.A., https://perma.cc/HE83-U4HW.

81 Riaz Tejani, LAW MART: JUSTICE, ACCESS, AND FOR-PROFIT LAW SCHOOLS (2017).

82 *2016 509 Reports*, A.B.A., https://perma.cc/HE83-U4HW.

83 Staci Zaretsky, *Law Schools Duel for the Worst Bar Exam Passage Rates Ever*, ABOVE THE LAW (Mar. 29, 2017), https://perma.cc/X4VL-4J5X.

84 Stephanie Francis Ward, *ABA Rejects Proposal to Tighten Bar-Pass Standards for Law Schools*, A.B.A. J., Feb. 6, 2017, https://perma.cc/ERR4-QKF7. The new text of the interpretation can be found here: Am. Bar Ass'n, *Resolution*, https://perma.cc/574K-8Z4R.

85 The Title VII rebuttable presumption is known as particularly easy to overcome because the defendant just needs to raise any nondiscriminatory purpose; *see* M. Isabel Medina, *Good Night, and Good Luck Sanitized Workplaces*, 29 T. JEFFERSON L. REV. 65, 68 & n. 22 (2006). By contrast, res ipsa is quite hard to rebut, since the accident is of the type that would not normally occur without negligence, so the defendant is put in the position of proving a negative (they were not negligent); *cf.* Richard H. Sugg Jr., *The Effect of Colorado's Comparative Negligence Statue on the Doctrine of Res Ipsa Loquitur*, 52 U. COLO. L. REV. 565, 566 (1981).

86 Am. Bar Ass'n, *ABA Standards, supra* chapter 6, note 1, at 52–53.

87 Karen Sloan, *ABA to Overhaul Law School Accreditation Process with Major Reorganization*, Law.com, July 31, 2018, https://www.law.com.

88 R. Lawrence Dessem, *The ABA/AALS Sabbatical Site Inspection: Strangers in a Strange Land*, 37 U. TOL. L. REV. 37, 37–38 (2005).

89 ABA Section of Legal Education and Admissions to the Bar, *Conduct Memo: Overview of the ABA Accreditation and Site Visit Process* (2016).

90 *American Bar Association Finds Ave Maria's Admissions Practices Lacking*, AVE HERALD (Aug. 11, 2016), https://perma.cc/U2BR-GEZB.

91 Olivia Covington, *Valparaiso Law Says It's Fixing School Admission Policies*, IND. LAW. (Nov. 17, 2016), https://perma.cc/PR8P-SJ5C; Jennifer Thomas, *Charlotte*

School of Law Placed on Probation by Bar Association, CHARLOTTE BUS. J., Nov. 17, 2016, https://perma.cc/X738-XV27.

92 Am. Bar Ass'n, *ABA Standards*, *supra* chapter 6, note 1, at 74–75.

93 *Complaint Filed with ABA Against Rutgers-Camden*, Law School Transparency, https://perma.cc/EMD4-PWK2.

94 If you do not agree with me, consider Ama Sarfo, *Rutgers-Camden's Recruiting Email Deserves Sanctions: Suit*, LAW360 (Jan. 2, 2013), https://perma.cc /EHL4-MWZ4.

95 Am. Bar Ass'n, *ABA Standards*, *supra* chapter 6, note 1, at 57 (Rule 14).

96 Am. Bar Ass'n, *ABA Standards*, *supra* chapter 6, note 1, at 70–73.

97 Lucille A. Jewel, *I Can Has Lawyer? The Conflict between the Participatory Culture of the Internet and the Legal Profession*, 33 HASTINGS COMM. & ENT. L.J. 341, 371 (2011).

98 *ABA Accreditor for Law Schools Recommends Expanding Distance Learning Opportunities*, ABA, https://perma.cc/EH67-6QRM.

Chapter 7. Why Haven't More Law Schools Closed? Part 3

1 *See* Suevon Lee, *The Explosive Growth of For-Profit Higher Education, by the Numbers*, MOTHER JONES (Aug. 13, 2012), https://perma.cc/3V8D-VBFN.

2 Craig Harris, *Arizona Cardinals' Glendale Stadium to Get a New Name: University of Phoenix Backing Out*, ARIZONA REPUBLIC, Apr. 11, 2017, https://perma.cc /VX5F-LUVP.

3 Seth Cox, *Arizona Cardinals Have a New Name for University of Phoenix Stadium*, REVENGE OF THE BIRDS, Sept. 5, 2018, https://perma.cc/488C-XEPS.

4 *See, e.g.*, Arthur F. Kirk, *Leveraging Technology to Increase Enrollment, Capacity, and Revenues*, UNIVERSITY BUSINESS, Feb. 1, 2010, https://perma.cc/3NDZ -5GQC.

5 Kaitlin Mulhere, *For-Profit College Students Are Defaulting on Their Loans at an Alarming Rate*, TIME, Jan. 12, 2018, https://perma.cc/MP8W-HZBZ.

6 U.S. Gov't Accountability Off., GAO-10–948T, *For Profit Colleges: Undercover Testing Finds Colleges Encouraged Fraud and Engaged in Deceptive and Questionable Marketing Practices* (2010), https://perma.cc/VGT6-UJUH.

7 United States Senate, Health, Education, Labor and Pensions Committee, *For Profit Education: The Failure to Safeguard the Federal Investment and Ensure Student Success* (2012), *available at* https://perma.cc/D5FK-H6SQ.

8 Charlie Sorrel, *What Would Happen if 40 Million Americans Defaulted on Their student Loans?* FAST COMPANY, June 2, 2017, https://perma.cc/LKZ9-U799.

9 Scatman Crothers, *Student Loans Are Worse than Herpes*, Twitter, June 25, 2016, https://perma.cc/HA79-8T7X.

10 Vince Martin, *For-Profit Education Stocks Are Not as Cheap as They Look*, SEEKING ALPHA (July 26, 2012), https://perma.cc/4X6H-YZ54.

11 *Id.*

12 *Id.* at 135–36.
13 Betsy Mayotte, *What the New Gainful Employment Rule Means for Students*, U.S. NEWS, July 8, 2015, https://www.usnews.com.
14 *Id.*
15 Andrew Kreighbaum, *Overburdened with Debt*, INSIDE HIGHER ED (Jan. 10, 2017), https://perma.cc/T6PD-ZBUA.
16 Matt Leichter, *What If the Gainful Employment Rule Were Applied to All Law Schools*, LAW SCH. TUITION BUBBLE (July 17, 2017), https://perma.cc/3 THV-A9SW.
17 Stephanie Francis Ward, *Department of Education Flags 5 Law Schools' Debt-to-Income Ratios, including 3 in Infilaw System*, ABA J. (Jan. 11, 2017), https://perma .cc/9N2W-VGHP.
18 Ass'n of Private Sector Colleges & Univs. v. Duncan, 681 F.3d 427 (D.C. Cir. 2012).
19 Allie Bidwell, *Gainful Employment Survives For-Profit Challenge*, U.S. NEWS, June 24, 2015, https://www.usnews.com.
20 Andrew Kreighbaum, *DeVos Allows Career Programs to Delay Disclosure to Students*, INSIDE HIGHER ED (July 3, 2017), https://perma.cc/LAL4-9FH7.
21 *Id.*
22 Education Department, *Program Integrity: Gainful Employment*, FEDERAL REGISTER, Aug. 14, 2018, https://perma.cc/XC6M-E9UN.
23 Sophie Tatum, *18 AGs Sue Department of Education Over Gainful Employment Rule*, Oct. 18, 2017, https://perma.cc/8S99-8VBB.
24 *See, e.g.,* UNC Chapel Hill, *Program Participation Agreement* (Mar. 31, 2017), https://perma.cc/G8Y4-EQ2S.
25 Jarrett Carter, *These 3 Charts Show the Collapse of For-Profit Education*, EDUC. DIVE (Oct. 13, 2017), https://perma.cc/MT2Q-F52D.
26 Letter from Robin S. Minor, acting dir., Admin. Actions and Appeals Service Group of Dep't of Justice to Jack Massimino, president/CEO, Corinthian Coll., Inc. (Apr. 14, 2015), https://perma.cc/B25L-AQ4N.
27 Anya Kamenetz, *The Collapse of Corinthian Colleges*, NAT'L PUB. RADIO ED, July 8, 2014, https://perma.cc/DKM9-BB5X.
28 U.S. Sec. and Exchange Commission, *Form 8-K*, https://perma.cc/U8RH-34PH (last visited May 11, 2018).
29 DOE Letter to Corinthian, *supra* chapter 7, note 26.
30 Doug Lederman, *Corinthian Campuses Getting Nonprofit Makeover*, PBS NEWSHOUR (June 5, 2015), https://perma.cc/VFU6-38BR.
31 *Id.*
32 The letter from the DOE to Charlotte Law School lays out the specifics: Charlotte School of Law Letter, *see infra* chapter 7, note 52, at 1–3.
33 Letter from Michael Frola, dir., Multi-Regional and Foreign Sch. Participation Div. of the Dep't of Educ., to Kevin Modany, CEO, ITT Educ. Serv., Inc. (June 6, 2016), https://perma.cc/N8WZ-6M9E; Annie Waldman, *Who's Regulating*

For-Profit Schools? Execs from For-Profit Colleges, PROPUBLICA (Feb. 26, 2016), https://perma.cc/89JF-96NG.

34 Secretary of Education, *Decision of the Secretary* (Dec. 12, 2016), https://perma.cc/E2XB-AFN5.

35 Matt Lehrich, *UPDATE: What College Accreditation Changes Mean for Students*, ED HOMEROOM, https://perma.cc/LJC3-WF75 (last visited May 11, 2018).

36 Doug Lederman, *Court Opens Door for For-Profit Accreditor's Future*, INSIDE HIGHER ED, Mar. 26, 2018, https://perma.cc/R4JB-NXSL.

37 Erica L. Green, *Betsy DeVos Reinstated College Accreditor Over Staff Objections*, N.Y. TIMES, June 11, 2018, https://www.nytimes.com.

38 Michael Larkin, *Trump Spares the Rod, Makes For-Profit Colleges Great Again*, INVESTOR'S BUS. DAILY, Sept. 8, 2018, https://perma.cc/V53Z-Z9YY.

39 Letter from Anthony Bieda, exec., Accrediting Council for Indep. Coll. and Sch., to Kevin Modany, CEO, ITT Educ. Serv., Inc. (Apr. 20, 1016), https://perma.cc/N4MQ-AY8K.

40 *Id.*

41 *Id.*

42 Letter from Michael Frola, *supra* chapter 7, note 33.

43 Ashlee Kieler, *Is ITT Tech Headed for a Collapse? School Required to Set Aside Funds Just in Case*, CONSUMERIST (June 7, 2016), https://perma.cc/83MZ-AB7T.

44 Letter from Ron Bennett, dir., Sch. Eligibility Serv. Grp. of the Dep't of Educ., to Kevin Modany, CEO, ITT Educ. Serv., Inc. (Aug. 25, 2016), https://perma.cc/7QMH-XQYG. A more readable DOE overview can be found here: *Department of Education Bans ITT from Enrolling New Title IV Students, Adds Tough New Financial Oversight*, U.S. Dep't of Educ., https://perma.cc/4WKB-Z2B6 (last visited May 11, 2018).

45 *ITT Educational Services (ESI) Says ACICS to Continue Show-Cause Directive for Review*, StreetInsider.com (Aug. 18, 2016), https://perma.cc/H9BN-YNNQ.

46 James Briggs, *ITT Clings to Accreditation, for Now*, INDIANAPOLIS STAR, Aug. 18, 2016, https://perma.cc/5PHF-M6UP.

47 Letter from Ron Bennett, *supra* chapter 7, note 44.

48 Dawn McCarty and Shahien Nasiripour, *ITT Educational Services File for Bankruptcy after Shutdown*, BLOOMBERG, Sept. 16, 2016, https://perma.cc/AJQ7-PT92.

49 Debra Cassens Weiss, *ABA Puts One Law School on Probation and Censures Another*, A.B.A. J., Nov. 17, 2016, https://perma.cc/27M7-Y9SR.

50 Am. Bar Ass'n Section of Legal Educ. and Admissions to the Bar, *Council Decision* (Oct. 2016), https://perma.cc/7X33-D5YJ.

51 Letter from Ron Bennett, *supra* chapter 7, note 44.

52 Letter from Susan Crim, dir., Admin. Actions and Appeals Serv. Grp. of the Dep't of Educ., to Chidi Ogene, president, Charlotte Sch. of Law (Dec. 19, 2016), https://perma.cc/6G32-U45W.

53 *Id.*

54 *Id.*

55 Letter from Susan Crim, *supra* chapter 7, note 55.

56 Peter Marchetti, *The Need to Regulate For-Profit Law Schools to Prevent Inherent Conflicts of Interest* (2018) (draft on file with author).

57 Debra Casseins Weiss, *This Law School Had a 30% Bar Pass Rate; Do Lower Standards Presage Troubled Times for Law Grads?* A.B.A. J., Oct. 26, 2015, https://perma.cc/VGP4-R58W.

58 *See infra* chapter 5.

59 Am. Bar Ass'n, *Council Decision* (Aug. 2016), https://perma.cc/C46C-PNDH; and Am. Bar Ass'n, *Council Decision* (Oct. 2016), https://perma.cc/E4Z2-XY4S.

60 *Id.*

61 Letter from Susan Crim, *supra* chapter 7, note 55.

62 Michael Gordon, *Details Emerge in Nasty Fight between Feds and Charlotte School of Law*, CHARLOTTE OBSERVER, Jan. 20, 2017, https://perma.cc/RE48-V8ND.

63 *Id.*

64 Letter from Barry A. Currier, managing dir. of accreditation and legal education, ABA Section of Legal Education and Admissions to the Bar, to Chidi Ogene, president, Charlotte Sch. of Law (Mar. 27, 2017), https://perma.cc/9TXA-XTZV.

65 Michael Gordon, *Charlotte School of Law Fires Dozens of Faculty*, CHARLOTTE OBSERVER, Jan. 19, 2017, https://perma.cc/HE5X-LK6K.

66 Lisa Worf, *Charlotte School of Law Enrollment Shrinks; Student Receives Violation over Email to Administrators*, WFAE, Feb. 2, 2017, https://perma.cc/U8T2-UG97.

67 *Id.*

68 Michael Gordon, *Charlotte School of Law Starts Food Drive so Students Can Get Something to Eat*, CHARLOTTE OBSERVER, Jan. 27, 2017, https://perma.cc/YJ7G-R7AK.

69 Karen Sloan, *With New Lobbyists, Charlotte Law Disperses Federal Student Loans as School Year Ends*, Law.com, May 22, 2017, https://perma.cc/89R7-B8AP.

70 Drew Griffin, *Hillary Clinton's For-Profit University Problem*, CNN MONEY (Aug. 29, 2016), https://perma.cc/5HDH-R8L4.

71 Alexander Holt, *Trump University Is Somehow Even Worse than You Imagined*, NEW AMERICA (Nov. 16, 2015), https://perma.cc/S7L4-XYQY.

72 Rosalind S. Helderman, *Trump Agrees to $25 Million Settlement in Trump University Fraud Cases*, WASH. POST, Nov. 18, 2016, https://perma.cc/EB9N-ENW8.

73 Patricia Cohen, *For-Profit Schools, an Obama Target, See New Day under Trump*, N.Y. TIMES, Feb. 20, 2017, https://www.nytimes.com.

74 Katie Lobosco, *Another Election Winner: For Profit Colleges*, CNN MONEY (Nov. 17, 2017), https://perma.cc/7GWP-R7VL.

75 Kaitlin Mulhere, *Donald Trump Proposes Student Loan Forgiveness after 15 Years*, CNN MONEY (Oct. 14, 2016), https://perma.cc/BA6K-BCBN.

76 Allesandra Lanza, *5 Possible Student Loan, Higher Ed Impacts of a Trump Presidency*, U.S. NEWS (Nov. 16, 2016), https://www.usnews.com.

77 Jackie Kucinich, *Will Trump Clamp Down on For-Profit Colleges—or Reverse Obama's Regulations*, DAILY BEAST (Jan. 17, 2017), https://perma.cc/8794-4WGG.

78 Jeff Crouere, *Liberal Indoctrination Trumps Education at U.S. Colleges*, TOWNHALL (Dec. 10, 2016), https://perma.cc/K5NZ-VDXE.

79 Kim Clark, *The White House Just Delayed Rules Meant to Protect Students from For-Profit Colleges*, CNN MONEY (Mar. 7, 2017), https://perma.cc/NS52-EA39.

80 *Public Notice regarding Probationary Status of Arizona Summit*, ABA Section of Legal Education and Admissions to the Bar, Mar. 27, 2017, https://perma.cc /WE67-RGRZ.

81 *Notice of Probation Thomas Jefferson School of Law*, ABA Section of Legal Education and Admissions to the Bar, Nov. 2017, https://perma.cc/C2Y2-HE3F.

82 Letter from Barry A. Currier, *supra* chapter 7, note 64.

83 Karen Sloan, *With New Lobbyists, Charlotte Law Disperses Federal Student Loans as School Year Ends*, Law.com, May 22, 2017, https://perma.cc/N57B-QLZS.

84 *Id.*

85 Karen Sloan, *Charlotte Law School Closes with a Whimper*, Law.com, Dec. 5, 2017, https://perma.cc/BWH4-X5SS.

86 William D. Henderson, *The Calculus of University Presidents*, NAT'L L. J., May 20, 2013, https://perma.cc/HNK5-NTM6.

87 Robert Frank, SUCCESS AND LUCK: GOOD FORTUNE AND THE MYTH OF MERITOCRACY (2016).

Chapter 8. The Middle Class Sweats It Out

1 *See, e.g.*, Alex M. Johnson Jr., *The Destruction of the Holistic Approach to Admissions: The Pernicious Effects of Rankings*, 81 IND. L.J. 309, 326 & n. 66 (2006) ("It is easy for law schools to be grouped and to be ranked because we are very similar."); Maimon Schwarzschild, *Foreword: The Ethics and Economics of American Legal Education Today*, 17 J. CONTEMP. LEGAL ISSUES 1, 1 (2008) ("At many if not most accredited law schools today the academic style is broadly similar, including an emphasis on faculty scholarship which was not characteristic of "non-elite" law schools before the 1970s or 80s."); Michele R. Pistone and John J. Hoeffner, *No Path but One: Law School Survival in an Age of Disruptive Technology*, 59 WAYNE L. REV. 193, 243–44 (2013) ("Law school culture—'heretofore remarkably static, non-adaptive, and resistant to change'—has not favored experimentation.").

2 *Member Schools*, AALS, https://perma.cc/ZBN8-SQBM.

3 Lyman Johnson et al., *Washington and Lee University School of Law: Reforming the Third Year of Law School*, in REFORMING LEGAL EDUCATION 11–40 (David M. Moss & Debra Moss Curtis eds., 2012).

4 James E. Moliterno, *A Way Forward for an Ailing Legal Education Model*, 17 CHAP. L. REV. 73, 78 (2013).

5 Ashby Jones, *The Boldest Move (to Date) in Legal Curriculum Reform?* WALL ST. J., Sept. 9, 2009, https://perma.cc/US4H-8PFE. *See also* Patrick G. Lee, *Law Schools Get Practical*, WALL ST. J., July 11, 2011, https://www.wsj.com.

6 Daniel de Vise, *Washington and Lee Takes Law Students from Class to Court*, WASH. POST, Dec. 18, 2009, https://perma.cc/SQ8J-DSJN.

7 Leslie A. Gordon, *Rodney Smolla: Running a New Play*, ABA J. (Sept. 25, 2009), https://perma.cc/794E-2Z8J.

8 Moliterno, *supra* chapter 8, note 4, at 78.

9 Bill Henderson, *Washington & Lee Is Biggest Legal Education Story of 2013*, Legal Whiteboard, Jan. 29, 2013, https://perma.cc/HGN2-56VW.

10 Elizabeth G. Olson, *And the U.S. News Law School Ranking Fallout Begins*, FORTUNE, Mar. 12, 2014, https://perma.cc/8HXB-FDU3.

11 *Id.*

12 *School of Law Strategic Transition Plan*, Washington and Lee School of Law, Feb. 9, 2015, https://perma.cc/ZWE8-9PG7.

13 *Id.*

14 *The Law School Class of 2016: By the Numbers*, ABOVE THE LAW (Oct. 10, 2013), https://perma.cc/UQV3-RCNY.

15 *School of Law Strategic Transition Plan*, *supra* chapter 8, note 12.

16 *Id.*

17 *See* Orin Kerr, *Changes at Washington & Lee Law School*, WASH. POST, Feb. 19, 2015, https://perma.cc/4TA6-D5SF; Katherine Mangan, *Law Schools Cut Back to Counter Tough Financial Times*, CHRON. HIGHER ED., July 1, 2016, https://perma.cc/T5UC-DL2N.

18 *See* Deborah J. Merritt, *An Employment Puzzle*, LAW SCHOOL CAFÉ, June 18, 2013, https://perma.cc/2NPV-QTDD.

19 Kathryn Rubino, *It's Official—There's a New T14 in Town (2018 USNWR Rankings Are Here)*, ABOVE THE LAW (Mar. 14, 2017), https://perma.cc/8YQW-2K3P.

20 *Second and Third Year*, Washington and Lee School of Law, https://perma.cc/9D9U-PL3Y (last visited Apr. 13, 2018).

21 Johnson, *supra* chapter 8, note 3, at 11–40.

22 Paul Caron, *Survey: Rankings Are the Most Important Factor in Students' Decision on Which Law School to Attend*, TAXPROF BLOG, Aug. 31, 2017, https://perma.cc/FNE9-5ZMG.

23 Dessem, *supra* chapter 6, note 88, at 37.

24 *See* AALS, *2017 Site Evaluators Workshop*, at 3–5, *available at* https://perma.cc/SDF8-QCNX (last visited May 1, 2018). All the remaining facts in this paragraph come from this document.

25 For a comprehensive overview of the history of the AALS and their membership requirements, see Stevens, *supra* chapter 1, note 10, at 173–99.

26 Stevens, *supra* chapter 1, note 10, at 114–15.

27 *Id.* at 173.

28 Robert W. Bennett, *Reflections on the Law School Accreditation Process*, 30 WAKE FOREST L. REV. 379 (1995).

29 *Member Schools*, AALS, https://perma.cc/HB55-KPF6 (last visited Apr. 16, 2018); *Official Guide to ABA-Approved Law Schools*, ABA, https://perma.cc/BF2Q-9M4X (last visited Apr. 16, 2018).

30 *AALS Fast Facts*, AALS, https://perma.cc/LQ4R-VRK8 (last visited Apr. 16, 2018).

31 *Mission Statement*, ABA, https://perma.cc/9GAN-A89U (last visited Apr. 16, 2018).

32 Espeland and Sauder, *supra* chapter 5, note 100.

33 Elizabeth Olson, *Cincinnati Law Dean Is Put on Leave after Proposing Ways to Cut Budget*, N.Y. TIMES, Mar. 30, 2017, https://www.nytimes.com.

34 Paul Caron, *Jennifer Bard Named Dean at Cincinnati*, TAXPROF BLOG, Mar. 4, 2015, https://perma.cc/FM76-SSMA.

35 Karen Sloan, *Ex-Cincinnati Law Dean Claims Her Removal Was Improper*, NAT'L L. J., Apr. 5, 2017, https://perma.cc/25SY-QHAN.

36 Olson, *supra* chapter 8, note 33.

37 Andy Brownfield, *University of Cincinnati Law Dean under Fire from Faculty*, CIN. BUS. COURIER, Mar. 19, 2017, https://perma.cc/QKV9-4UYT.

38 *Id.*

39 Kate Murphy, *UC Law Dean Gets $600k to Drop Suit, Step Down*, CINCINNATI ENQUIRER, May 8, 2017, https://perma.cc/6UKH-R47G.

40 *History*, University of Cincinnati College of Law, https://perma.cc/E27Q-WJLJ (last visited Apr. 17, 2018).

41 *Id.*

42 Nikil Saval, *If You Build It, They Will Come . . . Won't They?* N.Y. TIMES MAG., Sept. 10, 2015, https://www.nytimes.com.

43 *Ohio Law Schools*, Supreme Court of Ohio, https://perma.cc/8S3R-62EE (last visited Apr. 17, 2018).

44 Matt Leichter, *Law Graduate Overproduction*, LAST GEN X AMERICAN, https://perma.cc/8V94-8K4B (last visited Apr. 17, 2018).

45 Encarnacion Pyle, *Ohio's Law Schools Draw Fewer Students in Lawyer Glut*, COLUMBUS DISPATCH, Oct. 7, 2013, https://perma.cc/Q2HS-XLYP.

46 *Id.*

47 The 2009 data is from Pyle, *supra* chapter 8, note 45.

48 *Tuition and Fees*, University of Cincinnati College of Law, https://perma.cc/8UB2-KKCS (last visited Apr. 17, 2018).

49 Olson, *supra* chapter 8, note 33.

50 Bradley Areheart, *The Top 100 Law Reviews: A Reference Based on Historical USNWR Data* (2018), *available at* https://perma.cc/E5GN-XVZX. Kate Murphy, *Thinking About Grad School? Here's How Local Universities Rank Nationally*, CINCINNATI ENQUIRER, Mar. 20, 2018, https://perma.cc/Y6MH-YWLF.

51 *About CUA Law*, Cath. Univ. of Am., https://perma.cc/D932-MGVL (last visited Apr. 18, 2018).

52 Staci Zaretsky, *Open Thread: 2013 U.S. News Law School Rankings 76–99* ABOVE THE LAW (Apr. 11, 2012), https://perma.cc/M9XM-4AQZ.

53 Barton, GLASS HALF FULL, *supra* chapter 1, note 27, at 163.

54 Paul Caron, *Catholic University Provost Blasts Critics of Plan to Lay Off Tenured Faculty, Increase Teaching Loads: "Shared Governance Means Not Just Sharing, but Also Governing,"* TAXPROF BLOG, May 13, 2018, https://perma.cc/G4J4-HM8J.

55 Matt Leichter, *Which Law Schools Are Shedding Full-Time Faculty? (2016 Edition)*, LAST GEN X AMERICAN, https://perma.cc/TM5C-SSPJ (last visited Apr. 18, 2018).

56 Areheart, *supra* chapter 8, note 50, at 5.

57 Leichter, *Which Law Schools*, *supra* chapter 8, note 55.

58 Areheart, *supra* chapter 8, note 50, at 4.

59 Paul Caron, *University of Minnesota Increases Law School's Annual Subsidy to $12 Million Amidst Declining Applications, Enrollment (on Top of $40 Million Subsidy since 2012–13)*, TAXPROF BLOG, May 11, 2018, https://perma.cc/V53G-9UFR.

60 Josh Verges, *UMN Subsidy for Law School Soars as Applications Drop*, TWIN CITIES PIONEER PRESS, May 10, 2018, https://perma.cc/QR49-LUM8.

61 In 2015, before the announced merger, Hamline and William Mitchell had already shed half of their respective faculties; *see* Leichter, *Which Law Schools*, *supra* chapter 8, note 55. Further cuts and firings are very likely postmerger, resulting in a lawsuit (since settled) by two tenured professors; *see* Chao Xiong, *Professors Drop Lawsuit against William Mitchell in Tenure Fight*, STAR TRIBUNE, May 14, 2015, https://perma.cc/X5CN-5K7L.

Chapter 9. The Good News and the Bad News from the T14(ish)

1 Rebecca Flanagan, *The Kids Aren't Alright: Rethinking the Law Student Skills Deficit*, 2015 B.Y.U. EDUC. & L.J. 135, 175 n.229 (2015).

2 *See* Gregory L. Acquaviva and John D. Castiglione, *Judicial Diversity on State Supreme Courts*, 39 SETON HALL L. REV. 1203, 1245 n.205 (2009).

3 Joe Patrice and Elie Mystal, *Is T14 Dead? Is It T15? T13? Was T14 an Arbitrary Ranking All Along?* ABOVE THE LAW (Mar. 15, 2017), https://perma.cc/X6F5-VYFJ.

4 Areheart, *supra* chapter 8, note 50, at 4.

5 Tamanaha, FAILING LAW SCHOOLS, *supra* chapter 4, note 11, at 42–44.

6 Justin McCrary et al., *The Ph.D. Rises in American Law Schools, 1960–2011: What Does It Mean for Legal Education*, 65 J. LEGAL EDUC. 543, 545–46 (2016).

7 Brent E. Newton, *The Ninety-Five Theses: Systemic Reforms of American Legal Education and Licensure*, 64 S.C. L. REV. 55, 110 (2012).

8 Alexis de Tocqueville, DEMOCRACY IN AMERICA 315 (Gerald E. Bevan, trans., 2003).

9 *History*, Harvard Law School, https://perma.cc/5EW5-AZJ4.

10 The data from the years 2011–16 came from the ABA required Standard 509 reports, available here: https://perma.cc/2YPZ-VEPH. The data from 2004–10 come from here: https://perma.cc/3T7Q-T4H5. The 2017 data comes from each school's website. I use the out-of-state tuition for state institutions.

11 *See* Yale Law School, *Endowment Funds*, https://perma.cc/57Q7-VZRN (last visited Mar. 28, 2013).

12 Jonathan D. Glater, *Harvard Law, Hoping Students Will Consider Public Service, Offers Tuition Break*, N.Y. TIMES, Mar. 18, 2008, https://www.nytimes.com.

13 Christopher Danzig, *How Stanford Law School Could Cut Tuition and Save the World*, ABOVE THE LAW (Mar. 9, 2012), https://perma.cc/QU32-XWV9.

14 Karen Sloan, *Despite Jump to $180k for Big Law Associates, Median Salary Stalls*, Law.com (June 1, 2017), https://perma.cc/6WLQ-JFD6.

15 Matt Leichter, *Class of 2016 Employment Report (Corrected)*, LAST GEN X AMERICAN (May 15, 2017), https://perma.cc/7DKZ-YA9X.

16 *ABA Required Disclosures*, ABA Section of Legal Education, https://perma.cc/38U2-UBZ4 (last visited May 11, 2018).

17 Michael I. Krauss, *The Ethics of Law School Merit Scholarships*, FORBES (Apr. 3, 2014), https://perma.cc/5VD9-PSHR.

18 *Wake Forest Law Joins Two Other Schools*, *supra* chapter 5, note 36; Zaretsky, *This Law School*, *supra* chapter 5, note 36.

19 Caron, *Arizona Is the First*, *supra* chapter 5, note 37.

20 Sloan, *Harvard Becomes Second*, *supra* chapter 5, note 41.

21 *Taking the GRE General Test*, *supra* chapter 5, note 43.

22 Kathryn Rubino, *Leaked: Are These the 2018 U.S. News Law School Rankings?* ABOVE THE LAW (Mar. 7, 2017), https://perma.cc/4K79-HY9V.

23 Robert Morse and Kenneth Hines, *Methodology: 2018 Best Law Schools Rankings*, U.S. NEWS, Mar. 13, 2017, https://perma.cc/FNS9-DZ42.

24 Victoria Clayton, *The Problem with the GRE*, ATLANTIC, Mar. 1, 2016, https://perma.cc/JZN9-9JF7.

25 Patricia B. Campbell and Sandra L. Peterson, PREDICTING PHD ATTAINMENT: THE EFFICACY OF THE GRE (2012), *available at* https://perma.cc/6AY9-PFYR.

26 Harry T. Edwards, *Reflections (on Law Review, Legal Education, Law Practice, and My Alma Mater)*, 100 MICH. L. REV. 1999 (2002).

27 Richard A. Posner, *The Judiciary and the Academy: A Fraught Relationship*, 29 U. QUEENSLAND L.J. 13 (2010).

28 William M. Sullivan et al., EDUCATING LAWYERS (2007), *available at* https://perma.cc/79QL-WS8R; Roy Stuckey, BEST PRACTICES FOR LEGAL EDUCATION (2007), *available at* https://perma.cc/9K8A-B956.

29 Tamanaha, FAILING LAW SCHOOLS, *supra* chapter 4, note 11.

30 Becky L. Jacobs, *A Lexical Examination and (Unscientific) Survey of Expanded Clinical Experiences in U.S. Law Schools*, 75 TENN. L. REV. 343, 345 (2008).

31 Jerome Frank, *Why Not a Clinical Lawyer-School?* 81 U. PA. L. REV. 907 (1933).

32 Laura G. Holland, *Invading the Ivory Tower: The History of Clinical Education at Yale Law School*, 49 J. L. ED. 504 (1999).

33 Michael Genesereth, *Computational Law: The Cop in the Backseat, available at* https://perma.cc/385D-GWGD.

34 Access to Justice Lab at Harvard Law School, https://perma.cc/5D6X-F5ZD (last visited May 11, 2018).

Chapter 10. Should I, My Child, My Buddy, or Anyone Go to Law School?

1 Gillian Hadfield and Jamie Heine, *Life in the Law-Thick World: The Legal Resource Landscape for Ordinary Americans*, in BEYOND ELITE LAW: ACCESS TO CIVIL JUSTICE IN AMERICA (Samuel Estreicher & Joy Radice eds., 2016).

2 Paul Campos, DON'T GO TO LAW SCHOOL (UNLESS) (2012).

3 David Barnhizer, *Competitive Data Trends for Great Lakes and Midwest Law Schools, 2012–2015* 3 (Cleveland-Marshall Coll. of Law, Working Paper No. 16–294, 2016), *available at* https://perma.cc/K8ZV-9TCL.

4 Jerome M. Organ, *Reflections on the Decreasing Affordability of Legal Education*, 41 WASH. U. J. L. & POL'Y 33 (2013), *available at* https://perma.cc/YP2C-EL9Z.

5 Jordan Weissmann, *Apply to Law School Now!* SLATE, June 25, 2014, https://perma.cc/4LUU-HT3U; Jordan Weissmann, *Now Is a Great Time to Apply to Law School*, SLATE, June 30, 2014, https://perma.cc/K7DJ-S2NF?type=image.

6 Weissmann, *Apply to Law School Now! supra* chapter 10, note 5.

7 Judith N. Collins, *Jobs and JDs: Employment for the Class of 2016—Selected Findings*, Nat'l Ass'n for Law Placement, Aug. 2017, at 1, *available at* https://perma.cc/3MTW-XYG4.

8 Frank McIntyre and Michael Simkovic, *Timing Law School*, J. EMPIRICAL LEGAL STUD. (June 9, 2016), *available at* https://perma.cc/QV9X-63KA.

9 *Id.* at 1. For a description of the Access Group, *see* Maxine Joselow, *Access Group Releases Loan Calculator for Law School*, INSIDE HIGHER ED, July 25, 2016, https://perma.cc/WZ68-9NYR.

10 Jane H. Allen, Counsel on Call, https://perma.cc/4A4V-UGEC (last visited Apr. 30, 2018).

11 William D. Henderson, *How Managed Services Are Building Systems for Corporate Legal Work*, ABA J. (June 1, 2017), https://perma.cc/P5HB-T22G.

12 Daniel H. Pink, TO SELL IS HUMAN (2013).

13 Gillian K. Hadfield, RULES FOR A FLAT WORLD 127–95 (2016).

Conclusion

1 Peter Lattman, *Obama Says Law School Should Be Two, Not Three, Years*, N.Y. TIMES, Aug. 23, 2013, https://dealbook.nytimes.com.

2 Zac Auter, *Few MBA, Law Grads Say Their Degree Prepared Them Well*, GALLUP, February 16, 2018, https://perma.cc/3UN7-WGXU.

3 Deborah Jones Merritt, *IBR*, INSIDE THE LAW SCHOOL SCAM, October 6, 2012, https://perma.cc/M9L4-N5TL.

4 Deborah Rhode, ACCESS TO JUSTICE (2004); Gillian K. Hadfield, *Higher Demand, Lower Supply? A Comparative Assessment of the Legal Resource Landscape for Ordinary Americans*, 37 FORDHAM URB. L.J. 129 (2009), *available at* https://perma .cc/5RVH-T7NX; Gillian K. Hadfield and Jamie Heine, *Life in the Law-Thick World: The Legal Resource Landscape for Ordinary Americans*, https://perma.cc /E7DF-4WWM.

5 Clio, LEGAL TRENDS REPORT 4 (2016), *available at* https://perma.cc/E7UK -6ZH2.

6 Chicago-Kent College of Law, Illinois Institute of Technology, Center for Access to Justice and Technology, History and Research, https://perma.cc/B7GU-X8XM (last visited May 11, 2018).

7 *Id.*

8 *History of A2J Author*, A2J Author, https://perma.cc/XC32-55UG.

9 Clio, *supra* conclusion, note 5, at 5.

10 Task Force on the Future of Legal Educ., ABA, https://perma.cc/8SJV-BXB4.

11 Presidential Task Force on the Financing of Legal Educ., ABA, https://perma .cc/3GQF-SPE5.

12 Comm'n on the Future of Legal Serv., REPORT ON THE FUTURE OF LEGAL SERVICES IN THE UNITED STATES, https://perma.cc/RZD7-7ZY7.

13 Tamanaha, FAILING LAW SCHOOLS, *supra* chapter 4, note 11, at 8.

14 Katherine Mangan, *As They Ponder Reforms, Law Deans Find Schools "Remarkably Resistant to Change,"* CHRON. HIGHER ED. (February 27, 2011), *available at* https://perma.cc/9TFZ-U3BF.

INDEX

A2J Author, 57, 237–38

Above the Law, 51, 125, 135, 158, 199

Accrediting Council for Independent Colleges and Schools (ACICS), 166–68

After the JD Study, 44

Allen, Jane, 229

Altman Weil Report, 41

American Association of Law Schools (AALS), 15, 24–30, 101, 133, 180, 188–91, 202

American Bar Association (ABA), 19–26, 128–32; AALS, 24–26, 188–90; accreditation, 3, 8, 128–40, 155–57; acquiescence, 107–11; AMA, 19–20; antitrust concerns, 133–36; bar passage, 140–50; Department of Education, 136–40, 168–69; disaccreditation, 155–59, 171–72, 241; diversity, 100–103; employment data, 41–42; LSAT 103–7; House of Delegates, 147–48, 154; Standard 316, 4, 8, 146–51; Standard 501, 148–50; Standard 503, 103–7; Whittier Law School, 3–8

American Medical Association (AMA), 19–20, 26–27

apprenticeship, 17–26, 129, 213

Arizona Summit Law School, 132, 139, 153–157, 163, 172–74

artificial intelligence (AI), 53–66

attrition, 148–50

Auerbach, Jerold, 22

bar examination, 94–96, 102–3, 140–46, 151–52

bar passage rates, 140–46

Belmont Law School, 9, 73

Best Practices for Legal Education, 15, 215

BigLaw, 33, 41, 45–50, 60, 69–70, 205–9, 225, 238

Campos, Paul, 15, 51, 78, 220

Carnegie Foundation, 15, 26–28

Caron, Paul, 83, 96–97, 116, 143

case method, 15, 20–21, 203, 213

Catholic University of America, Columbus School of Law, 196–97

Charlotte School of Law, 73, 151–53, 163, 167–77

Chicago-Kent College of Law, 56, 68, 218, 236–27

Clio, 238–39

CodeEx, 217

Computational Legal Studies, 57

Cooley Law School, 10, 73, 91, 139

Corinthian Colleges, 165–66

Council on Call, 229

creative destruction, 11, 230

CUNY School of Law, 181

Department of Education (DOE) 160–78; program participation agreement (PPA), 164–69; recognition process, 138–40, 147, 169–71

diversity, 94, 96, 100–103, 129, 147, 213

ABOUT THE AUTHOR

Benjamin H. Barton is the author of *Rebooting Justice*, *Glass Half Full: The Decline and Rebirth of the Legal Profession*, and *The Lawyer-Judge Bias in the American Courts*, and is a Professor of Law at the University of Tennessee. He has worked as an associate at a large law firm, clerked for a federal judge, represented the indigent for twelve years as a clinical law professor, and now teaches torts, contracts, and the A2J Lab.